My American
Success Story

Melvin & Patria
Wish you two
the very best!!
Roy Roberts

My American Success Story:

Always the First, Never the Last

Roy S. Roberts

Monday
04/20/2015

Charles H. Wright
African American
Museum

By Roy S. Roberts

with Elizabeth Ann Atkins

This edition published in 2015 by Roberts Detroit Publishing.

ISBN 978-0-986-40670-6

Printed in the US by Lightning Source
Typesetting by *www.wordzworth.com*
Editing and book production by Anthony Neely
Cover image by Rogers Foster, *smugmug.com*
Back cover bottom image by Randy Piland, Boy Scouts of America
Book jacket design by Sydgrafix

Endorsements
of My American Success Story

Roy Robert's life began in abject poverty in a segregated southern town in the late 1930s. His future seemed extraordinarily bleak. Yet, against all odds, Roy rose to the senior executive ranks of General Motors. This remarkable American success story is explained here in Roy's own words. For young men and women on the verge of giving up, facing seemingly insurmountable challenges, this inspiring real-life story charts a course of hope and fulfillment based upon an unwavering commitment to education, integrity and hard work. It starts with a loving father who steered his son away from a path leading nowhere, and ends with a son's 55-year, ever-ascending success story that truly defines the American Dream!

HARRY PEARCE

former Vice Chairman, General Motors Corporation

Roy Roberts served as a Director for the BNSF Railway for over fifteen years. For thirteen of those years I was the CEO, and dealt with Roy on a number of different issues. Mainly, though, Roy was a mentor to me. He does have his "Roy-isms." Each one comes with a life lesson. I was blessed to serve under Roy's leadership at the railroad as well as the Boy Scouts of America National Board. Roy has had a huge impact in corporate America. Roy has had a huge impact in my life.

MATTHEW K. ROSE

Executive Chairman, Burlington Northern Santa Fe, LLC

My American Success Story is a must-read that will serve to remove any doubt about your ability to achieve the American Dream. Early in life, Roy Roberts accepted his father's mandate that he get a good education and commit to serving others. He worked hard and earned remarkable success. I have followed Roy's exemplary career since we met as students at Western Michigan University, and worked with him to solve some of Detroit's challenges. If Roy Roberts tells you something -- if he shares valuable, life-changing information, as he does in this book -- you can take it to the bank.

DENNIS W. ARCHER
former president, American Bar Association;
former Mayor of Detroit

From the depths of poverty to the heights of power and prestige, *My American Success Story* traces the life of an extraordinary man's journey to make a difference for himself and others. It is an inspirational book of trial and triumph for all of us.

JAMES B. NICHOLSON
President and CEO, PVS Chemicals Inc.

"I'm living proof of the possibility of the American success story. It's not a black story. It's not a white story. It's an American story, and that's powerful for everyone."

ROY S. ROBERTS

Contents

*My American Success Story is dedicated to Maureen,
my wife, who has been a great partner and the
best mother to our four kids and grandmother
to our six grandsons I could ever wish for.*

Acknowledgments

I want to express my infinite gratitude to Maureen for pushing me to write this book.

"Roy, don't you dare leave this earth without telling this story," she warned repeatedly, until I finally took action.

Next, I must thank Elizabeth Ann Atkins for writing my life story. With great enthusiasm and eloquence, she conveyed my experiences, emotions and opinions in captivating prose that will forever serve as the official record of my life. Thank you, Elizabeth, for your diligent professionalism from the start, and for sharing your gift to compose *My American Success Story*.

Also, I appreciate the contributions of Anthony Neely, an accomplished professional writer who edited the final manuscript and helped me bring the book to market.

In addition, I am immensely grateful to Reverend Leon Sullivan, who stands out as a giant in my life. He ranks amongst the many people who have been instrumental by offering opportunities for me to grow and make a difference. As such, I want to recognize the following individuals for their integrity and leadership: Matthew Rose, Chairman and CEO of Burlington Northern Railroad; Miles D. White, Chairman and CEO of Abbott Laboratories; Richard Gonzalez, Chairman and CEO of AbbVie, Incorporated; and Harry Pearce, former Vice Chairman of General Motors.

I must also thank the Boy Scouts of America, the National Urban League, the NAACP, and the United Negro College Fund. I joined these organizations to help others, when in truth, they helped me learn, grow and contribute in immeasurable ways. For that, I am immeasurably grateful.

i

Introduction

I have written this book because I don't believe I have a right to leave this earth without sharing my life story. When I was born in 1939 in racially segregated Magnolia, Arkansas, I stood a far greater chance of suffering a life of poverty, struggle and even deadly violence than making history as a trailblazer in corporate America, in education and in the civic arena.

Just two years after my birth, my mother died, leaving ten children to the care of my father. At times, we were so poor that I plugged holes in my shoes with cardboard and we scrounged food from a garbage dump.

Back then, neither my family nor the oppressive world around us could have ever fathomed that I would attain the power, prosperity and prestige that epitomizes the most opulent American Dream. Likewise, no one imagined that I would catapult to positions that enabled me to help people across America and the world.

My ability to wield positive influence for others accelerated exponentially when I became the highest-ranking African American *ever* in the automotive industry. This occurred when I was named Group Vice President for North American Vehicle Sales, Service and Marketing during my 24 years of service at General Motors Corporation, which was the world's largest and leading automotive company when I joined in 1977.

My prominence at GM crowned a pattern that distinguished my entire professional career that began in 1959 in the Aerospace division at Lear Siegler Inc. in Grand Rapids, Michigan. Then, and during my fifty-five years in the corporate world, I became the first African American to hold every job that I've ever had.

This trailblazing legacy manifests itself in other ways as well. When I was only nineteen years old, I became the first African American homeowner in our neighborhood. It was such an anomaly in 1959 that people would drive by our home as if it were a tourist attraction. When I was national president of Boy Scouts of America, I was the first person of color to do so. And I have been the first African American to serve on several corporate boards.

This life-long phenomenon inspired one of my trademark mantras that others affectionately characterize as "Roy-isms." I often say:

"It's not a sin to be the first; it's a sin to be the last."

Because I adhere so fiercely to this tenet, I found it appropriate to include in the title of this book. This title also celebrates the fact that each time I became the "first," someone opened the door. Those individuals were Caucasians who defied the norm by elevating me to positions where no African American had gone before.

"Roy, after all these years," a lifelong friend, Phil Saunders, recently remarked, "I've never heard you say anything negative about white people."

My response is that white people enabled me to do what I've done. And while I have witnessed racism first hand in my personal and professional lives, I refuse to blame or dislike anyone for "the sins of the father." Instead I have always glorified the good will of those who helped me, by proving that they did the right thing. In every position, I've made it my mission to perform far above and beyond anyone's highest expectations. I've done this by implementing an impeccable, self-styled Code of Conduct to demonstrate that African Americans are talented, productive and beneficial assets in the business world.

This Code of Conduct includes diligently "Reinventing Roy" to excel in every new assignment, while avoiding what I call "Silent Killers" — behaviors that hinder success.

These secrets are detailed on the pages of this book, along with countless examples of how I continuously impart this knowledge to help others.

Very importantly, when the mainstream opened doors for me, I always, always propped those doors wide open for women and other people of color to advance in along with me. Yet I did this not solely by virtue of race, gender or ethnicity; I demanded the same immaculate performance from those whom I helped as I did from myself.

I told every protégé: "You have to be sure that when you leave this job, the company can never say, '*Your people* can't do it.' They might be able to say, '*He* can't do it.' Or '*She* can't do it.' But never, '*They* can't do it.'"

I have passed along this self-imposed challenge to function at such a high level that people will never turn their backs on African Americans as a race.

This principle and my Code of Conduct rank as crown jewels in the treasure trove of knowledge that I now feel compelled to share with new generations that include my six grandchildren.

Because it was my father's wisdom that kept me on track as a rebellious teenager who was threatening to quit school. Though Papa was a factory worker and a barber with an eighth grade education, he had a vision for my future. Turner Ray Roberts saw something special in me, and he set me straight one cold winter morning in 1957. Papa had a way of sharpening his eyes and lowering his voice that we kids didn't dare disobey. In our stark apartment over a hardware store, he told me:

"You're going to go to school. You're going to get a good education. You're going to be somebody. And you're going to help other people."

At the time, I didn't understand anything beyond his admonition to stay in school. As for saying that I would "be somebody," my comprehension of that in our all-black, poor neighborhood in the factory town of Muskegon, Michigan, meant that I would become someone of importance and do something meaningful in the world.

Those were the only words *ever* spoken to me about my future. Not a single teacher encouraged me to attend college or pursue a profession. As for role models, our town had one black physician and one black pharmacist; African American businessmen were non-existent. We did not own a television; my father never owned a car or a house.

Despite this, the meager reality of my early years provided fertile ground for my father's four seeds of wisdom to take root and bear then-inconceivable fruit over the next six decades.

Now, as I reflect on my father's prophecy, my relentless hard work, and the people who have catapulted me to previously implausible heights for a black man in America, I am awed and overwhelmed with gratitude.

Yes, I earned my education. After graduating from Muskegon Senior High School, I received a bachelor's degree in Business Administration from Western Michigan University. Later, while serving as an executive at GM, I completed the Executive Development Program at Harvard Business School and the General Motors Advanced International General Management Program in Switzerland. I have also been awarded several honorary degrees.

As for my father's encouragement to "be somebody," an article in *Driven* magazine left no doubt about that. Over a two-page spread that included my photograph, the headline declared: "GM's BILLION-DOLLAR MAN."

Likewise, during our travels to dozens of countries around the world, my wife Maureen and I have dined with the King of Sweden, watched an inaugural performance of *The Phantom of the Opera* in London, and enjoyed a luxurious safari in Tanzania. *Black Enterprise* named me Executive of the Year, and President George Bush bestowed me with the American Success Award. Maureen and I live in a beautiful home in a Detroit suburb that is one of America's most affluent communities; we enjoy a second home on a golf course in Scottsdale, Arizona.

Very importantly, to "be somebody" also means being an exceptional husband and father. I have cherished nearly forty years of an idyllic marriage with Maureen, following 13 years with Ruby during my first marriage. I am extremely proud of our four children: Ricky, Robin, Ronald and Katrina, as well as our six grandchildren.

Lastly, I wish my father had lived to see the many ways that I continue to "help people," well beyond my retirement from GM in 2000. In May of 2011, we donated $1.1 million to the world-renowned Detroit Institute of Arts for the Maureen and Roy S.Roberts Gallery of Contemporary African American Art.

That same month, Michigan Governor Rick Snyder appointed me as Emergency Manager for beleaguered Detroit Public Schools; in just 18 months, I generated the district's first operating surplus in nearly a decade, and I accelerated the elimination of a $327-million deficit. This, while improving test scores and implementing a strategy for the district's long-term success.

From August until November of 2013, I served as Detroit's Chief Land Officer to help utilize a $300 million federal grant to remove blight. At the same time, I am involving myself in a variety of exciting, entrepreneurial ventures, while enjoying a robust social life and precious time with my family.

Now during my seventy-fifth year, I'm presenting *My American Success Story*. My motive is purely altruistic. I must share what I know with those who can contribute to, and benefit from, everything that makes America the land of opportunity for all. For that reason, I am including tough lessons learned during the many struggles and setbacks throughout my life.

In addition, though the election of President Barack Obama has shattered the color barrier at the highest level of government, a dearth of black leadership continues to plague corporate America. Thirty percent of the corporate boards of America's largest publicly traded companies do not have a single African American director, according to a 2013 *Black Enterprise* report. This is unacceptable; I want *My American Success Story* to serve as a framework for ambitious professionals to emulate. I also want to convince business leaders that promoting people of color to key positions benefits the company's culture, its public image, and its bottom line.

Now, as I reflect on my life, I wonder, "How did I do it?" I rose from abject poverty to the pinnacle of success. However, I don't believe everyone can replicate my success formula. Many people want the rewards — the salaries and bonuses, the beautiful homes, the designer clothing, the world travel, the luxury automobiles, the prestige, the accolades — but they are unwilling to take the long, tough journey. My message? There are no shortcuts. If you're not willing to do the work, you may never receive the perks.

"Roy, this is a long way from Magnolia, Arkansas, ain't it?" a long-time friend recently remarked about my life.

"You'd better believe it," I said with a smile, "and I wouldn't trade it for anything."

Now my wish is that you may mine the printed words hereafter for gems of knowledge that inspire your own American Success Story.

ROY S. ROBERTS
Bloomfield Hills, Michigan
January 2015

With former U.S. Secretary of State Colin Powell

Prologue

They Didn't Plant No Cotton, and They're Not Going to Pick No Cotton

My father, Turner Ray Roberts, was achieving as close to the American Dream as was possible for a black man in 1938. As owner of The Turner Roberts Delivery Company, which had several employees, he catered to the booming black community of Waxahachie, Texas.

Located thirty miles south of Dallas, the picturesque town was surrounded by the rich, dark soil of cotton plantations that had once made Ellis County the largest cotton producer in America. That industry had built this town after the Civil War. From then until the Great Depression, cotton was king, and the blood, sweat and tears of the poor, uneducated black folks continued to enrich white plantation owners.

Now, as my father drove his mule-drawn buggy to deliver groceries and goods around town, he would pass the cotton workers as they walked out to toil under the blistering sun. They were earning pennies; my father was raking in an impressive $25 per day (about $414 now). All those hopeless black faces were a constant reminder of the miserable fate he had escaped as a boy in Magnolia, Arkansas, thanks to his courageous determination for a better life.

Now, at age forty, he loved being his own boss, and taking care of his wife and eight children in a five-room house with plenty of food and clothing. He relished his good fortune every time he steered through the town square, past the Ellis County Courthouse, which looked like a castle. He'd navigate past the Victorian, Gingerbread, Gothic Revival, and Queen Anne homes. Known as The Gingerbread City, Waxahachie would one day inspire an annual tour of its turn-of-the-century architecture, and be the setting for the 1983 film *Places in the Heart* starring *Sally Field*; she won the 1984 Academy Award for Best Actress.

My father had arrived in the town that served as the county seat twenty years prior, with nothing but desire for a better life. Papa had picked Waxahachie because its flourishing black community offered opportunities for blacks who shared his entrepreneurial spirit. Every day, he and his employees delivered food and merchandise to steady customers who paid well and tipped generously.

These included the black businesses along East Main Street, built a few decades after slavery ended. Among them were The James Funeral Parlor at 441 E. Main; the second floor of the brick façade building housed the black Masonic organization called Pythagoras Lodge #87, founded in 1893. My father's delivery route also took him past the spiritual sanctuary of the black community: Samaria Baptist Church at 603 E. Jefferson, assembled after the Civil War, Joshua Chapel African Methodist Episcopal Church, and the New Mount Zion Baptist Church.

Papa's company also delivered to the black families who were his neighbors in "shotgun houses" around Wyatt Street. Like the Roberts home, these one-story, wooden houses featured a covered front porch with a single front window beside the door. It led to three to five rooms that, with no interior hallway, flowed one into another. They were called "shotgun" because a bullet could fly straight through.

Papa loved providing for his family, because he had never known his own father. One year after my dad was born on August 18, 1897, my grandfather died as a soldier in the Spanish American War. The U.S. Government paid a $10 death benefit to my grandmother, left alone to raise two girls and two boys. Though my father had earned enough education to teach black children at the one-room schoolhouse that he had attended in Magnolia, Arkansas, chances were greater that he would have to work in the cotton fields. The misery of such back-breaking work — to make someone else rich — activated within him a Roberts family character trait that endowed my father with entrepreneurial business savvy. This would later enable my uncle, Roger Roberts, to become the first black to own a cotton gin in Arkansas.

According to the family's oral history, a Roberts man had served in every war since Papa's great grandfather Will Roberts fought in the Civil War. This legacy continued through World War I, World War II, the Korean War, Vietnam, the Persian Gulf War and the conflicts in Iraq and Afghanistan.

At that time, however, in 1910, the only thing he saw in his future was the oppressive reality of life in a segregated Southern town. He hated that Jim Crow laws harassed and humiliated his people. Even worse, black men in Columbia County, Arkansas were prone to getting beaten and lynched.

My father wanted to survive — and thrive. So at age 13, he *walked* all the way to Texas! Some 233 miles westward, he settled in Dallas. As the Texas Oil Boom industrialized the agricultural Lone Star State, my father worked as a cook's helper at Standard Oil. The company, which had just begun drilling for oil in Texas, made owner John D. Rockefeller the world's richest man and the first American worth more than a billion dollars.

My father worked there from 1910 until 1917, when he was drafted into the U.S. Army to fight in World War I. Trained at Jefferson Barracks on the *Mississippi River*, south of *St. Louis* in *Lemay, Missouri*, he was scheduled to fight in France, but the War ended in 1918. So Papa returned to Arkansas to check on his mother, who never remarried. Two months later, he went to Waxahachie.

There, he fell in love with a beautiful fifteen-year-old girl who was tall, slim and dark complexioned. In 1920, he married Erma Lee Livingston, and their first child, a son named Cleo, was born on Christmas Day. The unique tone of his voice would earn him the nickname, "Tang." After Cleo came: Lessie Bee; Retha Mae; Turner Ray "Junior;" a stillborn girl; Erma Dean; Ludine; Minnie Ruth; and Robert, who was born on February 3, 1937 and nick-named "Bob."

Meanwhile, the Great Depression devastated local cotton farm-ers; they struggled to survive by using blacks for cheap labor. One day, when Bob was a baby, one of the town's biggest cotton farmers noticed that Turner Roberts' kids were old enough to work in his fields. This well-known white man stopped my father as he made deliveries around town.

"Why aren't your kids going out and picking cotton?" the farmer demanded.

In those days, when a white man spoke, the standard survival tactic among black men was to respond with subservience and obedience. Treating the white man like he was anything less than the boss could have put a black man at risk for legal trouble, violence or even death. But Turner Roberts lived by his principles, not by the unjust ways of the world.

"Boy, can't you hear?" the farmer snapped. "I asked you a question! Why aren't your kids going out and picking cotton?"

My father kept his head held high and his shoulders squared as he declared:

"They didn't plant no cotton, and they're not going to pick no cotton."

The white man was outraged that a black man would dare to speak with such defiance.

"Boy, I want those kids down at my farm to start working on Monday!"

My father did not flinch. "My kids didn't plant no cotton, and they're not going to pick no cotton."

The farmer glared at Papa and accused, "Well, you're gonna be a smart nigger!"

"I'll be anything I have to be," my father retorted, "but my children will not pick no cotton. They're going to school." With that, my father steered his mule-drawn buggy into the street, to carry on with his business.

Meanwhile, the farmer was so furious, he sent word that a confrontation was imminent. He was going to come after my father, and force the Roberts children to work on his farm. Undaunted, my father called eight friends who, like him, were experienced hunters who brought their guns.

At the same time, the farmer assembled his own posse of armed men, and they went to the Roberts home.

"Turner, come on out!" the farmer yelled.

The front door remained closed. Papa stayed in the house.

"C'mon out here!" the farmer commanded.

Still, my father refused to leave the house.

"We're comin' in to get you!" the farmer yelled.

Cha-chink! Click! Cha-chink! Clink-clink!

The sound of eight shotguns and pistols cocking filled the air, while as many gun barrels appeared in the front window and doorway of our family's home. The farmer and his men backed away. The next morning, the Mayor of Waxahachie arrived with the Ellis County Sheriff and said, "Turner Roberts, you should leave town."

"Otherwise," the Sheriff added, "somebody's gonna get killed. And whether it's you or him, it won't serve you or your family well."

So my parents packed up the children and moved back to my parents' hometown of Magnolia, Arkansas.

ONE

Roy S. Roberts is Born into a World of Loss and Love

I cherish my first memory as prophetic, because it illustrates two powerful themes that have distinguished my life. It happened when I was two-and-a-half years old, attending my mother's funeral. As the service ended, gospel music filled the Baptist church, while throngs of people hugged, cried and milled around the pews.

The noise and commotion were frightening, as I was unaccustomed to seeing so many men in suits and women in their Sunday dresses, hats and gloves, as was the style during July of 1941 in Magnolia, Arkansas.

I could not see my father in the crowd. Nor was I able to spot my five older sisters, or my four brothers, including nine-month-old Gene. Complications from his birth had resulted in our mother's death at age 36. At the time, I was too young to comprehend the tragedy of losing our mother. My only thought was that I felt scared and bewildered, standing amidst this spirited crowd of foreign faces in an unfamiliar place.

I burst into tears.

"Don't cry, little fella," a well-dressed man said with a comforting voice and a tender look in his eyes. He picked me up, reached in his pocket, and pulled out something small and shiny. Then he placed the round object in the palm of my hand.

I blinked away tears. It was a quarter! No one had ever given me so much money. I was deeply touched by the kindness of this man whose name and face I did not know, though I had a vague sense that he was a distant relative. Not only did he soothe me at a frightening time, but he made me feel special, and rewarded me for it.

I treasure this memory because it encapsulates several important characteristics that, I believe, made my success possible.

First, for as long as I can remember, I have always refused to dwell on the negative. I was born with what seems like an automatic delete button in my brain; it erases negative thoughts, feelings and experiences from my mind. This has enabled me to focus on rising onward and upward from any situation. As a result, this character trait precluded me from lamenting the loss of my mother. And thankfully, I always felt loved and nurtured by my sisters, some of whom were old enough to be my mother.

Second, the man who picked me up at my mother's funeral was the first of many people who would single me out of a crowd, then offer me opportunities and rewards. I believe this has occurred time and again because people have seen something special in me, and felt compelled to help me.

I have no doubt: it was by divine Providence that I was endowed with these two qualities that would ultimately bless my life beyond measure. This is all the more powerful because the era and circumstances into which I was born offered no hint of my future success.

Roy Stewart Roberts, Ninth of Ten Children

I was born on Sunday, March 26, 1939, in Magnolia, Arkansas.

At the time, Franklin D. Roosevelt was President, Adolf Hitler and Benito Mussolini were spreading tyranny across Europe to usher in World War II, and Jim Crow segregation kept black people in the American South poor, oppressed and terrorized. In fact, the month after my birth, Billie Holiday recorded the haunting song called *Strange Fruit* to focus attention on widespread lynching of black men.

Though life for most blacks in Arkansas was bleak, Papa supported the family as a concrete finisher, laying highways for the WPA. The Work Projects Administration was a New Deal program that President Roosevelt used to put nearly eight million Americans to work after the Depression, by hiring them to build bridges, roads and buildings.

When I was born, we lived in a newly constructed house on Vinegar Hill at the corner of Calhoun Road. My mother worked as the head chef at the Magnolia Hotel. Starting early every morning, she supervised breakfast, then lunch. After that, she'd come home, still wearing her blue uniform that had a white collar and buttons down the front. At 4 p.m., she would return to the hotel to oversee the dinner shift. Our mother was also a talented seamstress who made all of the family's clothing. This skill enabled her to earn extra money by working as a seamstress for many whites in town. While she worked, the older siblings took care of the smaller children; Bob and I were the youngest, and she was soon pregnant with Gene.

On Sundays, our mother took us to church, with the goal of imparting good Baptist values to each of us. At home, she demanded an impeccable work ethic by teaching the oldest children how to do chores. Bob's recollection of watching how the family washed clothes is a telling example of the discipline and high expectations that our parents instilled in us.

Back then, doing laundry was quite a production — outside in the yard. First, the clothes were scrubbed on a ridged, metal board in a large tub of soapy water. Next, the clothing was bleached and boiled in a giant pot on an open fire. Then the clothes were hung on lines to dry in the breeze and the sun.

"You've never seen clothes come out so clean," recalls Bob, now 76 and retired after owning successful businesses in California. "But our mother was a strict disciplinarian, and if you were going to wash clothes, you were going to do the best job possible. So she used to walk around the clothesline, inspecting the clothes as they hung to dry in the sun. "Anything she found that wasn't clean enough," Bob says, "she'd pull it off the line, throw it on the ground, step on it and say, 'Do it again!'"

Life Without Mother

About six months after our mother died, my father married a younger woman, Ethel Thomas, whom he had met at a sanctified Baptist church.

"Nobody could have had a better stepmother," Bob recalls. "She was great, by the way she treated us. We called her Mom, and she did everything for us."

Together, she and my father had three children: Joyce Ann, Larry and Betty.

"We all loved each other like brothers and sisters," Bob says.

"Roy always carried me around on his hip," recalls my sister, Joyce Dawson, now CEO of a security company in Nevada. "He called me his baby. He still does. If we went into town, all the boys would take turns carrying me. I was so spoiled, because my brothers loved me so much."

Our home had three bedrooms, and I shared a bed with Bob and Gene. While my sisters Minnie Ruth, Erma Dean and Ludine still lived at home, Retha Mae and Lessie Bee had houses nearby and were my caregivers. Retha had one son, Ray, who was two months younger than me.

We have no photographs of our early years, because we were too poor to own a camera. However, my most vivid memories include an incident with the potbelly stove in our living room. Made of cast iron, it was round with legs; when we got the fire blazing with wood, that stove would glow red-hot! One cold winter morning, I was standing around the stove with my brothers to get warm. Gene, who was nude, said something to me, and I inadvertently pushed him into the red-hot stove.

It seared his rear end! He screamed something terrible. Thankfully, the burn did not require medical attention, and family members nursed him until it healed. As I feared, I got a real whuppin' from my oldest sister and my father. Spankings back then were customary, as Bob recalls:

"Everybody whupped me. My sisters, my daddy, everybody who was older than me. If I did something wrong, I got five whuppin's before noon."

"It Takes a Village to Raise a Child"

I'll never forget the terror of seeing all five-feet, ten-inches of Papa's solid brawn charging at me like a military tank.

"Go get me a switch!" he ordered. It was customary for black families to augment a child's punishment by forcing him or her to retrieve a spanking stick from the ground or a tree branch. "And don't get me one that'll break!" I did as told, and Papa wore my little butt out with that switch.

"Boy, don't you ever do that again!" he shouted with every lash.

Sometimes Papa was the *second* person to spank me. Back in the early 1940s, black neighborhoods exemplified the African proverb, "It takes a village to raise a child." In the unspoken way that socialization was conveyed, it was the accepted norm that parents authorized neighbors to scold and spank a child for misbehavior. If I got into a fight or said a bad word, Miss Smith or Mr. Applewhite down the block would spank me. Then they'd bring me home and tell Papa what I had done, and he'd whup my tail once more.

Once, a police officer arrived at the home of a neighbor who was spanking a child for misbehaving. "Keep whuppin' him," the officer commanded. Then he turned his back and left.

This punishment was effective, because fear is a powerful motivator to make a child follow the rules of good behavior. Likewise, mothers and fathers did not lavish children with affection or warm, fuzzy declarations of love. I cannot recall ever seeing a black man — Papa included — hug his child or say "I love you" while I was growing up.

It was a tough, racist world, and parents were training their kids to overcome the inevitable challenges they would face. My father never said, "This is a harsh world and you've got to learn how to live in it." Instead, he showed me that it would be tough all the way. That was his form of love. Those were the times we lived in; I did not feel deprived or neglected. In fact, I always felt that I was loved and that I was somewhat special.

Similarly, if you look at the animal kingdom, ruled by "survival of the fittest," this tough love enables offspring to thrive and survive. My father had been fending for himself since age 13; he wanted his children to become independent, self-sufficient individuals. That's why, for as long as I can remember, Papa drilled into us his realistic, core philosophy about life. He used the "three-strikes-you're out" rule of baseball.

"Being black in America," he often told us, "you only have one strike. Everybody else has three strikes. You have to manage your one strike. If you ever lose that one, you will never get it back again." Our father warned that if we ever got ourselves into trouble, we would have to get out the same way — by ourselves. "I'm not coming to the police station," he frequently warned. "I'm not going to lie for you. Now you know what the rules are, and that's it." Papa's warning haunted me with chilling visions of getting thrown in jail — and having to stay there.

Papa's Principles and Entrepreneurial Spirit

Though he needed to support the youngest of his thirteen children, my father's entrepreneurial spirit made it difficult for him to take orders from anybody very long. I'll repeat fifty times, Turner Roberts was the most principled person I've ever known. He had a personal belief system that worked for him, and he let no one and nothing sway him from conducting himself otherwise. As a result, my father was driven by the need to be his own boss, as he'd been during his professional heyday in Texas. Now in Arkansas, he was always working a deal and trying to sell something to people.

He was a barber in the local barbershop, and he became a farmer, growing tomatoes, beans and corn. Most notably, he was "The Watermelon Man," because he purchased wagonloads of watermelons and sold them from our front porch for a quarter or 50 cents to everyone in the neighborhood. It was such a joy to help my brothers unload the delivery wagon. We'd always get our youngest brother Gene to "accidentally" drop one. It would crack open and, since Papa couldn't sell damaged goods, all of us kids would devour the sweet fruit right then and there.

Less fun, however, was my first day of kindergarten. My sisters, Ludine and Minnie Ruth, along with Bob, were walking me to the schoolhouse for black children. Though we were in different grades, all of us were taught in the one room where our father had learned years ago.

The idea of going to school terrified me to such an extreme that, en route, I had "an accident." I soiled my pants! My siblings took me into the woods and used leaves to clean me as best they could. That did not make for a happy start to my education. Nor did I enjoy the grim reality that fistfights were a normal, accepted part of childhood. In those days, fights were just little dusters. You got up, said, "You win," and everybody went home. Still, I didn't like hitting, kicking or rolling around on the dusty ground.

"You have to take care of each other," our father warned. "We're a tight-knit family, and you have to protect your brothers and sisters." Papa's motto for anyone who wanted to fight us was, "If you pick a fight with one Roberts, all the Roberts are coming after you!"

This was important, because my family perceived me as a nice, little guy who was easy-going and vulnerable to getting beaten up. While I was not physically aggressive, I was pretty smart, and could take care of myself verbally. I soon learned that my aversion to fighting would cost me — painfully. Once, Bob and I got in a fight with two guys, but I stepped back and wouldn't help Bob.

"Come help me!" Bob shouted.

"I ain't in it, man," I answered. "I'm not gonna get my clothes torn off!"

When we got home, Bob jumped on me and beat my behind.

"I sure did jump him," Bob recalls. "I was kickin' his butt, and the old man didn't say a word. Daddy's attitude was, 'He ain't in it.'"

Both my brother and my father taught me that failing to defend a Roberts was unacceptable and punishable by an even worse beating at home. Because representing the family and the Roberts name with courage, pride and respect meant everything.

TWO

Following the Great Migration for a Better Life

When I was five years old, Papa decided to move our family to Michigan. How we traveled there reflected one good reason that we were leaving the South.

"We rode at the back of the bus during our trip from Arkansas to Michigan," recalls my sister Joyce. "I was only two years old at the time, and I'd never been on a bus. But to this day, I can almost tell you where everybody was seated — my sisters, my brothers and my mother. I didn't understand the significance at the time, except that it was a big trip and all of us had to go to the back of the bus."

The year was 1944, and moving North promised to liberate our family from inferior, segregated schools, the humiliation of "white" and "colored" sections, and the hardscrabble economy that left few opportunities for blacks. Papa had heard that the abundance of automotive industry jobs in Michigan provided steady work, paid good salaries and offered benefits.

So we joined the six million African Americans who would flee the South during the Great Migration between 1910 and the 1960s. It had started with Henry Ford's unprecedented, $5-a-day wages, which drew people from around the world to work in Detroit's automobile factories. The industry expanded across Michigan, as car plants and foundries were constructed to supply automobile manufacturing.

Three hours west of the Motor City, along the breathtaking, white sand shoreline of Lake Michigan, rose the smoke stacks and boxy metal structures of factories in Muskegon. Settled by French fur traders and trappers in the 1700s, it was named after the Ottawa Indian term of "Masquigon," which means "marshy river or swamp." As the biggest city on the western edge of the state, Muskegon borders Muskegon Heights, where black factory workers settled in cheap housing built to accommodate the working class.

When we moved there, the Big Three were dominating the economy, usurping western Michigan's dominance as the "Furniture Capital of the World." As a result, furniture companies were relocating to the Carolinas, because they could no longer compete for workers while Ford, General Motors and Chrysler paid high wages with good benefits. The auto industry and its suppliers became our region's main employers.

Our father had actually moved to Muskegon Heights ahead of us, and my sister Retha Mae and her husband already lived there. At the time, World War II was raging on; my sister Lessie Bee lived on the U.S. Army base in Newport News, Virginia, while her husband served in the war. Papa secured a job at Campbell, Wyant and Cannon Foundry, which made four-cylinder engine blocks for Continental Motors. He rented a basement apartment, where we lived with him for four months.

Then, like the growing number of blacks who moved to the town of 16,000 people, we lived in government housing. The Muskegon Heights Housing Projects consisted of long, one-story buildings, each containing four to six units. At the center of the complex was a playground and an administrative office where residents were taught how to follow local laws and ordinances.

Our end unit — 921A Hinman Street — was considered pretty nice, because we had extra outdoor space. Entering through the front door led to the small living area, which had off-white walls and an olive green couch. It was possible to walk straight into the small kitchen and exit through the back door.

A coal heater in the living room warmed the apartment during the winter. A truck would dump coal into a bin in the back alley, and we boys had to retrieve the coal with a bucket and put it in the stove. Down a small hallway were two more bedrooms; one for the girls: Joyce and Betty; and one for the boys: Bob, Roy, Gene and Larry. Ray was in the home for a short while, until he left and married, as the older siblings had done. To the right of the living room was our parents' bedroom; in the corner was a baby bed for my youngest sister, Betty.

Everyone shared one bathroom.

Unlimited Potential, Despite Poverty

Despite the harsh reality for blacks during the 1940s — ten years before the Supreme Court desegregated schools and two decades before the 1964 Civil Rights Act desegregated public accommodations — our father and stepmother conveyed the idea that we all had unlimited potential.

"We had so much love," Joyce recalls. "Our family structure taught us early on that you could be anything you wanted to be, and that you could do anything you wanted to do. Any limitations were between your ears. As a result, when I got into the outside world, I never bought into what other people thought I should feel or be. I always wanted to lead and not follow, and these same qualities were apparent in Roy."

We learned these qualities from our father's rugged individualism, industriousness and indomitable need to be his own man. His seasonal factory work included shakeout jobs at Lakey's Foundry, making molds from molten metal. Once the mold formed, he would "shake it out" to remove the burned parts. It was strenuous, sometimes dangerous work because the heat and dust were injurious to the lungs.

Papa also obtained a barber's license which, unlike in Arkansas, was mandatory in Michigan. Oftentimes, he would work a factory job until seven in the evening on weekdays. Then, on weekends, he would earn extra money in a local barbershop.

When the automobile industry boomed, Muskegon boomed. And when the Big Three caught a cold, so to speak, the factory towns of Muskegon, Saginaw and Flint got pneumonia and really suffered.

This imposed a cycle of poverty and prosperity on working class families like ours. When Papa was out of work, we received welfare, like many families around us. At the time, depending on the government for money and food was considered a temporary necessity during tough times — not a lifestyle. Our family would only receive welfare for four or five months at a time, until the economy improved and Papa could find work. Sometimes, however, his unemployment resulted from his refusal to take orders from white people. Papa often declared that he was better than whites: "I don't *think*, I *know* I am."

Despite hardship, our family enjoyed fun times that included snowball fights.

"There were a lot of us," Joyce remembers, "so we could divide up in teams: my father on one team, my mother on another. We'd all throw the snowballs at each other. That was great, great fun!"

At Christmas time, we attended our Baptist church as a family. At Halloween, Joyce recalls, "The boys would go trick or treating, and they'd come back with bags bursting with sweet potatoes, candy and gum. I loved Juicy Fruit gum, and one time all of Bob's goodies fell on the floor, including a pack of Juicy Fruit. He wouldn't let me have it, so we had a tussling match. I took the gum and socked him. Roy would have just given me the gum."

Bullying was the Norm

Bob, Gene and I started off at Lindbergh Elementary School, where we had great teachers who set the standard for the remainder of my grade school education. Ironically — in our all-black community

— we did not have a single black teacher, ever. Due to overcrowding, we were transferred from Lindbergh to another school. It was farther away, forcing us to walk through some woods, but we had some pretty tough guys in our group.

Muskegon Heights was a rough environment. What's considered bullying today was the norm in our predominantly African American neighborhood.

If I didn't fight everyday, I was watching somebody else fight. Like in Magnolia, fighting was about honor, not inflicting major pain or physical injury. If someone had you down, you'd say, "I give," and they'd get up and leave. The fight ended there, but everyone knew whether you won or lost. Fighting was about reputation, and boy, did I tarnish mine the day I fought with a girl.

"C'mon, Roy!" she taunted. "If you're too scared to fight me, I'm gonna beat your butt in front of everybody!"

I restrained myself.

"Chicken!" she shouted. She flapped her arms and made chicken noises. "Bawk! Bawk! Bawk! Chiiiiiiiiiiiii-cken!"

She got in my face, and with all the neighborhood kids watching, I had to defend my reputation.

"Roy Roberts is scared of a girl!" she yelled.

The fight was on. We started throwing punches like two men. Bob, who was in sixth grade, walked up on the fight.

"Bob, get this damn girl off me!" I shouted.

"I ain't in it," Bob responded as punishment for when I had not helped him during a fight.

"That girl pulled Roy back and kept whuppin' him," he says. "This chick whupped him good!"

I hated losing, so I mustered the strength to pin her to the ground. I was winning! What I didn't realize was that while she was looking up at me, she was scratching my face and body. Despite that, being in the dominant position gave me the official victory.

"Roy, you won!" my friends declared. But I looked like a plucked chicken, and I was reeling with shame that, in my opinion, I had lost a fight against a girl.

The Roberts brothers: (L-R) Roy, Bob, Gene and Ray

Church: Dressing Up For the Lord and Life

When we first moved to Michigan, our stepmother made sure that the family attended Bible study on Wednesday evenings, and service at our Baptist church on Sunday mornings. In the African American church, the tradition is to wear your nicest clothes to give the Lord your best look. While I loved the music and the celebratory feeling with family and neighbors, I especially loved dressing up. I vividly remember wearing gray slacks with a blue sport coat, a white shirt and a multi-colored, reddish tie. I thought that outfit, which I wore to a funeral once, was really special.

As I got older, the sermons began to reinforce my value system about right and wrong. Looking your best at church reinforced these lessons. There we would see our neighbors, our relatives, and people from around town. I was acutely aware that each of us represented the Roberts family, and we were taught that it was important to do that with good manners, pride and appropriate behavior.

Church was also a very social place, where news and gossip were exchanged. Overhearing how information about people — whether good or bad — passed so quickly from lips to ears, taught me that it was best to avoid being the subject of such chatter, especially if the reports were negative. I viewed dressing well and behaving in a polite, respectable manner as the best way to keep my name off the gossip grapevine.

"Roy always wanted to dress nicely," Joyce remembers. "He would find a way to make things happen for himself. If he wanted to wear that certain thing, even if it was someone else's, he had a way of making you see that it was beneficial to you, to let him wear your things."

1948 – A Rough Year For Turner Roberts

My father's "dancing eyes" for other women prompted our step-mother to move — six years into the marriage — with her three children back to Arkansas. I was nine years old, and their departure left just me, Bob, Gene and Papa. Subsequently, my father never invited dates or girlfriends into our home or around the family.

Being in a small, all-black community, kids saw and heard everything. As a result, the neighborhood became my classroom on life, and it was as important as everything I was learning at school. For as long as I can remember, my natural curiosity and keen observation have enabled me to study my surroundings, learn how people behave, and model myself accordingly. Of course, I saw plenty of examples of how *not* to conduct myself.

All the black people were sequestered in a few areas, so the pimps, the prostitutes, and the hustlers lived amongst the everyday working folks, most of whom were factory workers. The few black professionals in our community included one black physician and one black pharmacist. African American businessmen or businesswomen were nonexistent.

It was fascinating to watch individuals develop a hustle to survive and thrive in a world that offered few opportunities for advancement. I saw men abuse women, and women who behaved irresponsibly. I watched people cheat and gamble. These observations taught

15

me "street smarts" and lessons on human nature that would prove invaluable later in life.

Meanwhile, my father's life was also providing many lessons about the world. Papa became known as "MacArthur," like the U.S. Army General Douglas MacArthur, who was credited with helping the Allied Forces bring a triumphant end to World War II. My father earned this nicknamed because during cold weather, he wore a big, Army overcoat. It was dark green, and reinforced his reputation as a big, tough man who disliked taking orders from others.

At the time, he was working at the Campbell, Wyant and Cannon Foundry. In 1948, the company suffered a big strike, and all ten thousand workers were laid off. Back then, a man would rather feed his family by taking government assistance, than by crossing a picket line to keep his job.

"People didn't cross a picket line," Bob remembers, "unless you wanted to get your head busted. Then, if a strike ended and the employees came back, they refused to work alongside the 'scab' workers, so the company had to fire them."

The strike ended about six months later, and Papa went back to work. But six moths after that, he was laid off, and went to work at Continental Motors, which manufactured military products. Clean and located on a hill, Continental was considered by the black community as a good place to work.

"Nigger!" shouted a white male co-worker as he kicked my father in the behind.

Papa picked up a piece of steel and struck the man repeatedly, nearly killing him. My father had stood up for his principles, but it cost him. He was blackballed. Factories around Muskegon would not hire him for quite some time.

Food, Fun and Fights

As a boy, one of my favorite foods was the cheese that we received in our monthly package of milk, bread, butter and other groceries through the welfare program. That cheese was delicious! The only

16

way to improve it was to eat it with Spam.

The craving for that combination would send us kids on a mission! A group of us would walk through the woods to Miss Ann's all-purpose grocery store. There, we'd buy something small, like a pack of gum. At the same time, we'd steal a can of the processed, ham-like meat. Then we'd hurry back to the house and devour slices of Spam and cheese. Boy, that was a great day for us!

Those were joyous times in Muskegon Heights.

Other times, however, when the monthly food ration ran out, and Papa had no money, we scrounged food in the same place as many other families: the garbage dump. Every day, trucks would transport discarded food from stores and restaurants to a particular spot at the dump.

I distinctly remember a few times when we retrieved food there, then ate it at home.

When our father had money to buy food, he'd show off his excellent cooking skills. Papa made delicious chili with beef and beans, melt-in-your-mouth corn bread, and outstanding pork chops with gravy.

Unfortunately, our portions were always limited. That sparked fierce competition at the dinner table. When Dad fried a chicken, Bob, Gene and I would battle for our favorite pieces. If they grabbed the last thigh — my favorite — I would almost cry. Other times, when Gene and I were in school and Bob was working, the first person to arrive at home had the best pick of the food. Sometimes, if Papa had prepared beans and rice, and everyone ate before me, they might leave a small portion that would be my meal for the night.

We had food, clothing and shelter, but little more. My father never owned a car. We did not have a television. Back then, televisions were black and white, and the screens were in big, boxy, wooden consoles. Only about five percent of American households had a television, and programming was limited.

An exciting occasion for me, my brothers and friends, occurred when World Heavyweight Boxing Champion Joe Louis would fight for the title that he held from 1937 until 1949. We would all gather to witness his historic, global domination in the boxing ring at the one house in the neighborhood that had a television. The small, black-owned store in our community also allowed us to line up and enjoy "the TV room" — if we purchased something first.

Other times, Gene and I would stand outside a neighbor's window and listen to radio broadcasts of "The Brown Bomber" as he pummeled his opponents. Meanwhile, we received most of our news via word-of-mouth, radios, newspapers and magazines.

When Papa's income was sporadic, I don't remember receiving gifts on my birthday or on Christmas morning. Once, I received a play pistol, and that was a big deal. Likewise, when it came to clothes, we did our best with what we had. Holes in my loafers or tie-up shoes were repaired by inserting just enough cardboard to cover the exposed area. When the cardboard wore out after a day or two, I replaced it. I did this until Papa was able to buy me new shoes.

As I entered my adolescent years, our father's lack of steady income pushed us into an extremely unstable and difficult period. Forced to leave the projects, we moved frequently and changed schools each time. Leaving our friends in Muskegon Heights and suffering white children's taunts in new schools was horrific. For that reason, I cannot remember a single, enduring friendship from that stretch of my life.

However, this blessed me with an important character trait: adaptability. I became adept at observing my environment, then adjusting and conforming in ways that would enable me to thrive and get along with everyone. When I was twelve years old and our father was having a particularly difficult time, my sister Retha took me, Bob and Gene to live with her.

Here, it's important to note the hierarchy in Muskegon's black community. The Heights, where most African Americans lived, were tough. Those who had somewhat "arrived," lived downtown, though this was purely perception because the socioeconomic status of blacks downtown was equally poor. As for North Muskegon where Retha lived, that growing area was considered "country" and even "hick." For us boys, this move was viewed as a major downgrade from the Heights.

Retha was doing quite well as a hospital worker. She and her husband had two daughters, Shirley and Betty, and one son, Ray, who was two months younger than me. They were building a house, which was half-finished. The lower level was complete, but they were still working on the upstairs, so it was closed off.

During the year that we lived with Retha and her family, we attended Reeths-Puffer Middle School in Muskegon. One day, I passed a Boy Scouts of America meeting in a classroom. I peered in, admiring the fifteen boys' crisp uniforms adorned with badges and medals.

I want to be part of whatever is going on in there, I thought. But I was immediately overwhelmed by discouragement. *We could never afford that. So I won't even ask for something that I can't have.* I quickly stepped away, aching with a deep yearning to join the Boy Scouts of America.

THREE

A Teenager Explores the Larger World

When I was thirteen, Papa began making more money when he resumed steady work at the Campbell, Wyant and Cannon Foundry. That job enabled him to rent a one-bedroom apartment over General Plumbing and Hardware at 506 Ottawa Street in downtown Muskegon. Ours was one of five small units accessible by a door and stairwell next to the hardware store entrance. The building, which included the store and apartments, was owned by Mr. Harold, a terrific guy who had a wife and two sons. They attended private school and doted on me.

Meanwhile, people in the Heights regarded our move as a step up, because we no longer occupied government housing, and downtown was perceived as more prestigious. In reality, the place was quite stark. With a beige, lackluster decor, its single, all-purpose room had with a small partition that separated two, full-size beds from a sink, a stove and a table. The bathroom and closets were outside the apartment, across a hallway that led to other units.

As was true throughout my childhood, I never had my own bed, nor did my brothers. Instead, I shared a bed with one brother, while another brother occupied a bed with our father. All the while, each of us learned how to wash and iron clothes, clean and cook.

After school, if I came home and Papa wasn't there, I could prepare a meal. In the morning, I rarely ate breakfast.

When I left for school, it was a good day if I had a little money in my pocket to buy lunch. To say Papa valued a dollar would be an understatement. If you asked him for money, and he actually agreed to give you some, he would hold out a dollar. He'd grasp it hard, staring at it. If you reached out to take it, he would turn his head away, to avoid watching the dollar being taken from his grip.

Working Hard to Avoid Looking Poor

As a teenager, I was extremely conscious of my appearance, my family's lowly status, and the image I was projecting to the world. This was especially important when I attended Angell Junior High School. I wanted to have a positive experience at this new, predominantly white school. Unlike the old neighborhood in Muskegon Heights where everyone was poor and our poverty was no secret, I saw attending Angell as an opportunity to present myself as a studious, well-dressed person worthy of respect.

My teachers were excellent, and the school was clean and orderly. Always observing and studying how people behaved and dressed, I was eager to learn and have fun.

My greatest worry as a ninth grader was for my brother, Bob, who had enlisted in the Korean War as an Army Ranger paratrooper. That was the equivalent of the Navy Seals; Army Rangers were the toughest of the tough, handling some of the most dangerous assignments.

My teachers initiated frequent classroom discussions about the war and why it mattered. At the time, I lacked understanding about the global and national implications of war. My only concern was that my brother would come home alive and in good health. I gleaned understanding about how wars started, who paid for them, and who profited from them. I came to understand that old men make the war, young men fight it, and millionaires double. I also concluded that nations didn't necessarily make peace by making war, and that intelligent conversations were a more logical, effective and human way to resolve global conflicts.

Thankfully, Bob returned home when the war ended in July of 1953. I've never given anyone a bigger hug than when I first saw him after his long absence for training and service.

Sports Boost My Courage, Confidence and Competitive Spirit

Sports played a starring role in my development as a young teenager, both at school and in the neighborhood. I was fortunate that Angell Junior High was one of four public schools across Muskegon that participated in the Junior High Athletic League. Our school excelled in the conference, with the greatest rivalries against Central Junior High School and Bunker Junior High School.

I fell in love with sports, especially football. Though I was small, I was really fast, and began to play running back. The big, tough guy who played tackle, George Lindsey Lake, became one of my best friends for life. All the while, my growing circle of friends included many athletes. Brothers Oscar and Lester German were great athletes and good friends who remain so today. Dave Brooks and his brother, Otis, would both become Golden Gloves boxing champions in Michigan.

Despite his boxing skills that took him to national championships, Otis was known for mischief that kept us entertained. Once, he entered a neighborhood store, wearing a jacket with the goal of stealing a pint of ice cream. He shoved it under his arm, but as he creeped past the cashier, it got so cold, he dropped it.

"Who threw that ice cream at me?" he shouted.

The cashier, wise to his ploy, laughed and said playfully, "Go put that away!"

Otis was always pulling stunts that kept us rolling with laughter.

Meanwhile, when we weren't playing sports at school, African American boys of all ages and skill levels competed at Green Acres

Park in Muskegon. This was where relationships and reputations were built. The courts and fields were our proving ground, where we were challenged to "man up." Failing to do so would jeopardize a boy's all-important standing in the neighborhood. As a result, Green Acres became a battlefield of wills, where boys competed and developed their "armor" to wear into a victorious manhood.

The park's run-down, dreary condition accentuated this harsh, character-honing atmosphere. The basketball court was not cement; it was hard dirt. The baseball diamond had some semblance of bases and a home plate. A large expanse of grass enabled us to play football. But we avoided the "water" flowing through the park. We called it Stink Creek, for its bad odor that everyone believed came from toxic chemicals dumped by factories.

When we were playing basketball, we selected teams and played in rotations. The best two players — who were well-known by all the guys — would select their teams, with five players on each team. Getting selected announced that you were a good player. I was always anxious about whether I would get chosen because I was small. In basketball, people usually equate height with skill. Importantly, I was always selected. That always made me feel good, and I would try harder. My younger brother Gene was always chosen as well; quite often, we'd be on opposite teams.

When we played baseball, I rated myself as an average player. Some people thought I was better than that. They wanted me to pitch, but I was not a good pitcher. I preferred to play shortstop. Regardless of the game, playing sports was a catalyst for toughening up.

"Get your little ass out of the way before I run you over," someone might say to me.

My response: "If you think you're big and tough enough, just try it, dammit."

That would spark a face-off or a fight, with the high drama of rolling on the ground. If someone said, "I give," the duel was over.

At this age, I never backed down from a fight. It was imperative to defend your honor, or your mother's or your family's, depending on what insult had caused the fight. The competitive atmosphere at

Green Acres included "playing the dozens" — lobbing insults back and forth until someone failed to retort. The mental rigor of "the dozens," always with your honor at stake, honed our ability to be quick-witted *and* fast on our feet.

Some of us were faster than others. Once, I got into a fight with Oscar German, who became one of the Michigan's best Golden Glove boxers a few years later. He was so fast, I think he hit me three times before I realized what was happening.

Another way to provoke a fight was for a small guy like me to score against a big guy. I learned I could best preserve my personal safety by mastering a jump shot, as opposed to driving to the basket, embarrassing the big guy, and having hell to pay later. Little did I know, this challenging environment was boosting my courage and confidence, while training me to relish competition.

As a result, I couldn't get enough of sports. We finally had a radio at home, and Gene and I would lie in bed listening to hockey matches. We had never seen a hockey game, and we didn't know the rules or regulations. We just loved to listen because hockey was such an aggressive sport, with players attacking each other. After the match, Gene and I would discuss sports in the context of the larger world. We'd draw parallels between hockey, football and basketball.

"There are no black hockey players," I remarked.

"It's too expensive," Gene said. "All that equipment costs an arm and a leg. And when's the last time you saw an ice rink in the black neighborhood?"

I chuckled. "Blacks usually play team sports that are cheap to play, like basketball."

"Hey," Gene said, "get me 22 guys and we can use a can as the football, and we've got a game! Easy as that."

Maureen Robinson Inspires Love at First Sight

One day, my friend Bobby Tates took me to meet a girl that he liked. We went to her house, and when Maureen Robinson greeted us on the porch, I was absolutely smitten.

Pretty and poised, she was the most sophisticated, studious and respectable girl I'd ever met. Slim and shapely, wearing a crisply pressed white blouse and pleated skirt, she carried herself in a way that announced that she was not impressed by the bevy of boys vying for her attention. A semester older than us, she attended Central Junior High School in Muskegon.

"I'm going to graduate from high school, attend college and have a career of my own," Maureen declared as we sat on her big front porch. With a creamy, caramel-hued complexion and large, attentive eyes, all framed by a mane of thick, black hair, her beauty mesmerized me.

Even more importantly, however, was that Maureen was by far the classiest girl I'd ever met. Her family, headed by her Native American grandfather, instilled her with excellent values and a strong, independent work ethic. Her father worked in the foundry, and her mother occasionally performed day work for well-to-do white families in town.

Though they did not have a lot of money, Maureen's clothes were clean and proper. She attended church, but she was not preachy or holier-than-thou. Her demeanor declared that she was not one to follow the crowd or engage in certain behaviors to gain others' approval. She was marching to her own tune, and I couldn't have been more awed.

I liked that Maureen and I shared Southern roots; she was born in tiny Philadelphia, Mississippi, which was settled by Choctaw Indians. Maureen was very quiet, almost introverted, but I loved that she only spoke when she had something relevant to say.

"Roy was very attentive, even at that age," Maureen recalls. "All of my girlfriends liked Roy. Maybe not romantically, but just as friends, because Roy always made you feel like you were special. He'd ask, 'How do you feel?' Or he'd say, 'You look nice' or 'That's a pretty dress.' He talked a lot, and he said things that impressed young girls when they're thirteen."

It turned out that Maureen knew Bobby Tates because her family had also lived in the projects. As a result, she'd met some of my sisters and brothers before her grandfather purchased their house across town.

26

At the time, I did not reveal my romantic feelings.

"Bobby may have had a crush on me," Maureen says, "but I didn't have one on him. I was naïve. I thought Roy was nice, and he dressed well, but I wasn't looking for a boyfriend. I wanted to focus on school."

I was so excited the first time I met Maureen at the NK Theater in Muskegon. We considered this "our" movie theatre, where black teenagers felt comfortable and welcome. Everyone knew a lot of kids gathered there, so no one spoiled the fun by telling us to be quiet. Less frequently, we would go to The State Theater, and rarely, The Michigan Theater. Every Sunday, groups of girls walked to the theater to meet boys. It was 15 cents to enter. Another dime would buy popcorn.

"Roy and I would sit together, either in the upper balcony or on the first floor," Maureen recalls. "It was very innocent, with no hugging or kissing. In our generation, kids were more naïve. It seemed like there was always someone watching you, and they could go back and tell your mother. That kept you from doing things you weren't supposed to do. Roy and I would also see each other at dances on Saturdays. We listened to a lot of blues, and dance music and be-bop songs that were popular at the time." The biggest hits of 1953 included: a Nat King Cole song called *Pretend*; *Please Love Me* by B.B. King; *Mess Around* by Ray Charles; *You're the One* by the Spiders; *Hound Dog* by Willie Mae "Big Mama" Thornton; and The Drifters' hit, *Money Honey*.

Roy Becomes a Working Man at Age 14

When I turned fourteen, I wanted new clothes, food, and cash to go to the movies. Papa had no extra money to give me. In our community, nothing was given. You had to go out and get what you wanted.

So during the summer of 1953, I went to the bus terminal downtown Muskegon. That was the bustling hub for all buses that entered the city, dropped off and picked up passengers, then dispersed on routes around town. I had heard that the man who owned the shoeshine stand was hiring, so I asked him for a job. He hired me and I began working immediately. Even as a kid, I was aware of the subservient nature of this job. The fellow who's having his shoes shined sits on chair on the elevated shoeshine stand — above the man who's hunched over his feet, vigorously working to make the customer look his best.

That I was black, and the man above me was usually white, symbolized the subordinate position where African American men were generally relegated on every level of society. As a youngster, I didn't find shining shoes as demeaning as if I were grown, but I wanted better. I didn't know how, or when, but deep in my heart I knew that someday, with hard work and determination, I would be in a dominant position to benefit myself, and to help others rise with me.

This realization, along with my innate curiosity and keen observation of the larger world around me, helped me experience that bus station as a microcosm of the world. I began to see the bleakness of my reality. I wanted more than anything to escape it. I believed that if I kept my head down and worked hard, I could attract good fortune and opportunities.

The common thread of my early work experience was that the world offered no gifts to a black boy from the lowest rungs of the socio-economic ladder. Yet at the same time, I received invaluable gifts of knowledge, motivation and determination. Sometimes those gifts came in the form of making a mistake, taking constructive criticism, and learning how to become better.

If I felt any bitterness about my lot in life, I didn't dwell on it. Instead, I focused on the sweet fact that I was earning money as a reward for my hard work. I remember saving $40 for a new, blue bicycle. The day I purchased it, I rode to Green Acres Park to show my friends. I was so proud and excited, I came speeding down a hill, hit a bump, and flew head over heels in front of everybody. Skinned knees and elbows notwithstanding, I was terribly embarrassed, but I played it off so nobody could see my hurt.

My next job was at a company that rented trailers. My responsibility was to connect the trailers to cars. It required a meticulous touch because many recent, fatal car accidents had been blamed on cars pulling trailers that were not properly secured. After three weeks on that job, my boss refused to pay me, so my father confronted him.

"You're going to pay him," Papa threatened, "and you're going to pay him today. Or I'm going to call the police right now."

The man paid me that day, but fired me two weeks later.

Another job involved helping Mr. Harold, who owned the hardware store and our apartment, to build the swimming pool behind his beautiful home. That broadened my horizons to see new possibilities for how I wanted to live one day.

Henry "Sticks" Green, M.D. — Role Model Extraordinaire

One job that had a profound impact on my life was washing cars. At age fourteen, I began washing cars at a service station on Western Avenue across from Seattle Hall in Muskegon. I washed Studebakers, Ford Crestliners, Dodge Meadowbrooks, Coronets and Royals, and Chevrolet 150 Specials, Delrays and 210 DeLuxes.

Amidst the soap and spray hoses, I encountered one of the most powerful role models of my young life: Henry "Sticks" Green, M.D. He was the most impressive African American man I had ever seen. Tall, handsome and impeccably dressed in tailored suits, he was a physician. The consummate bachelor, he carried himself in a way that was classy and cool, and he always had a beautiful woman at his side.

Even better: he bought one of the first Ford Thunderbirds in 1955, and I had the privilege of washing it. I marveled at this car. Someday, somehow, I vowed, I would own this same vehicle. Two years later, I was equally awed when Sticks Green pulled into the car wash with his new, 1957 convertible Ford Thunderbird.

I had seen Dr. Green around the black neighborhoods, because he liked to socialize and gamble with people in the streets. Though no one else was in his class educationally or financially, he was a man of the community. Though we had no relationship other than saying "Hi" when he came to the car wash, Sticks Green made a life-long impression on me as a great motivator, because he was the most extraordinary example of black success that the world of Muskegon, Michigan in the 1950s offered to young Roy Roberts.

At the time, Sticks Green was everything I could ever imagine being: accomplished, educated, wealthy, desirable, classy, sophisticated, and the best-dressed man in town. I quietly made up my mind right then: *If I ever get any money, I want to be just like Sticks Green.*

FOUR

Racism and Sports Offer Life Lessons

If I had to summarize my three years at Muskegon Senior High School, and the two summers in-between, I would offer two words: "Treasure trove." That period was difficult, but it laid a solid gold foundation for my personal development. My high school years polished me from a diamond in the rough into a person who could shine in any situation. And, just as the pressure of the earth literally squeezes rock into diamonds, the pressures on a black male teenager between 1955 and 1958 deposited gems of wisdom into my young mind.

It all started on the first day of school. I was dressed to impress. As one of only five blacks who would ultimately graduate with our class of 550 students, it was extremely important to project my best appearance and behavior. As I walked through the front doors with my best buddy, George Lake, we were eager to shine on the football field, playing for the legendary, Class A Big Reds.

"Man, I hope the coaches aren't as bad as everybody says," George said as we navigated the hallways. "How do we stand a chance when the athletic director is so racist, he won't let blacks on the starting line?"

I shook my head, remembering how guys at Green Acres Park had filled our heads with ominous warnings that Muskegon Senior

High School Athletic Director Harry Potter was reputedly so racist, that star athletes would actually move back to Muskegon Heights so they could play on the starting line for their high school football team. For many African Americans, earning a football scholarship to college was their only hope of furthering their education and sprinting toward a dream of playing professional ball in the NFL someday.

"Maybe things will be different for us," I said, fearful that a little guy like myself — at just 5'7" and 150 pounds — would be banned from the team altogether.

"Good luck, Roy," George said. "I'll see you at lunchtime."

"Later," I said, as we headed to our first classes. There, I had the good fortune of being seated alphabetically, behind blond-haired, blue-eyed Linda Roberts. Slightly taller than me, she was attractive, quiet and serious. She liked me, and I liked her.

But during the 1950s, interracial dating was taboo, so we would secretly meet in my brother Bob's car, or in one of her father's automobiles. Other times, I would visit Linda's home by foot, passing stately homes near Lake Michigan. Her family was wealthy; her father, Frank Roberts, was president of S.D. Warren Paper Mill Company, one of the biggest employers in town. While her parents were away, Linda would invite me into her family's mansion. I dreamed of living in such a grand home, earning an impressive education, owning many cars and taking trips to Europe as she did with her family.

One morning during my junior year, I was sitting in class when the public address system clicked on and the school secretary announced:

"Roy Roberts, report to the principal's office immediately."

My gut cramped with apprehension as I hurried through the halls. The office had an outer reception area; Linda was sitting there, bawling. My heart pounded with panic.

Oh shit! I thought. *I am in big trouble!*

It looked like I was stepping into one of the worst moments of my life. I didn't know what was wrong, but I knew it was bad. I remembered Papa's warning that a black male had only one strike.

Was I about to use mine up and be struck out of the game of life for good? The secretary took me into the office, where the principal awaited with Athletic Director Harry Potter and a big, tall white man — Linda's father! His face was stern as he sized me up.

"Are you Roy Roberts?" he demanded.

"Yes," I said as firmly as possible despite my wobbly knees.

"Son," the man said, "let me tell you something. Don't you ever let anybody tell you who your friends are." He shot a dead-serious look down at me. Then he was silent.

"Is that it?" I asked.

"Yes," he answered.

I left the room. That bad feeling still clenched my stomach, but I was perplexed about what it all meant. I later learned that the football coach had called Linda's father to report that she was dating a black guy.

As for what Mr. Roberts had said, I didn't decipher the power of that teachable moment until many years later. Linda's father had very cleverly used reverse psychology to stifle the natural human craving for forbidden fruit. If he had ordered me to never see his daughter again, that would have driven us closer together. But as most high school romances do, this one ran its course — with a little help from my good friend, unbeknownst to me.

"Roy, you shouldn't be going with Linda," warned Thurman Brown. "That white girl is gonna get you in trouble."

I quit Linda. And he married her! After graduation, they moved to California.

Maureen Holds a Special Place in My Heart

When I saw Maureen Robinson on my first day at Muskegon Senior High School, I was head over heels in love once again. In fact, my very first high school date was with Maureen at the NK Theater. She was the classiest girl in town. Negative words about others never passed over her lips, and she had an unshakable moral compass that could not be swayed by smooth-talking boys. When she wasn't studying, she worked part-time in a drug store. During her junior year, she played clarinet in the band. Our classmates respected Maureen, and I was her number one admirer.

"All of the black kids sat at one lunch table," Maureen remembers. "There was not a lot of mixing. In class, you did feel out of sorts because you'd be the only one. You were self-conscious, but they were nice to you in class. I don't remember any hostility."

As a result, being one of only a few fostered close bonds with the other black students. Janet Tony was a dear friend; I knew her family from the neighborhood. Back in junior high, she'd been the only black cheerleader at her school when we competed against their team in football. Likewise, she was the first to integrate the cheer team at Muskegon Senior High. Perky with a nice shape and short hair, Janet stood about 5'2". Her magnetic personality earned our classmates' adoration.

My friendship with her exemplifies how I have always gravitated to positive people. I have an innate aversion to negative people; they are an absolute drain on my being. As a result, I avoided classmates who bemoaned academics, and I disregarded those who complained about what "the man" had done to us.

I have always believed that there's more opportunity ahead of me than behind me, so I was not going to waste my time on history. I wanted to understand it, and avoid pitfalls. Likewise, I wanted to surround myself with individuals who would lift me up, not drag me down.

Thurman Brown was one of my best friends, and the wealthiest African American teenager I had ever met. His father owned real estate, as well as a nightclub, and that afforded Thurman the opportunity to flaunt the best clothes and a brand-new Buick. In contrast, my second most well-to-do black friend was Bob Flowers. His parents had good factory jobs, but he never flaunted the middle class trappings provided by their relative affluence.

Meanwhile, George Lake and I developed an unbreakable bond, fortified by our mutual passion for football. Big, strong George was elevated to the varsity football team as a tenth grader, while I remained on the junior varsity team. Many days after practicing on the hard, clay field, I would walk home with George. Since we passed his house first — where he lived with his mother and his brother, Robert "R.L." Lake — they would invite me in for dinner. George's appetite was as big as he was. He could eat half a skillet of corn bread and leave me a small slice. His mother was a great cook, and we shared a lot of wonderful times around their table.

Football Teaches Life Lessons on the Gridiron

High school sports taught me teamwork and further developed my competitive spirit, because I was forced to toughen up and prove that I was worthy to compete. When I first arrived at Muskegon Senior High School, my small build made the coaches question whether I would play at all.

"If Roberts can't play," George Lake said, "I'm not playing."

Since George was all-state material, his influence enabled me to join the team. One day during a practice scrimmage, I was goofing around with the guys. One of the coaches, former Detroit Lions player Joe Garlonni, said, "Roberts are you gonna play football or are you just gonna piss around?"

"Well I'm playin'," I answered.

"Get down here," Coach Garlonni ordered, getting on all fours. "We're gonna play football! I'm gonna show you how to block. Get down here!"

I faced him on my hands and knees.

"One, two, three, hike!" he shouted. His right forearm smashed into my jaw! The impact rattled my head. Blood dripped from the left side of my mouth.

"Now get down," Coach Garlonni commanded. "I want to show you how to block."

I followed his instructions.

"One, two, three, hike!" he yelled. His left arm rammed into the other side of my head. Dizzy and stunned by searing pain, I struggled to get my bearings.

"Now get your butt in there and play defensive halfback," the coach ordered.

Something miraculous happened as I walked to the backfield. I told myself, "The next person that comes through the line, they're going to have to hurt me, or I'm going to have to hurt them. They'll either kill me, or I'm going to kill them."

Sure enough, a guy came at me, and I tackled him! I mean, I really hurt him. He was removed from practice due to bruised ribs. From that day forward, I made up my mind about how I would play football, and how I would approach every challenge in life:

I'm going to compete, and you're going to have to take me out to beat me at anything that I do in life.

My intention was not to hurt anyone. Instead, my goal was to compete — physically and intellectually — to demonstrate all that Roy S. Roberts could be in the world. This has been my *modus operandi* since that fateful day nearly six decades ago.

After that defining moment, my game improved significantly. In 1957, I became the first African American to start in the backfield for Muskegon Senior High School, which played in the Class A Division. For some reason, Harry Potter took a liking to me, and gave me a chance to shine, thus beginning to erode his reputation for never allowing African American players to succeed.

I proudly wore my red-and-white Big Reds uniform, emblazoned with "50" on the back. That was usually a linebacker's number, but I chose it after seeing it on a star player in the National Football League.

Our team was big-time, playing tough teams from schools in Pontiac and Lansing. My brother Bob attended my games, overjoyed that I was starting for Muskegon Senior High. My father never attended. In fact, I don't recall him ever voicing an opinion about my participation in sports (I also ran track). Back then, it was not customary for black families to travel to away games, due to the expense of gas and demands of work schedules.

One of my most memorable games occurred when we played Flint Northern High School. Our whole school was geeked up because we were playing the Vikings, ranked as Michigan's top Class

A team. Their star player, Jim Sharp, was an outstanding runner. Before the game began, whispers spread through the crowd in Atwood Stadium that I was a decent player. It would be tough competition, because we were the state's number three-ranked team.

Once the game began, I had a lot of success running the ball in the first half. It was looking like a game the Big Reds could win. In the second half, I took the kickoff, and ran it back a pretty long way. But I did not score a touchdown.

Instead, a bunch of big guys tackled me — and broke my arm! While I was being transported to Hurley Hospital, where I would stay four days, our team lost the game by one point.

Well after my arm healed, and I turned eighteen, I went to the Muskegon Post Office to register for the Draft. I flexed my arm and told the woman taking my registration:

"This arm was broken about eighteen months ago. I should be classified as 4F." That classification would rank me as "Not Qualified for Military Service due to medical reasons."

"Do that again," the woman ordered. "Let me see." I flexed my arms up. She laughed. "That's perfect for digging ditches! Young man, I've seen it all. You are fit to serve."

Roy Roberts: Best Dressed and Most Friendly

Performing on stage as part of our school's Thespian Group enhanced my ability to hone my character as a well-behaved, well-dressed person who wanted to rise above my circumstances and become someone great. In fact, I conveyed such a convincing image of success, that most of my classmates never knew that I was probably the poorest student among the 500-plus graduating seniors who voted me "Most Friendly" and "Best Dressed!"

My people skills were self-taught. No one ever taught me manners and etiquette. Instead, I drew upon all the lessons I had learned on proper behavior from my family and neighbors as a kid. I discerned negative behaviors such as: a grumpy demeanor; a negative, complaining and critical spirit; and bad or gruff manners.

My "best dressed" status was thanks to my brother Bob, who returned from the Korean War and worked at the West Michigan Steel Foundry. He would often take me and Gene shopping, buying us each two or three shirts and shoes. This helped me achieve "best dressed" status. Since Gene and I were close in size, I'd talk Gene into his suit choices, while I'd get my first choices. Then I'd wear his other choices to school first — brand new before he even wore them! Bob's clothes didn't fit me, but his shoes did, and I would wear them to go dancing with my friends.

Meanwhile, I kept my wardrobe in good repair. I washed and ironed my own clothes, making sure that my button-down shirts were crisp, my dress pants were sharply pleated, my sweaters were smooth, and my loafers or lace-up shoes were shined. When I wore a sport coat, it matched to a tee and hung just right. My hair was neatly groomed and my fingernails were clean. It helped that during my senior year, I worked in Vet's Men's Clothing Store, where I could purchase clothes at a discount. I later became a fashion model.

"Roberts, You're Not Going to Make It!"

My biology teacher, Mr. Troutman, was like all of my teachers at Muskegon Senior High School: excellent. They were passionate about teaching, and committed to nurturing our young minds.

"Everything we've learned in biology this year will culminate in dissecting frogs today," Mr. Troutman said, standing in front of the class with a dead frog.

"First," our teacher said, pinning the frog's legs to a board, "you secure the frog." He picked up a scalpel. "Then, you cut it across the chest and down the center." The class watched attentively.

"Then," Mr. Troutman said, pulling back the quarters of skin and piercing each one with a metal pin, "you secure the skin to the board to expose the organs."

He sent us to the lab tables, where I confidently got to work. Somehow, my scalpel found its way to the frog's throat — and I cut off its head!

"Roberts," Mr. Troutman said, examining my mutilated frog, "you're not going to make it."

Earlier in the year, when we'd studied the one-celled organism called an amoeba, our assignment was to draw one.

"Roberts, is that your picture of an amoeba?" Mr. Troutman asked incredulously. "The shape of an amoeba is free-formed, and you can't be wrong. But yours is wrong!"

I survived his class with a B, consistent with my 3.0 grade point average at graduation, which was higher than my four African American classmates.

However, no one recommended that I attend college. Back then, blacks took unspoken messages from the mainstream that told us where we were — and were *not* — welcome. The Michigan Theatre epitomized that. The cold stares and chilly reception that we had received declared that blacks were not welcome. No WHITES ONLY signs were posted, but that feeling was palpable, so we stayed away.

This unspoken communication manifest in the void of encouragement that I received from my teachers and guidance counselors about attending college and pursuing a career. By saying nothing, they were saying: *"College is not for you. A professional career is not in your future."*

"You're Going to be Somebody"

One frigid, snowy morning during my junior year, I felt frustrated that our poverty made it such a struggle to dress well and fit in with my affluent schoolmates.

"Papa, I really want that new sport coat for school," I snapped. "I have to look nice—"

"I don't have the money for that, son, so you'd better just make do with the clothes you have."

"I really want that jacket!"

"Roy, I can't afford that jacket, and that's that."

"Then I'm not going to school! I'll quit!"

My father's expression announced that I had roused the wrath of Turner Roberts.

"You're going to go to school," he said, sharpening his eyes. "We're not going to debate that." Then he said with a commanding tone befitting his nickname, "MacArthur": "You're going to get a good education. You're going to be somebody. And you're going to help other people."

"Yes, sir." My cheeks stung as if he'd smacked me. He deserved my respect, and he could whup my behind if he so desired. I promptly found an outfit and hurried to school.

What had he meant that I would "be somebody?" The most prominent black men in America included a lawyer named Thurgood Marshall, who represented the 1954 Supreme Court decision *Brown v. the Board of Education of Topeka, Kansas*. I'd read news reports about a preacher from Atlanta named Dr. Martin Luther King, Jr.. who was leading protests in the South. He was working alongside Rosa Parks, who just two years before had refused to give up her seat to a white passenger on a bus in Alabama. But the Civil Rights Movement seemed far away from Muskegon, Michigan.

That morning, I needed to get to class, looking my best in clothes that I already owned.

Fast, Fun and Fearless

My friends and I were typical teenaged hell-raisers. We never wanted to hurt anyone; we just wanted to have fun. One night, Bob Flowers was driving us home from skating in Grand Rapids. He was racing down the highway at one hundred miles per hour!

As we approached Muskegon, a County Sheriff's deputy got on our trail. The blaring siren and flashing lights curtailed our playful mood. Bob pulled into a corner gas station. I assumed he was going to cut through it to dodge the police. But suddenly Bob stopped. The squad car pulled up behind us. Bob jumped out and hurried toward them.

"Sir!" he told the police officer approaching our car. "I'm so glad you're here! Those guys chased us all the way from Grand Rapids. They said they were going to kill us!"

I watched Bob's convincing performance in disbelief. How in the world had he thought up a lie that fast? And what gall, to lie to the police!

"Son," the sheriff's deputy said, "if you're lying, you got a problem."

"I'm not, sir."

"Then I want you to come down to the station and press charges, or else," the officer said. Somehow, we finagled out of the situation, and all that became of it was a funny memory.

Summer Work and Play in Idlewild

I knew I had stepped into some kind of paradise during the summer of 1956, when my friend Bobby Tates first drove me to Idlewild. Our official duty in this black resort town, located ninety minutes north of Muskegon, was to help his father build the Sweetheart Motel. I had taken an architectural design class in school, and had drawn the floor plan for the one-story, cement block structure that would become a popular destination for newlyweds and couples.

Each day, Bobby and I worked hard to dig the motel's foundation on a wooded lot facing the blue lake that sparkled under the sun. After work, it was time to play, and we couldn't have been in a better place for that.

Idlewild felt like a hedonistic oasis, far from the rest of the world. Thousands of people and nearly as many cars would pack "the island," which was a strip of land between two lakes. This was the hotspot, where, nightclubs, the beach and the roller-skating rink were absolutely electrified with African Americans in all their finery.

Fancy clothes, flashy cars and the hottest performers made the Paradise Club and the Flamingo Club glamorously reminiscent of

The Cotton Club in Harlem. During the day, the beach pulsed with people while boats zigzagged the lake. I had never seen so many black folks in one spot in my life. Everyone was laughing and loving, styling and profiling.

At the time, during segregation, blacks were barred from mainstream vacation destinations. That created an indescribably joyful feeling in Idlewild, where black people enjoyed the common bond of enjoying life and love in a sanctuary free from the oppressive reality of mainstream society. Blacks from across the United States flocked to this lakeside town to enjoy lakes and forestland that were so pristine and beautiful that the area became known as "Black Eden."

Joy and love electrified the air, and it was customary for folks in Idlewild to open their homes and kitchens to complete strangers. In fact, Bobby and I stayed in a cottage owned by his family's friends. Many of the cottages were built by African American men who made good livings on the assembly lines of Ford, Chrysler and General Motors. They purchased cheap land and constructed cottages that symbolized the Black American Dream that would be cherished by future generations.

Linking the cottages through the woods were dirt roads with names such as Joy Boulevard, Miracle Drive and Wealthy Road. On these tree-lined roads, Bobby taught me how to drive his black, 1936 Chevrolet. It was old-looking, but ran pretty nicely. Somehow through trial and error, I mastered how to use the stick shift, change gears and maneuver the vehicle.

Knowing how to drive made me feel mature and grown-up, and that boosted my confidence as we hit the hotspot for teenagers in Idlewild: the roller-skating rink. Amongst folks from places like Chicago, Detroit and Saint Louis, I flaunted my best skating moves like never before! I loved to team up and do fancy moves with Delores Smith, whose father owned the skating rink. I did well in the contests, but the all-time best guy was a lanky dude from Flint, who did some fabulous maneuvers on wheels. Another guy, who lived between Detroit and Idlewild, won often as well.

These guys were older, so Bobby and I hung out with them and gained entrée into the nightclub scene. We loved to go to the

Paradise Club and the Flamingo Club, to watch black showgirls that included the Fiesta Dolls and the Zigarettes who performed with Ziggy Johnson. The girls wore elaborate costumes of sequins, satin and feathers as they graced the nightclub stages. Those clubs were a launch pad for black superstars: Cab Calloway, Louis Armstrong, B.B. King, the Four Tops, Della Reese, Aretha Franklin, Bill Cosby, Sammy Davis, Jackie Wilson and many others.

One night, I was attending a show with my friends. We were riding in my buddy's new Cadillac. He was the slick guy from Flint, and we'd been in a skating contest together earlier that day. When we pulled up to the club, his new car turned heads among the white folks standing in the roped-off area at the entrance, where a doorman was taking tickets. My friend parked his Cadillac within view of the arriving patrons, and we all stepped out, dressed to the nines in suits, ties and shiny shoes.

"Sir!" someone yelled to my buddy. "Sir, your lights are on!"

"Oh yeah," my friend said. He turned back toward the Cadillac, then blew, as if blowing out a candle. The car lights went out — and the crowd went wild! The newfangled timer on the car's lights made them turn out as he had blown.

We felt like superstars! And we were amongst many performers who would become global legends in the music industry. At the time, The Four Tops were one of the hottest acts in Idlewild, and I became good friends with Levi Stubbs, Renaldo "Obie" Benson, Abdul "Duke" Fakir and Lawrence Payton, well before they became Motown legends. They were really fun, regular guys who loved boating, hanging out on the beach, and playing sports.

One shining star amongst them was songstress Freda Payne. A few years younger than me, Freda was a big city girl from Detroit who would later perform on Broadway, host a TV talk show, and become best known for her 1970 hit single, *Band of Gold*. Her younger sister, Scherrie, performed with the Supremes. Freda often joined our group as we socialized on the beach, went roller-skating and attended shows.

It was the summer of 1957, and I was having the time of my life. My father's wintertime admonition to stay in school was a distant memory amidst the glitz and glamour of this summer paradise. One day, while I was hanging out with the Four Tops, I announced:

"I'm going to quit school." This decision was inspired by emotion rather than reason, as well as by my persistent belief that I would make it under any condition. I've often said, "If I had been born in Russia, I'd be the best Communist you've ever seen, Comrade."

So I told my friends, "I'm having too much fun to go back to Muskegon. I'd rather hang out with you."

"Roy, you get your ass out of here!" Obie ordered, echoing the objections of Levi, Lawrence and Duke. "You're going back to school!"

I recently saw Duke at the Detroit airport as I was returning from Las Vegas. "Hey, there's the guy we saved!" he announced. He says it playfully now, but back in 1957, he and the other Four Tops were dead serious.

One Strike: Was Roy Already "Out?"

Though I started driving at age fifteen, I never applied for a license. I didn't own a car, nor did my father, so I never felt the need to go to the Secretary of State's office.

"Go get your license, boy," Papa would often say.

"I'm alright, Dad," I would answer.

But my typical teenaged sense of invincibility had convinced me that getting caught without a license was a problem that only happened to other people. Besides, I was a cautious, responsible driver, and that earned me the privilege of borrowing vehicles owned by my brother Bob, my friend Bobby Tates, and my sister Minnie Ruth Wesley's husband, Jeff.

"Roy, you can take the old station wagon to the skating rink," Jeff often said. "I don't have insurance on it, but I know you're responsible."

I never wanted to disappoint him, so I made certain that I returned the car, unscratched, at the appointed time, and expressed my appreciation for his generosity. At the same time, since I often lacked money, Minnie Ruth would put some cash in my hand so I could go skating. She and Jeff were my saviors. They made me feel more loved and special than anybody on the face of the earth.

When Minnie Ruth cooked for me, it was like she was serving love on a plate. My sister put her heart and soul into the food she prepared for her legendary family dinners. Her melt-in-your-mouth corned beef brisket was so good, it could make you cry. Her signature, southern-style cuisine included barbecued ribs, collard greens, potato salad, beans and big tossed salads. She also made incredible apple pie and peach cobbler, which especially pleased Jeff's sweet tooth.

Minnie Ruth's passion for food was profitable; she was a celebrated waitress at the Sayfee's restaurant in Grand Rapids. Upscale with an all-white clientele, it was owned by Mr. Sayfee, who adored Minnie Ruth.

The fact that Minnie Ruth and Jeff thought I was a responsible, mature young man, reinforced my belief that I would never get in trouble for driving without a license.

Bobby Tates shared my nonchalance when he frequently loaned me his car. "Here's my license," Bobby would say, handing it over as casually as if it were a stick of gum. One day during the Fall of my senior year, I was whizzing through Muskegon, driving Bobby's car, with his license in my pocket. I was excited because I was about to take a trip with my father and brothers down to Arkansas to visit our relatives. I was also thinking about how I would play my best in the next football game.

A siren wailed. Red and blue lights flashed in the rear view mirror.

"Oh, shit." I pulled over, my heart pounding.

I cursed again. Because Officer Spencer was approaching the car. He was the only black policeman in town, and the popular belief was that he was tasked with keeping the black people "in line."

"Is this your car?" he demanded.

"No, sir. It belongs to Bobby Tates."

"Show me your license, registration and proof of insurance."

I gave him the proper documents from the glove box, along with Bobby's license.

"You're breaking the law, driving without a license of your own," Officer Spencer said. "You're under arrest."

Panic exploded inside me as he put handcuffs on my wrists and guided me to his squad car. During the ride to the station, I prayed that my father or brother would bail me out immediately. When we arrived at police headquarters, Officer Spencer said I was charged with driving with someone else's license, in someone else's car.

"You'll have to pay a hundred-dollar fine," he said.

I didn't have a hundred of anything. All I had was hope that Bobby Tate would clarify the situation and come to my defense. Instead, when I phoned him at home, he spoke with Officer Spencer. When they finished talking, the police officer turned to me and accused: "Your friend denies that he loaned you his license. And he says you stole a hundred dollars from his mother."

I was stunned!

"Now, Roy," the officer said, "if you'll confess that you took the license and the money—"

"No! Bobby loaned me his car and his license, and I have never stolen money in my life!" It was unbelievable! On top of the shock, I was reeling with worry, because I didn't know the extent of the trouble that I was in, or whether I could be prosecuted on false allegations.

Oh please let Bob or Papa bail me out...

I called home. Bob answered. I told him my dilemma, which he relayed to our father.

"Daddy says you'll have to get out of jail the same way you got in," Bob said. "By yourself."

My older brother was sympathetic to my plight, but under our father's orders, he stayed home and prepared to drive Dad and Gene down to Arkansas.

"Time's up," Officer Spencer said, taking the phone. He walked me to a jail cell. I'll never forget the eerie echo of those metal bars sliding, then clanking shut, before he stuck in the key and locked me inside.

Dinner was terrible — a bologna sandwich. I was so terrified, I laid on the hard cot, staring wide-eyed at the ceiling until dawn. While I did not feel physically threatened, my 17-year-old mind was spinning with Papa's warning that as a black man, I had only one strike, and when I used it up, my life would be ruined. Was this my strike? How long would I have to stay here? Would I be kicked off the football team? Expelled from school? Prosecuted and sent to prison? All I wanted was to escape this place and the awful feeling of being in trouble with no one willing to help me.

In the morning, someone slid me a bowl of horrible-looking goulash. I refused to eat it.

Finally, my principal and coach paid a five-dollar court fee, and I was released. I don't know what happened to that hundred-dollar fine. I had never been happier to go home, clean up, and walk through the doors of Muskegon Senior High for an ordinary day of school.

As for my father, he personified the wise adage: *Actions speak louder than words.*

When he and my brothers returned from the week-long trip, Papa never mentioned my night in jail. Yet his refusal to bail me out taught me a tough lesson about being responsible for my actions. The bottom line was that I had done something wrong, I got caught, and it was my responsibility to get myself out of it.

From that moment on, I resolved to behave in a manner that would keep me on the good side of the law.

One Bad Apple Can Spoil The Bunch

Unfortunately, my personal resolve to stay out of trouble did not shield me from the bad behavior of people around me. One cold, winter night, a group of us gathered at the pool hall in Muskegon Heights, where we would all pile into a car for the ninety-minute drive to go skating in Lansing.

On this night, a man selling fruits and vegetables parked his truck alongside our car. One of the guys in our group — R. L. Lake, the brother of my best friend, George Lake — grabbed a bushel of apples off the truck and put them in our car.

"Man, these are some good apples," R.L. said as all six of us crunched the fruit as we drove on Grand River Road en route to Lansing. Unbeknownst to us, the driver of the apple truck had called the police. As soon as we neared the skating rink in Lansing, police sirens rang. Lights flashed. Officers surrounded our car.

"You're all under arrest for stealing apples back in Muskegon Heights," an officer said.

They loaded us into an open-air vehicle. It was like a police van — with no glass in the windows! On this frigid winter night, we were exposed to the sub-zero wind for the sixty-minute drive back to Muskegon Heights. It was inhumane! I have never been so cold in my life. We huddled together, but failed to keep warm. Perhaps the police thought that damn near freezing us to death was part of our punishment. Thankfully, we survived without injury.

Back at the police station, we were questioned. I was terrified that this time, I would go to jail and stay there. My thought was, *One more strike, and Roy Roberts is out!*

Thankfully, R.L. spoke up: "I admit, I took the apples."

We were all released, and assured that this incident would be expunged from our records.

Proms, Graduation, and Growing Up Quickly

During our senior year, Maureen had a serious boyfriend who attended another school, so she and I no longer registered on each other's romantic radar screens. Still, I maintained immense admiration for her high morals and ambition.

Meanwhile, I attended three senior proms. I escorted girls whose mothers perceived me as an exemplary young man, so they trusted me with their daughters. First, I attended the Muskegon Senior High School prom with Janet Tony. Then I was off to Grand Rapids for two more proms. Driving Bob's Oldsmobile, now with my own license, I picked up a buddy, and we drove to Sandra Hollerman's house. She was my date, and my friend was escorting her girlfriend.

"Sandra, I want you home by midnight," warned her mother, Inez, who was raising Sandra and two brothers without a father.

"And Roy," she said, shooting a *don't-mess-with-Momma* glance my way. "You know I am very protective of my daughter, so you need to respect her curfew."

"Yes, Ma'am," I said, with every intention of doing just that.

After the prom at Central High School, my buddy and I brought the young ladies back to Muskegon to show them the beach along Lake Michigan. Then we went to a restaurant. While we were waiting to eat, an insect ran across the table.

"Hey, Mister," I told the waiter, "there's a bug."

"Be quiet," he snapped. "That bug is well fed. You're not."

We roared with laughter.

But the wee hours of the morning were hardly humorous. When I took Sandra home, her mother was irate! I had kept her out well past her curfew. Not only was Inez furious with Sandra, but I had betrayed her mother's trust, and I hated feeling like a disappointment.

(Both Tony and Sandra have remained dear friends. Maureen and I have seen them with their spouses many times over the years at social functions).

After that, attending the South High School Prom in Grand Rapids with Ruby West was the most significant, because I truly loved Ruby. Classy and beautiful, she came from a good family with strong moral values. Ruby embodied all the good qualities that I desired in a wife.

"Roy, I'm pregnant," Ruby said a few months after I received my diploma from Muskegon Senior High School.

"Let's get married!" I proposed. "I love you, Ruby."

My excitement turned to panic. I had no money, no job, and no plans to attend college or a work-training program.

After a small wedding in August of 1958, Ruby and I moved into her parents' home in Grand Rapids. They worked in the factories, made a good living, and were very generous. I was grateful, but I urgently needed a good job so that I could buy a home.

"Sorry, we're not hiring," employers told me and a half-dozen friends during our daily job searches as we filled out applications at factories around Grand Rapids.

A few months before our baby was due, I received a letter from Blodgett Hospital.

"Dear Mr. Roberts," the letter said. "Your wife is scheduled to arrive here to have a baby in March of 1959. This letter is to inform you that you must make a $300 deposit before she can be admitted." For an unemployed teenager, that was a small fortune. I needed a miracle, and I needed it fast.

FIVE

Grace under Pressure: Responsibility at a Young Age

The cold, damp wind off Lake Michigan seemed to slice right through me as I exited the factory with my job-hunting buddies.

"Sorry fellas, we're not hiring," the personnel manager had just told us.

"Man, that's all we hear!" lamented my friend as we huddled in the cold.

"Times are tough, my brotha," another guy groaned as we stood united in our common plight as unemployed teenagers. Most of us had recently graduated from high school; others had dropped out.

"Now where do we go?" asked one friend. "Seems like we've been to every factory in Grand Rapids, and the answer is always the same. No damn jobs!"

Frustrated, I shoved my hands into my pockets, where I felt the letter from Blodgett Hospital. They wanted $300, but I didn't have a single dollar. Plus, that was just the down payment for Ruby to give birth to our child in a few months. I would need hundreds *more* to cover the delivery and hospital stay. My heart pounded with panic.

"I have a wife, and a baby on the way," I announced. "I have to find a job!"

"I feel for you, Roy," my buddy said. "It's rough when you gotta feed a family."

Without a job, I couldn't even do that.

"Hey," one guy said. "We haven't been to Kelvinator's yet."

"Naw, I heard you need ten years of factory experience," another guy added.

"That can't be right, knucklehead," another teen said. "My uncle works in the plant and he quit school. Just like your sorry self!" They launched into a lively round of the dozens as we walked to the Kelvinator Company, which manufactured refrigerators. Their loud banter continued as our group's lead guy opened the personnel office door. The white male personnel manager was at the counter, wearing a shirt and tie.

"Are you doing any hiring today?" our guy asked.

"No, we're not doing any hiring," the personnel manager responded.

"Aw, man," one guy groaned as our group headed outside.

Suddenly I realized how a group of young, black men must have appeared to the personnel manager. Grand Rapids was a conservative, Republican city of 177,000 people. About 10 percent of the population was African American; most were very poor. Perceptions of blacks, especially male teenagers, were hardly favorable in 1958.

How could I make myself stand out as a desirable job candidate? And if jobs were few and far between, wouldn't one person score a better chance of getting hired – alone – than as part of a rambunctious group?

"Hey," one guy said. "Let's go try again at that other factory down the street."

"Man, get ready to lose!" one teen taunted. "Soon as that ball goes up in the air, you're jacked!" The guys noisily proceeded down the street.

I stood alone in front of Kelvinator's. Determination propelled me inside, exuding an amicable expression as I approached the man at the counter.

"Sir, I see you're wearing a wedding ring," I said. "You're probably married with a family, and you want the best for them."

Slightly annoyed, he nodded, sizing me up.

"I'm married and my wife is going to have a baby. And here's a letter I received from the hospital," I said, placing it on the counter. "They said I have to make a deposit of three hundred dollars. Sir, I need a job, because I want to pay the three hundred dollars for my child."

He stared with a serious glint in his eyes. I feared he might order me to leave, but I had to give it my best shot.

"Sir," I said, "I don't have three hundred dollars." Then I remembered my buddy's comment about needing experience to work at this particular factory. "And sir, I don't have ten years of experience at anything but breathing."

The man smiled — then laughed, almost hysterically.

"Son, you want a job?"

"Yes, sir."

I was hired! I began working — that day! — at 3 p.m. on the second shift, driving a forklift in the Material Handling Department. (Since then, I have never applied for a job, and I have never been out of work, having been continuously employed at three corporations and having founded two additional corporations).

Operating a forklift at Kelvinator's didn't demand brainpower or brawn. All it required was the ability to drive the "hi-lo" in a safe manner. It was good pay, and I was able to cover the down payment and ensuing bills for my wife's labor and delivery.

A Doting Dad Lands a Better Job

I had always thought babies were ugly. But when Ricky Stewart Roberts was born on May 25, 1959, I thought he was the most beautiful baby I had ever seen. Ruby and I and his grandmother doted on him like he was a little prince.

Six months after Ricky was born, Ruby's uncle helped me get a better job. He was an orthopedic doctor and had graduated from high school with a fellow who became the Personnel Director at Lear Corporation, which manufactured precision instruments for aircraft, missiles and spacecraft.

Having passed the company's lovely campus on Eastern Avenue many times, I had always been impressed by its modern-looking, light gray buildings and manicured grounds. And like the nearby Steelcase furniture manufacturing company, Lear was ranked as one of the best places in Grand Rapids to work.

However, very few African Americans were employed there. As a result, it felt out of reach, so I had never envisioned myself working at Lear.

"I've got a young nephew who's married to my niece," Ruby's uncle told Lear's Personnel Director. "Roy Roberts is smart, he's sharp, and you ought to consider hiring him."

"Send him over," the Personnel Director said.

I met with him, and he hired me. In fact, I went to work at Lear without filling out an application. I earned a little more money, but the work environment was worlds above my previous job.

Quite honestly, I thought I'd gone to heaven! Lear was an incredible place, on a beautifully landscaped campus with two main buildings. One housed Administration and Manufacturing, which included offices for the president of the division and several vice presidents of manufacturing. A long passageway connected those offices to the Research and Development building, where engineers were developing cutting-edge, aerospace technology.

It was an exciting time to join Lear because the "space race" was going strong, after the Soviet Union launched Sputnik, the first artificial Earth satellite. That would, in just a few years, prompt President John F. Kennedy's vow to land an American astronaut on the moon, and return him safely to Earth, during the 1960s. Lear benefited and profited tremendously from this race to the moon because the company secured government and aviation contracts for controls, navigation systems and instruments.

Here's where this fascinating piece of American history and my first job at Lear intersected, because I was hired as an Instrument

Assembler. The instruments were so sensitive that the smallest foreign object — even an eyelash — could make the instrument faulty or defective.

So, to maintain the extremely sterile atmosphere in the laboratory, I would start my shift in a locker room, where I was required to don a silk smock that tied at the side. Then I placed booties over my shoes, and a nylon hat over my head. To access the laboratory, I would walk through an air duct where strong gusts of air blew any foreign material — such as lint, dust or a single hair — off of me. Inside the lab, everything was spotless. I loved it!

This felt futuristic and intelligent in contrast to the grease and noise of the forklift I had left at the Kelvinator factory. Plus, Lear's space-age atmosphere was exciting and made me feel like I was part of something big and important. I was constantly learning, intrigued by the instruments that we were building for spacecraft and *Lockheed L-1011* commercial aircraft.

One of the instruments that I assembled was a three-axis gyroscope, which is installed in the nose of an airplane. It measures the plane's orientation by keeping track of its movements — called the pitch, roll and yaw — through the indicator, which tells the pilot where the plane is going. I also assembled altimeters, which measure an airplane's altitude. It was especially interesting to construct instruments for moon shots. These were control systems for the spacecraft that NASA sent into space. In fact, these instruments would, a decade later, be on board the spacecraft for the Apollo Moon mission that sent Buzz Aldrin, Neil Armstrong and Michael Collins to the moon in 1969. This was exhilarating!

I mastered my duties, and performed them with meticulous precision. In short order, I was promoted to an Instrument Inspector, then a Calibrator Tester, the highest position in the lab. On average, I made $75 or $80 a week, which calculates to $632.21 in today's dollars. Other times, when I was working on special government projects, we were compensated for teamwork. Three of us could earn $1,000 in one week. That meant $333 — or $2,631.55 in today's dollars — for me. On top of excellent compensation, I received great benefits that included health care and life insurance.

Lear was a great place to work. It was not high pressure and, unlike many of the factory jobs that my father had worked, it required no sweat. Lear didn't need my back; they needed my brains. Many hours on those team assignments involved sitting and waiting for the instrument to "bake" in a special oven before we could remove it and apply a label.

I loved everything about my work! Ambition to advance to higher positions and greater income motivated me to apply myself with great enthusiasm. Thankfully, my natural ability in each position was attracting attention from people in high places.

Among them were the engineers in the next building. When they were developing a new product model, they would come to me to test it and provide thorough feedback on its quality and performance. This, and their praise for my work, made me feel special. And because the conventional wisdom of the day urged young men to get one job with a company and stay there until retirement, I hoped to enjoy lifelong employment at Lear.

Buying a Home for Our Growing Family

Every day, I marveled at our thriving baby boy, and I was thrilled that Ruby was a devoted mother. At the same time, several factors accelerated my ambition to purchase a home for my family. Most importantly, when Ruby went to her six-month check-up after Ricky was born, her doctor had a surprise.

"Well, Mrs. Roberts," the doctor said, "you're pregnant again!"

We were shocked. While I was confident that I could pay the hospital bill this time, living with my wife's parents and two children was simply unacceptable. Around the same time, Ruby's mother bought Ricky a pair of shoes, and I — perhaps overly aggressively — took offense.

"Shoes and other necessities are my responsibility," I told Mrs. West. "I don't want you or anyone else buying shoes for our child!"

All the while, I had been saving money by making deposits every payday in the credit union. And rather than bearing the expense of a car, I paid two women who worked at Lear and lived in our neighborhood to drive me to and from work every day.

One day, Ruby and I saw a house that we wanted to purchase. Unfortunately, I did not have enough money for the down payment.

"I need a loan," I told my father-in-law.

"How much are you going to pay down?"

"Sixteen hundred dollars," I said.

"How much of the down payment do you need?" Mr. West asked.

"Sixteen hundred dollars," I said.

He loaned me the 20 percent down payment on the $8,000 house. Ruby and I purchased the two-story, traditional-style home with an attractive porch and detached two-car garage. With three bedrooms, three bathrooms and a nice lawn, it was perfect for a growing family.

We even had money for furniture. It just so happened that I was a friend of the Chief Financial Officer at Lear, whose uncle was the chief designer at John Widdicomb Furniture in Grand Rapids. This uncle was moving into a smaller home and wanted to sell his furniture. Ruby and I purchased several pieces from him that included a stereo console. Inlaid with blond wood, this furniture was so exquisite, it had been featured in two magazines.

Meanwhile, when word spread through Grand Rapids that we had purchased a home in an all-white neighborhood, a steady stream of cars drove past to see our place.

Just ten months after Ricky was born, we welcomed our daughter, Robin Rene, into the world on March 13, 1960. She, too, was an absolutely beautiful baby.

Being a husband, a father of two, and a homeowner before my twenty-first birthday was especially remarkable in the context of the financial plight of blacks at the time. Because many African Americans lacked the freedoms that were proferred in Michigan and the North, the Civil Rights Movement was gaining momentum in the South. That year, demonstrators held the first sit-in in Greensboro, North Carolina. I followed their progress in newspaper, radio and television news reports.

The country was changing. I was part of that change by providing a positive example of a young black man for my neighbors and for the majority of my colleagues at Lear who had had little or no interaction with African Americans. At work, I felt the sky was the limit. And owning a home, something my father had never done during my lifetime, inspired me to work harder to continue to provide a solid financial foundation for my wife and children.

I had purchased the home on a land contract, even though Michigan law prohibited anyone under age 21 from buying a house. The penalty for breaking this law stated that if a minor purchased a home, and the seller wanted to negate the purchase, the underaged buyer would have to return all the money and the property.

In my situation, the sellers were a Lithuanian couple, and the wife handled their business. Their daughter was a student at Michigan State University and a part-time summer employee at Lear. She was getting married, and her parents wanted to sell our house after we had lived there four years.

"I'm going to sell the land contract to another party," the mother told me. "I'm going to bring them through the house for a showing."

"I've made every payment," I protested. "I'm surprised you wouldn't give me first option to buy the land contract."

"I have the right to sell to anyone," she said.

"I won't let any potential buyers come through the house," I told her. "The contract states that you can come through the house twice a year for inspection with a sixty-day notice. Therefore, I'm not letting anyone I don't know come through this house."

Then I remembered when I first bought the property, the land contract said she had sixty days before vacating the premises. At this point, it was fifty days into the contract, and she needed an extra sixty days.

"It will cost you," I told her. "You'll have to pay."

I calculated that she would have to pay me $100 a month. She agreed. When the first payment was due from her for one month, she gave me $100.

"Now give me a check for one hundred dollars because you owe me," she said.

I did not realize that my agreement was overlapping with me paying her my $100 a month. Unfortunately, she got to stay two months free.

"Young man, these are the things you learn as you go through life," she said with a condescending tone.

Apparently, her new buyer balked at buying the land contract, and she offered it to me for a 15 percent discount.

"No, I will buy it at a 20 percent discount," I said.

After some gnashing of teeth, she agreed to my 20 percent. I bought the land contract. Then I had the pleasure of saying to her: "Ma'am, these are some of the things you learn as you go through life."

I felt I had gotten even because I was able to get a significant discount on the home and move forward. This included paying my father-in-law back for all of the money he had loaned me to purchase the home.

That incident taught me the importance of reading the fine print and understanding every clause in a legal contract before signing it.

Enjoying a Happy Home Life with My Family

I took pride in the fact that we owned a lovely home in a safe, pretty neighborhood. The local public elementary school was outstanding, and our three children were learning in a nurturing environment. Ruby and I especially appreciated the small class sizes and harmony amongst the mostly white students and a handful of other African American children.

At home, we ate dinner together, and I cherished the joy of having a solid family unit. Taking care of my family, and enabling Ruby to stay home to take care of the children, made me feel responsible, mature and fulfilled on every level. We doted on our children, and time together was delightful.

My children as youngsters:
(L-R) Ricky, Ronald and Robin with Santa

"I remember when I was very young, in a high chair and stroller, and my parents were always around me," recalls my daughter, Robin. "Our parents were very young, and they were a lot of fun. And since Mommy didn't drive back then, we did a lot of things together as a family."

Taking the children to see Santa Claus at Herpolsheimer's department store downtown Grand Rapids was an annual tradition.

"I remember doing that as early as two or three years old," Robin recalls. "We would sit on Santa's lap, get a kiss and a picture, then we would ride the Santa Express, a child-sized train on a monorail that was suspended from the ceiling of the store. After that, we'd go to the Christmas parade."

Back at home, I would make snowmen with the kids. Inside, Ruby challenged them with flashcards to learn math and reading, and she played card games with them, such as Old Maid and Go Fish.

"In the summer," Robin remembers, "Daddy drew the hopscotch grid with chalk on the sidewalk for me and my friends. Or we'd be jumping rope outside while he was cutting the grass. He'd take a break and teach us how to double-dutch, which is jumping rope with two ropes at once. My friends used to say, 'Robin, your dad can jump double-dutch better than any of us!'"

Ruby and I also took the kids roller-skating in Grand Rapids.

"This man can roller-skate!" Robin recalls. "If he hadn't gone into business, he could have easily become a professional roller-skater."

Her fondest memories occurred during family trips.

"They took us to Idlewild. I remember waking up in the morning in the cabin on a lake. We'd go swimming and splash around with other little kids. We'd ride a paddleboat, then go into town for Jones Ice Cream. We had a ball up there!"

Of course, roller-skating also took center stage.

"I remember we'd watch Mommy and Daddy roller-skating at the rink in Idlewild," Robin recalls, adding that Ruby and I were in our mid-twenties. "They'd be out there, going around and around, dancing to all the Motown hits of the 1960s. The wooden floor was so dusty, you'd leave with dust in your hair. But we had so much fun together as a family."

Another special memory was our trip to the World's Fair in Montreal, Canada, during the summer of 1967.

"I was seven years old," Robin recalls, "and I remember being dazzled by all the beautiful people from around the world. I was just staring at these ladies from India who wore gorgeous saris that were brilliant reds, purples and lavenders. We also went inside this big glass ball to watch a movie about a helicopter ride. It was very high tech for the day, and it was so realistic, I remember being afraid, as if we were actually in a helicopter! I later learned that ball was taken to Disney World in Florida to become Epcot Center."

Our vacations closer to home involved driving to Cleveland to visit my sister, Minnie Ruth, and her husband, Jeff. She worked as a nurse at the Cleveland Clinic and he was employed by United Airlines. My other siblings lived in distant states, so we rarely saw them. We did occasionally visit my father, who remained in Muskegon.

When we were home in Grand Rapids, family outings involved getting dressed up on Sundays and going to church. After the service, we would take the children to brunch or dinner at the Pantlind Hotel, where the lobby boasted one of the world's biggest gold-leaf ceilings. This downtown Grand Rapids landmark was named "One of the Ten Finest Hotels in America," and later became the AAA Four-Diamond luxury Amway Grand Plaza Hotel.

We enjoyed delicious meals while Ruby and I taught our children proper etiquette: how to order, how to cultivate impeccable table manners, and how to present oneself with pride and dignity in public.

"I wore white gloves to church as a little girl," Robin recalls. "My brothers were in their little suits with ties and hats that matched their tweed coats. Our parents taught us to be meticulous about our clothing and grooming. We were always clean!"

The clientele in the Pantlind Hotel's dining room was all white and much older than our young family.

"Daddy has always done things ahead of himself, ahead of his age, and ahead of anyone around him, black or white," Robin says. "His motivation for the way he lived his life was 100 percent internal, because he had no one to set this example for him."

During these outings, as I gazed at our beautiful, well-dressed and well-behaved children, I couldn't help myself from reflecting back on my own childhood, when such an experience would have been unimaginable. Now being able to provide this lifestyle for my family filled me with pride, joy and a sense of accomplishment. It was extremely rewarding that I was rising above my life circumstances and doing something much more substantial than I had seen anyone in my family do.

"One Day I'm Going to Have an Office Like This"

Family Day at Lear was a special occasion for our family. The kids loved this annual event, because they visited my workplace to enjoy a picnic with food and games. I was proud to introduce Ruby to my colleagues, and take our family on tours of the building, which included displays of airplanes.

I cherish a photograph of Robin with me as we're standing in line to get a soda. Her little skirt is flared out to the side, and she's beaming with joy.

"I vividly remember that day," Robin recalls. "I was five years old, and Daddy took me and my brothers inside the building to show us where he worked. First, we were in a little room with a wooden table and fold-out chairs, and we sat down to eat our cookies and punch. The room felt like a maintenance closet, with clocks on the walls, no windows, and lockers. 'This is where I put my lunchbox and my coat,' Daddy told us at a time when he was still an hourly worker. 'Hurry up and finish your snack. I want to show you guys something.'

"We walked down, down, down this long hall. It seemed like we walked forever. Daddy opened these big, fancy doors, and inside was this huge office. Models of jet airplanes are sitting on this huge table, and there's a big chair pushed up to this massive desk, and behind it are big pictures on the wall.

"I remember so clearly," Robin says. "Daddy let us sit in the chair. We were twirling around in it. Then he looked at us and declared: 'You see all of this? One day I'm going to have an office like this.'"

"Roy, You Need to Go to College."

At work, I was getting along with everyone, and delighting the engineers. They continued to consult with me whenever they were creating a prototype or model.

All the while, I was intrigued by the fact that none of the people I met were any smarter than me. They may have come from different life circumstances, or attended college, or had better opportunities. But they were not smarter. And that motivated me to believe that I could achieve as much as — or more — than the men and women in my workplace.

One symbol of my increasing success was the ability to purchase my first automobile at age twenty-one. And yes, I had a driver's license. My first car was a blue and white 1957 Chevrolet. This enabled me to drive myself to work.

Cultivating excellent "people skills" had always been a top priority for me, and talking about sports is an appropriate and endearing conversation topic in the workplace. I had plenty to brag about, because my younger brother Gene was a star on the Muskegon Senior High football team. After joining the varsity team in tenth grade, he made All-State for three years straight. Like me, Gene was a running back, and he also wore "50" on his red-and-white jersey. This caused some fans to believe that I had spent six years in high school.

"Roberts!" people would yell from the stands while Gene was playing. "When are you gonna graduate?"

While I was generally faster than Gene, he gained more yards than I did, and was stronger. He had great vision and maneuvered well on the field, quickly making cuts and fooling opposing players. I was so proud of him that I would bet my coworkers at Lear over how many touchdowns Gene would score on the weekend. It was incredible. While I advanced at work, I continued to live my football dreams vicariously through Gene. After high school, he played defense for Colorado State University and did quite well.

Meanwhile, my colleagues were praising my abilities. This caught the attention of Miles Nishiyama, assistant to the vice president of administration for Lear. A native of Hawaii, Miles recognized that my potential was far above and beyond my current position.

"Roy, you need go to school."

"I've been to school."

"No, no, you need to go to college," he insisted. "You're pretty smart. You would do very well if you had a college degree."

He engaged me in this conversation many times. Each time, I balked. I told him that I had a wife, two small children, a full-time job, a house, and an increasingly demanding social and civic schedule. How in the world could I attend college on top of that?

Still, Miles badgered me relentlessly. Finally, just to get him off my back, I enrolled at Grand Rapids Junior College. When I signed up for one or two classes, I had no intention of completing a degree there. I soon discovered that Grand Rapids Junior College was no cakewalk. It ranked as one of the top junior colleges in the nation. I surprised myself by doing quite well. This infused me with encouragement to pursue more education.

Still, attending college, excelling at work and balancing family time was very difficult. If I had a morning class, I would work an afternoon shift. If I had an evening class, I would work during the day. This left Ruby alone to handle the demands of taking care of the children and our home.

"He's Going Blind"

On February 25, 1963, Ruby and I were thrilled to bring our third child, Ronald, into the world. For his three-month check-up, I drove Ruby and Ronald to the pediatrician's office. Because I was scheduled to work afterward, I waited in the car.

A short while later, I glimpsed the rear view mirror. Ruby was approaching, carrying the baby. Her strange expression startled me. Then she slumped down in the passenger seat with Ronald in her lap and sobbed:

"He's going blind!"

I reeled as she bawled uncontrollably.

"The doctor said he was born with congenital glaucoma," she explained. "He was born without certain membranes in his eye. The fluid can wash onto the eye, but it can't wash off, so that hardens up and will blind him."

I consulted with the pediatrician, who informed me that this was a rare disease, and that he would refer us to the top doctor who was treating it. We drove two hours to Ann Arbor, where Dr. Frehlich at the University of Michigan Hospital recommended a series of surgeries. He wanted to cut a slit in Ronald's eye, which would heal to allow fluid to drain off the eye. Over the next two years, Ronald had four surgeries. To say he was turned off to doctors and white coats growing up would be an understatement.

After his final surgery, as we were checking out of the hospital, the late President Kennedy's father was checking out in front of us! I surmised that Joseph P. Kennedy, Sr., surrounded by bodyguards, was receiving treatment in the wake of a massive stroke that he had survived.

Concurrent with Ronald's surgeries, President Kennedy delivered his celebrated *civil rights address* on June 11, 1963, on national television and radio. In doing so, he proposed his vision for legislation that would be included in the Civil Rights Act of 1964. Sadly, his assassination on November 22, 1963, would preclude him from witnessing the historic day when President Lyndon Johnson signed it into law.

Also during this time, we found it extremely inspiring that Dr. King delivered his "I Have a Dream Speech" in Detroit in June of 1963, two months before he recited it during the March on Washington, D.C. His message instilled hope in Ruby and me, as we prayed that our children would inherit the egalitarian society that Dr. King envisioned.

President Kennedy's support of Dr. King's message was encouraging. As a result, Ruby and I found it auspicious that the senior Mr. Kennedy was present at the conclusion of our son's medical treatments. We hoped the surgeries would restore his vision.

However, as the late president's father was escorted from the University of Michigan Hospital, Ruby and I learned that the bill for Ronald's four surgeries totaled $45,000! That would equal $344,000 today. I certainly did not have that kind of money, so I shared my dilemma with my bosses at Lear.

"Roy," the managers said, "you keep going to school, and you take care of your family and your job. We'll take care of this bill."

Lear negotiated a settlement with the insurance company, and the bill disappeared. At the same time, while Ronald was legally blind in one eye, he regained pretty good sight in the other eye, which he continues to enjoy today. Ruby and I were immensely grateful for these two miracles!

Advancing My Education at Western Michigan University

After eighteen months at Grand Rapids Junior College, I graduated with an associate's degree, then transferred to a four-year university for my bachelor's degree. I was accepted at Michigan State University and Western Michigan University. I chose Western, thinking the 120-mile, round-trip commute would be easier.

I was wrong. I narrowly escaped deadly accidents at least six times as I cruised north and south on U.S. Highway 131 in my used, 1957 Ford Mustang, which was dark blue with a lighter blue top. Once, I hit a slick spot on an underpass. My car spun 380 degrees across an embankment, finally stopping head-on with a cement wall. By the grace of God, I survived.

Later, my commute became more enjoyable because I realized a dream: I bought a new Thunderbird. (A few years later, I would purchase a second one).

Meanwhile, my schedule was arduous. If I had a morning class, I would work the afternoon shift, and vice versa. My routine was simple:

Get up at 6 a.m.

Leave for school at 7 a.m.

Arrive at school at 8 a.m.

Leave school at 2 p.m.

Arrive at work at 3 p.m.

Work until midnight, 1 a.m. or 2 a.m.

Repeat the routine the next day.

I was one of a few blacks in the Western Michigan University School of Business, and I excelled. Today I still enjoy friendships with former classmates who include: Dennis Archer, who would become an attorney and Mayor of Detroit; William Pickard, who would found Global Automotive Alliance, one of the country's leading minority-owned supply companies; Ron Hall, CEO of Bridgewater Interiors, one of the largest minority automotive supply companies; and S. Martin Taylor, former executive vice president of DTE Energy Company who, prior to that, had significant assignments with the state of Michigan. As we made our marks on the world, Western Michigan University called us "The Fabulous Five" and showcased our accomplishments as a recruitment tool. Today, pictures of us are all over the WMU campus.

When we attended, Dennis, Bill, Ron and Marty were traditional college students: enrolled full-time and free from the pressures of a full-time job, a family and home ownership. They could pursue the traditional pastimes of campus life, which included pledging a fraternity. While my schedule did not permit the investment of time and energy to do that, several of my peers agreed that when the time was right, we would pledge the graduate chapter of Kappa Alpha Psi Fraternity, Incorporated.

Meanwhile, I applied myself wholeheartedly to my classroom lessons about business. I was enthralled by every facet of how companies operated. My professors often referenced corporate giants such as IBM, General Electric and the Big Three automakers, whose world headquarters were in Detroit, just a three-hour drive across Lower Michigan.

I was especially intrigued by classroom discussions about the world's biggest, most profitable corporation: General Motors. Growing up in Muskegon, I had known people who worked in the factories that supplied parts to General Motors. I frequently drove past GM's massive metal fabrication plant on Thirty-Sixth Street and Buchanan Avenue. It fascinated me that this 96-acre facility was part of a global network of factories, offices and dealerships that comprised the world's top manufacturing company.

GM's chairman and 23-member Board of Directors, as well as its top executives, were all white, running the corporate behemoth from GM's executive offices in Detroit. (GM's first African American member, Reverend Leon Sullivan – who was also the first black board member of *any* major U.S. corporation -- would not be elected until 1971.) I often wondered if Roy Roberts would ever have the opportunity to succeed in that kind of environment.

School, Work, and Commute Take Toll on Family and Finances

Working full time and commuting 120 miles every day to college was difficult. I was so exhausted most of the time, my definition of "joy" was a twenty-minute break from work to take a short nap in the men's room.

Attending WMU was also taking a financial toll, due to tuition and the purchase of automobiles, fuel and maintenance. I needed help, so I talked with Lear's vice president of operations, who prompted Human Resources to ask me what I needed.

"I propose a tuition reimbursement program," I answered. "The employee should pay the tuition first, then after completing a class, he or she should submit a request to Human Resources for reimbursement. A grade slip from the college should be attached to the request, and reimbursement should be based on performance. Earn an A and receive 100 percent reimbursement." I continued to explain that a B would garner 85 percent reimbursement, while a C would be rewarded with 75 percent of the employee's tuition cost.

Lear liked my idea. The company implemented this policy for me personally. Later, when I headed up Hourly Personnel and Labor Relations, I negotiated this benefit for all UAW Local 330 employees, and Tuition Reimbursement became an official Lear Siegler policy for all salaried employees.

"Ask, and Ye Shall Receive"

I had never worked harder in my life, and I felt that after eighteen months at Western Michigan University, it was time to advance in the company. I made an appointment with the vice president of Human Resources. When I entered his office, Milt Stinstrom was talking on the telephone. Tall, handsome and impeccably dressed in a business suit and cufflinks, Milt placed a close second behind Sticks Green in terms of clothing style and sophistication. As I sat in a chair facing his desk, I couldn't help overhearing his conversation with a friend.

"My son Jay, he's down at the University of Michigan," Milt said. "He's doing well. We bought him a new car, and we took the car down to him last week, so he's got transportation. He's getting good grades in his classes, then he's going off to grad school."

Intrigued, I decided that someday I would attain the financial stature to have a similar conversation about my own children.

"And my daughter," Milt continued, "she's at Michigan State University, doing really well. We just bought her a car, too, and took it down to her."

I thought this was the most beautiful conversation. I had never heard anything like it while growing up. Finally, Milt hung up and turned to me.

"Now, Roy Roberts, what can I do for you?"

"Mr. Stinstrom, I've been working hard, and I've been going to school, doing the best that I can," I said. At the time, I was an hourly Instrument Calibrating Tester and a member of UAW Local 330.

"Someday," I told Milt, "I want to be in a position to talk to a friend about my children, and say what you just told your friend about your kids. But I don't want a gift. I want to earn it, just like you did."

Milt smiled. "Son, you want a different job?"

"Yes, sir."

Many people ask where I found the gumption to advocate for myself. The answer is that I know in my heart that I'm as good as all the people who are doing a particular job. With the right training, I can do it better. When you know this, you do not hold back. You run with it.

At the same time, I have always been driven by the belief that I have more opportunity ahead of me, than behind me. However, it's not anyone else's job to bring opportunities to you. You have to go get them. And I have always been one to go get them. When you put forth effort to achieve, people will gravitate toward you to help you. A lot of people helped me, often in ways that I would not know until years later.

In this particular situation, Milt Stinstrom recommended me for a promotion. At the same time, several other people in powerful positions were advocating for my advancement, because they had witnessed my hard work and dedication to the company. Bill Zollmer, Lear's vice president of manufacturing, was having discussions with the company's power players about promoting more people to supervisory positions.

"The company's rapid growth has exhausted our personnel options for supervisors," a personnel manager told Bill. "We need to test more people."

Bill Zollmer was a big, strong, smart, positive leader. Very importantly, he was aware of my reputation amongst the engineers as the "go-to guy" for testing and calibrating new products. That made me a natural recommendation, in his mind, for one of the new supervisory positions.

"How about Roy Roberts and Andy Perry?" Bill Zollmer said. "They're two performers."

"Yeah, but they're black," another manager said.

"So what," Bill said.

Just two weeks after my meeting with Milt Stinstrom, Bill convinced them to hire me as the first African American to work in management for Lear's Financial Department. My salaried position as a time keeper did not require extraordinary talent, but it exposed me to the inner-workings of the financial aspect of Lear, and provided new opportunities for growth and promotion.

Concurrently, management elevated Andy Perry as the First Line Supervisor in Manufacturing. Andy was the perfect choice. He had a milquetoast demeanor, while I was somewhat of a firebrand, out front, telling people what I thought and believed in. My promotion showed that Lear was high on Roy, and Roy was high on Lear. This inspired a strong sense of loyalty, and I envisioned a lifelong career with the company.

Learning From the Ladies

My excellent performance as Time Keeper in the Finance Department earned another promotion. I became an Expeditor in the

Production and Control Department. My job was to orchestrate the logistics of products and parts to make sure they were coming together at the right place. After that, I was elevated to a pivotal position that educated me on so many levels, it was unreal.

As was the case with every job I would hold throughout my 45-year career in the corporate world, I was the first African American to become the First Line Supervisor in the Gyroscopic Lab at Lear Corporation. As I ascended the ranks, I embarked on a personal quest to exceed the expectations of managers who hired me.

Since most of the managers and my colleagues had experienced little, if any, interaction with blacks in the workplace, I had the power to influence their perceptions of African Americans from that point forward. I felt that everything I said and did represented the entire race, and that our future opportunities within Lear Siegler hinged on my performance.

Therefore, my appearance and behavior were always impeccable. Likewise, I cultivated a friendly, upbeat personality with every man and woman whom I encountered. I could tell jokes with anybody and get along with everyone, and I could object without being objectionable. Those are vital skills in the corporate world. My goal was to ensure that every time I left a job, the company could never say, '*Your people* can't do it.' They might say, '*He* can't do it.' Or '*She* can't do it.' But never, '*They* can't do it.'"

Instead, I wanted to prove that African Americans could excel in any position, so that managers would be agreeable to hiring more of us. This personal commitment underscored the immense responsibility I felt as a pioneering African American in a predominantly white company. This status endowed me with the power to help other blacks get hired at Lear. Lear believed that I would know these individuals well enough to discern whether they were ideal job candidates. At the time, Lear was really starting to boom, and they were looking for talented, trustworthy people to hire. Meanwhile, a steady stream of black men and women were approaching me about the possibilities of getting into Lear. I recommended some of the best people in the city. All were hired, and they tended to progress in the organization.

My performance at work and my involvement in the Grand Rapids community was not just about Roy Roberts and his family; it was about doing my part to help elevate and advance the race. My growing success at Lear was establishing me as a respected role model in the black community in Grand Rapids. I didn't dare do anything that would be reflect negatively on my family, community or my employer.

These dynamics came into play when I was promoted to First Line Supervisor in the Gyroscopic Laboratory, which built gyroscopes, altimeters and controls for moon shots. I supervised thirty-five women. They were all white, all smart, and all older than me. Lear employed a lot of women because the work was not physically demanding, yet it required intelligence and attention to detail.

While I felt I was teaching the company something about African Americans' ability to perform, these women were educating me on how to supervise. If I mistakenly had a burnelled bearing in a gyroscope, I didn't dare go over and say, "Mary, fix this." Instead, it was more effective to ask, "Mary, do you know what's wrong with this? Can you figure this out for me?" Also, I had to balance the amount of time I spent on workplace issues with each employee. There was a high degree of competition among the women. It was an experience that taught me that successful managers must develop a sensitivity to their environment and understand how to inspire and motivate people.

This idea inspired one of my favorite Roy-isms: "When you find someone who can jump tall buildings, don't stand on their cape!"

At the same time, the women were always talking about saving money. That inspired me to become more aggressive about designating a certain portion of my income to my savings account at the credit union.

(Years later, when I was an executive at General Motors, I encountered seven of these women in Detroit's airport. They were stranded due to a cancelled flight, so I took them home with me. Maureen joined us as we told stories all night long, recounting our work together at Lear. The women playfully took credit for my success.)

Silent Killer: Romance on the Job

"Roy, we want you to become General Supervisor of the night shift in the Service Repair Order Department," Bill Zollmer said. "We have a lot of supervisors who are fraternizing with the women, and we want you to stop it. This is a big problem, and it's causing costly disruptions. We're confident that once you take charge of the second shift, you'll set a standard for our employees to stop mixing business with pleasure."

"Consider it done," I assured him with a handshake and confident look in his eye. In my new management position, I supervised twelve to fifteen foremen. All the while, I witnessed how the initial thrill of workplace romance often ended with dangerous consequences that could shatter marriages and families and destroy careers.

To this day, I warn young, ambitious professionals never to have romantic workplace relationships. The day after you do, the other person is the boss. They own you! They can blackmail you or file a sexual harassment claim that could tarnish your reputation at the very least.

In fact, workplace romance is a "Silent Killer" — a sure-fire way to kill one's career. The Killer is "silent" because oftentimes, it would be inappropriate or politically incorrect for someone to tell you to refrain from a particular behavior. While you may not get fired for having an office romance, the potential gossip, distraction and disruption justify classifying this behavior as a Silent Killer. The boss does not want that drama, and will be eager to get rid of the culprit. Therefore, let me emphasize: romance on the job will get you fired, and curtail your career.

If you glean anything from *My American Success Story*, know that you should never mix business with pleasure.

Creating My Personal Code of Conduct -- Without a Mentor

Early on, I cultivated a personal code of conduct that has served me well. Now, I recommend that you do the same, and adhere to it, no matter how alluring the temptation might be. Because you better believe, the higher you rise, the more frequently you will encounter temptations. At that point, however, it's less enticing, because you really know it's trouble.

Disciplining myself to maintain the highest integrity has always been fundamental to my success. Discipline comes from within, and I recognized its importance by observing managers, executives and individuals who rose from lowly positions to prestigious ones. Each of these individuals shared the common denominator of discipline to work hard, follow the rules and ignore distractions.

No one taught me this. Never did I have a mentor who took me under his wing to say, "Roy, let me tell you about the corporate culture here, and what you should do to succeed."

In fact, when I began at Lear, no black managers or executives worked there. Nor were any blacks employed in high positions at the other big companies in town, such as the Steelcase office furniture company and General Motors. Senior African American managers or executives simply did not exist to warn me about the traps and how to avoid them. This is not a complaint; it is simply a fact.

An important truth about my ascent in corporate America is that many white people did help me. Remember, my career began during the early 1960s, when segregation was still legal in the South. Without the help of the majority — and Reverend Leon Sullivan — I never would have been hired, promoted, or presented with so many golden opportunities for advancement.

At the same time, many people in the black community helped me in ways that I appreciated as extremely protective. For example, one Friday night, after working a full shift at Lear, attending college classes, and commuting back to Grand Rapids, I wanted to have some fun. I was exhausted, and felt bogged down by my many responsibilities.

So I stopped by the gambling joint in the neighborhood where I had grown up in Grand Rapids. Little had changed, and all the black people – professional, working class and hustlers alike – still lived together in the same area. Now, just as I had observed as a boy, all kinds of people were congregating amidst loud music, prostitutes and a sandwich stand. They were playing cards, drinking alcohol, shooting dice and much more. The energy was exciting, and I relished the familiarity of the neighborhood.

I was really enjoying myself — until three of the regular guys confronted me.

"You get your little ass outta here!" one of them ordered. "You got no business in here." By putting me out, they were helping me. They knew I was trying to "be somebody," as my father had said years before. They were proud of me for that, and didn't want to corrupt me. Today people won't do that. They drag you down deeper into trouble.

Because I was always being blessed with so much help from others, I became deeply committed to helping people excel, personally and professionally. To do this, I identified areas that were important to me, and important to the world: education, young people and civil rights.

Roy, that's where you need to be, I told myself. *Anything pertaining to those areas outside the corporate world, that's your place.*

Making a Personal, Positive Impact During the Civil Rights Movement

My first decade at Lear coincided with some of the most momentous events of the Civil Rights Movement. While I did not participate in sit-ins, marches or protests, I was doing important work to advance our people by setting an impeccable example in corporate America and helping to open doors for other African Americans to gain employment and advancement. At the same time, I was also providing strong leadership in the black community.

Because I held a prominent position in the highly respected Lear Siegler corporation, the community asked me to serve as president of the Grand Rapids NAACP chapter. In that position, I interfaced with Paul Philips, who was the oldest reigning president of a National Urban League local chapter in America. He was so respected that later, when he died, former U.S. presidents attended his funeral. Paul and I met every other Monday evening in his office to strategize how to help the community. We'd talk about current events and specific conflicts that required our attention, and we decided what role each of us would play in addressing them.

Paul was viewed as a senior statesman, while I was a young trailblazer. This association gave me a lot of power. As a result, we were ultra-successful. For example, a Grand Rapids radio station was for sale, but its owner refused to consider a bid from an African American buyer. As president of the Grand Rapids NAACP chapter, I blocked the sale until the station owner agreed to consider bids from everyone.

However, I refused cases that lacked merit. If someone came to me with a complaint, and I believed it was invalid, I would tell them that we would not represent them.

"Roy," my brother said one day when he came to see me at the NAACP office. "I have this problem. I want you to do this as NAACP President."

I refused, because I believed he was wrong. My discernment -- based on merit, not race, drew criticism because some black people assumed that the NAACP would defend their situation under any condition.

"No," I often responded. "I'll defend you if you're right. If you're wrong, you won't get defended here."

Steadfast adherence to my principles garnered respect in political circles, and I was drawn into local politics. With the help of many people, including book publisher Bill Erdman and Federal Judge Doug Hillman, I was elected County Commissioner for the Eighteenth District of Grand Rapids. This district spanned a significant portion of the African American community, as well as a nice part of town where we lived, and an impressive swath of the middle- and upper- class white community.

In addition, I had a chance at being appointed mayor of Grand Rapids by the city council, but my minister successfully blocked me and was himself appointed. An opportunity to run for the Michigan Legislature was squashed by having witnessed the financial and energetic toll that such campaigns and careers wreaked on individuals. I asked myself, "Do I want to feed my family or run for public office?" I opted for a compromise: staying active on a local level, while still meeting my financial obligations with a corporate job.

My commitment to civic involvement presented a litany of opportunities that seemed to evolve organically. The Boy Scouts invited me to speak, and the United Negro College Fund asked me to participate in their fundraising efforts. Meanwhile, our home became a bustling hub for my many endeavors.

"Phone calls were always coming into our house like it was an office," Robin recalls with a reminder that during the late 1960s, land-line telephones were the quickest means of communication. The use of cell phones, email and text messaging would not occur until decades later.

"When my father was the County Commissioner for the Third Ward – the entire southeast side of Grand Rapids – people would call him about any problem they had in the neighborhood. If the trash wasn't picked up, or the police did or didn't do something, or the snow wasn't plowed, they called our house at all hours of the day and night. On top of him working, taking college classes, raising a family, being president of the NAACP and the County Commissioner, Daddy was always in motion."

As such, my endeavors became a family affair.

"I remember my mother going door-to-door, campaigning for him and passing out leaflets," Robin recalls. "The whole family would be at his campaign office, really late at night, and Daddy would bring Mommy and us kids home, then he'd go back to work more."

Community work came to the house as well.

"Every Thanksgiving, volunteers for the NAACP would bring donated food to our house," Robin remembers, "and we would help them pack bags and line them up in the living room and den. Then other NAACP members could come, pick up the food packages, and deliver them to families around town for the holiday."

1967: Close Call in Detroit

My work with the NAACP was especially important in the wake of the 1967 riots, which devastated Detroit and sparked mini-insurrections in Grand Rapids. This was a frightening time, and my family narrowly escaped the deadly destruction in Detroit.

On Saturday, July 22, we were driving back from a wonderful vacation at the World's Fair in Montreal, Canada. After we crossed the Ambassador Bridge, back into the United States, I was too exhausted to make the three-hour drive from Detroit to Grand Rapids.

"Kids, we're going to check into a motel, get a good night's rest, and head home after breakfast in the morning," I announced.

We had dinner, then Ruby took the children to swim in the motel's pool. A friend of mine named James stopped by.

"We're going to ride around the city and check things out," I told Ruby. Racial tensions were simmering in Detroit, due to unemployment, poverty and complaints of police brutality. I was eager to witness conditions for myself.

But that night, a police raid on an illegal, after-hours bar sparked one of the worst riots in American history. Gunfire and flames erupted as people looted stores, burned businesses and battled with police. Word spread quickly as the sound of gunshots thundered and flames lit up the night sky. James and I sped back to the motel.

"Wake up!" I shouted, running into our room, where Ruby and the kids were sleeping. "Wake up! Wake up! They're rioting down the street!"

Robin, who was seven years old, says, "I remember getting up and my mother putting our clothes on really quick. I was afraid because we were rushing and leaving fast. It was semi-light because the sun wasn't even up yet."

Ruby and I hopped into the front seat while the kids were in the back.

"We trapped Ronald in the middle because he was the smallest and we always fought not to be in that seat," Robin remembers. "Ricky and I were on our knees on the back seat, looking out the back window as Daddy raced down the expressway."

"Oh, Momma!" Robin exclaimed. "Smoke is going up in the air!"

"Momma, we see smoke!" Ricky said.

Ruby and I were speaking quietly, terrified that the rioting might have closed the freeway and trapped us there. Thankfully, we returned to Grand Rapids safely. But in the following days, we were horrified by news reports that the riots were prompting Governor *George W. Romney* to send the *Michigan National Guard* while President Lyndon Johnson called in the U.S. Army. Sadly, forty-three people were killed, and looting and fires caused an estimated $60 million in damage.

Detroit's civil disturbance convinced me that my community work was more important than ever. Subsequently, my prominence proved invaluable as racial conflicts simmered in Grand Rapids, especially in the public schools. Unfortunately, mini riots forced the district to shut down the schools on several occasions. In an overall atmosphere of unrest, these insurrections could erupt over one student's expulsion, rumors, arguments between teenagers, or students' criticism of how teachers were dealing with racial matters. When this happened, the superintendent and the mayor of Grand Rapids would call on me.

"Roy, we need to you come and speak to the kids," Bobbi Butler, the city's Community Relations Director, would say as her first call for help. "We know you'll say what needs to be said. But most importantly, just seeing you has a calming effect on the kids."

As I stood in the auditorium facing hundreds of teenagers, I would remind them that two of the greatest civil rights leaders of the decade offered very different ways to deal with racial inequality and injustice.

"Stokely Carmichael said, 'Let's fight!' And Dr. King said peaceful protests will solve our problems," I announced. "I'm here to tell you that fighting will not do anything but get you in more trouble."

The young people were rapt when I spoke, because I was a respected member of the community who was showing that I and the teachers and the principals all cared about their well-being and their futures.

"We need to establish a truce between the parties involved in the conflicts here at school," I said.

Just as the students might follow a rabble-rouser who wanted to incite a mini-riot, I offered a better alternative by convincing student leaders to preach peace. Because most people are followers, those student leaders could then encourage others to find peaceful ways to resolve their conflicts.

At the same time, I was proud to present an example of a black businessman who was successful in corporate America. I knew all too well that many of the black students went home to parents who were uneducated and impoverished. And those parents who worked probably did so in blue-collar jobs in factories.

Therefore, my mission to inspire young people required me to project the image of success through my clothes, my cars, my speech, and my behavior. I wanted Roy Roberts to inspire them just as Sticks Green's impeccable clothing, sophisticated air and sports cars had demonstrated to me how a successful man should look and carry himself. Young black kids who come out of poverty and deprivation need to witness how successful, professional men and women look and act. They need to understand that appearance matters.

For that reason, clothes are really, really important to me. They go a long way to speak about *who* you are. As do one's actions.

However, never allow your clothes to subordinate your intellect. Instead, make sure that your intelligence always outshines your clothes.

It's important to note that I did not consciously set out to help people because my father had told me that I would. It was something I felt compelled to do naturally. Helping people is MY BEING. Helping to quell conflicts among young people in the wake of the

1967 riots is one example of that. And quite honestly, it brings to mind that old adage that you've heard a million times: "Situations make heroes out of people."

An Open Door to the Social Elite

Concurrent with my corporate ascent and community activism, I nurtured a vibrant social life that complimented my other endeavors. On one level, I inherited a certain social status through professional prominence. At the time, the expectation was that if someone formed a social organization for black men, the top people in the community would be selected for membership. Roy Roberts would be one of those persons.

Membership in these private social clubs distinguished men and their wives as the crème de la crème. It went without saying that I wanted acceptance from such an august body of doctors, lawyers and other professionals. Membership validated Roy Roberts the citizen. While I enjoyed the camaraderie, participation in these social groups broadened my sphere of influence in Grand Rapids. The city had two or three clubs, and 80 percent of the same people belonged to them. These clubs had a reputation for being rather icy to those who had yet to elevate to the level of accomplishment that they deemed worthy of their time and attention.

After a certain degree of promotion at Lear Siegler, I became the youngest person to join one of the most prestigious groups in town. I was only twenty-seven years old when Dr. John English invited me to a club meeting at his spectacular home. To provide perspective on this privilege, Dr. English had a son, John Jr., who was my age. However, the young man's lack of achievement cost him an invitation to join the club.

Meetings were held in members' homes; this provided an opportunity for people to brag about their success without verbalizing it. And Dr. English certainly had earned bragging rights; he lived two doors down from the home that was the birthplace of then-future U.S. President Gerald Ford. While I felt proud that this neighborhood was only six blocks from the home I had purchased, Dr. English's home was worlds away from mine in terms of size, value and décor.

As I walked through Dr. English's home to reach the basement for the meeting, I was awed by the opulent gold fixtures, crystal chandeliers, and expensive-looking vases. My immediate thought was, *I want a house like this.*

My membership in this club — sponsored by Jim Eddy, a principal and coach — convinced me that such a dream was wholly attainable if I continued to work hard and earn it. This mindset, along with my naturally inquisitive nature, inspired me to listen and learn from club members such as Dick Drew, a dental technician, and noted attorney Floyd Skinner.

When the clubs hosted formal events, I would don a tuxedo and Ruby would wear a beautiful evening gown. One year, *The Grand Rapids Press* published an impressive spread featuring three of the wives. Half the page showcased a photograph of Ruby! She was stunning, posing in her gorgeous dress on a grand staircase at the luxurious hotel lobby where the event was held. That was an extremely memorable experience as Ruby and I were celebrated by our African American peers, as well as the mainstream Grand Rapids community.

Educational Pursuit

As my professional life, social stature and civic involvement advanced, I wanted Ruby to pursue her education and career. This, I believed, would enable us to remain intellectually compatible. To do that, I encouraged her to take classes at Grand Rapids Junior College during the day, while our children attended the excellent public school in our neighborhood.

Our plan was that Ruby would study education, and secure a teaching position with the help of my friend, the superintendent of the Grand Rapids Public School system, Phil Runkel. Then she would earn her bachelor's degree from Western Michigan University and continue teaching. We set this plan in motion. Meanwhile, I was working long hours, commuting to college, participating in politics, and engaging in community endeavors.

I was not home much. Some days, I would see Ruby in the morning when she made breakfast. However, breakfast meetings at the office often required my attendance, so I would leave the house early. In the evenings, after returning from school, I would sometimes visit with Ruby.

"Roy, you should spend more time with Ruby," her mother warned. "She feels like you're never home and that you don't have time for her."

My feeling was that my full-time career was enabling me to support the family and cover college tuition for both of us. I believed my time was well invested because the journey would secure a solid financial future for our family.

In 1970, I graduated with honors from Western Michigan University with a bachelor's degree in Business Administration. As desperately as I wanted to celebrate, I could not attend the commencement ceremony, because I was scheduled to work at Lear that day. However, when I had the time, I drove to the highest point on campus, and stepped out of my car. There, I shouted up to the sky:

> *"Nobody on the face of the Earth is going to stop me from being successful!"*

This declaration accompanied the fact that I was not looking for gifts. I wanted to work hard, with focus and discipline, to earn all the accolades and abundance that I believed I could attain.

Playing Hardball with Owen Bieber

Not long after my graduation, I was in my office, tending to my duties as General Supervisor of Manufacturing, a position I held after serving in Quality Assurance.

"Mr. Roberts," my secretary announced, "I have a conference call for you with the president of the company, the vice president of the instrument division and the vice president of Human Resources."

When I took the call, the president said, "Roy, we're in a real bind here, and we're hoping you can step in and save the day in a big way."

"You know I love a challenge," I answered eagerly.

"We've got ninety-five days," the head of HR said, "to negotiate a new labor agreement for three-thousand Lear Siegler employees."

They explained that this national labor agreement would impact a major strategic and financial division of the corporation. I wondered why they were calling upon me to manage the responsibilities of the Labor Relations Manager.

"You know Jack Steel with the local UAW is as tough as his name sounds," the VP of the Instrument Division said. "But our Labor Relations manager, considering his penchant for rounders, is not the ideal person to square off with Steel."

"This is a 'do or die' situation," the HR director said. "Failure is not an option, or we'll have one ugly strike on our hands."

The vice president of the instruments division added, "And with a tough guy like Owen Bieber heading up the region for UAW Local 330, this is will be a real game of hardball."

"Roy," the President said, "we believe you can finesse these negotiations to make Lear Siegler stay on strategy, while keeping the UAW happy at the same time. Understand?"

I understood that they were glossing over some important information about why the labor relations manager was not fit to negotiate the labor agreement. The term 'rounder' suggested a drinking problem, and I suspected that he could not be trusted with this responsibility. For now, more importantly, I sensed a fantastic opportunity to learn and make my bosses look good by delivering results above and beyond their expectations.

"I'll do it!" I announced.

"Good deal," the three men responded.

"Now here's a little background," the vice president of Human Resources said. "Our first hunch was to hire a lawyer to come in and negotiate the agreement. But the legal firm recommended that we anoint someone inside our organization, someone who understands our people and who our people understand."

The president added, "Someone who can mix it up with the best of them, but understand where we're trying to go with our goals and objectives with the company."

"Our best success will come," the VP of manufacturing said, "when we put that special person in charge of negotiating the agreement. We agreed that person should be Roy Roberts."

The president continued: "Roy, you're well-known, well-respected, and you've had a lot of interface with the unions over the years. Sure you've had your share of squabbles with them, but you have a way of disagreeing without being disagreeable. You know how to maintain respect on both sides. So you're the man to get this job done."

I concluded the call with the proper decorum, then sat quietly to contemplate the exciting honor of this new assignment as Labor Relations Manager.

This was big time! This was one of the most monumental things that could happen to a person in his early thirties.

Next, I studied the calendar, imagining the word STRIKE DEADLINE looming in giant red letters, as the actual day of reckoning was only ninety-five days away. Researching and negotiating an agreement in such a short period of time was unprecedented. Adrenaline and nervous energy propelled me into an intensive work mode. By the time I assembled my seven-member team, we would have ninety days to prepare for and agree upon a major national agreement for Lear Siegler with the UAW. That was an impossibly short time period, even for seasoned negotiators.

And I had never negotiated before! Making matters worse, these negotiations could potentially put me face-to-face with a notorious titan of labor relations: Owen Bieber. As the UAW's Region One Director, which included Grand Rapids Local 330, his reputation was as imposing and intimidating as his large, physical stature. He was tough and razor-sharp.

That meant I needed to assemble the best and the brightest for my team. I needed people who really understood what had transpired since the last three-year agreement, which was about to expire. What were the grievances? What were the problems that the union had presented to us? What were the problems that Lear Siegler had experienced with the contract? What would we give and what would we take, this time around? We needed to answer and resolve these questions within the next thirty-five or forty days to avoid a strike that could devastate Lear Siegler and possibly the union.

That said, the first person to join my team was a First Line Supervisor who had impressed me when we had once worked together.

"I want to work with you in labor relations," he said. "All my life I've wanted to do this, and I feel that my work experience and my business classes at Aquinas College have prepared me for it."

He joined me and six other highly capable people when we began negotiations in a big conference room at a nice hotel on Cascade Road near affluent East Grand Rapids. It was important to take the union members out of their environment, into a semi-luxurious setting; this forced the union to look up to the company. It also made my team — which set up a workspace in a separate meeting room — feel like they were being rewarded for their hard work.

Because negotiating with UAW veteran Jack Steel was a Herculean task. This man was used to getting what he wanted, exactly as he wanted it. Backing him up was a team of 15 equally hard-nosed people. As a result, we jockeyed back and forth on all the issues for weeks. The day before the 7 a.m. strike deadline, we came to loggerheads about pay and benefits — the two most important parts of a labor contract.

We became very vociferous on both sides. Our exchanges were downright contentious. Anger, anxiety and nervous energy charged that conference room like one hundred tons of dynamite. Then, the night before the deadline, as the clock ticked toward midnight, it felt that our disagreements might set off a catastrophic strike.

Suddenly, without warning, a huge man charged into the room.

"Roy Roberts!" he shouted, "you don't treat my people like the scum of the earth!"

The shock of his appearance, and his threatening tone, startled me so much that I stood frozen in place, struggling to comprehend what was going on.

"I don't know who the hell you think you are!" the man yelled with an onslaught of expletives that are not fit to print. At six-feet, five inches tall and nearly 300 pounds, this irate fellow was nearly a foot taller than me, and almost twice my weight!

It was Owen Bieber — meaner and tougher than even his reputation had warned.

"You don't treat my people like they're unimportant!" he shouted.

I turned to my team and said, with as much confidence as I could muster, "I'd like you to go back to our meeting room."

After they exited the room, Owen Bieber continued his verbal assault in front of the UAW team. I sat down at the table and leaned forward to hide my trembling hands and shaking knees. I was physically afraid of this big, imposing guy.

"Roberts," he ordered, "come out in the hall. I want to talk to you."

With the contract on the line, and the strike deadline just seven hours away, I found the courage to stand up and stride into the hallway. Owen Bieber continued to yell and scream at me as we walked for a good seventy yards. Then, out of earshot of his team, he became silent and looked at me. With a kind, respectful voice, he asked, "Hey, partner, you got something for me?"

I was stunned. But I understood it right away.

"You've got to have something for me," he said, "so I can deliver it to my people back in the room, so we can get this thing done."

"Yes, sir," I answered.

He and I sat and talked about everything that was going on in Grand Rapids and the state of Michigan. For about three hours, we enjoyed a warm, engaging discussion about everything under the sun.

At 3 a.m., he said, "Let's go back down to the room."

The strike deadline was four hours away, and we had yet to negotiate a deal. When we arrived within earshot of the UAW team in the conference room, he launched another verbal assault. This time, I understood the game, so I played along with his strategy to deliver a deal to his people. This involved blocking me from entering the room.

"Can I come into the room?" I asked.

"No!" he shouted. "You can't come in the room! We don't want you in this room. When you learn how to treat my people with respect and decency and understand their needs and wants, then we'll consider letting you in!"

"Okay." I returned to the company meeting room with my team. For nearly three hours, I urged Owen and the union team by phone to allow the two parties to get back together and finalize an agreement before the strike deadline. Both sides were exhausted and frustrated after twenty hours of negotiating. Ultimately, Owen and the team agreed that I could return at 5:45 a.m., so we headed back to the conference room to negotiate. There, within a short period of time, we agreed to increase pay and some benefits for UAW members. With that, we had a labor agreement. It was 6:30 a.m., a half-hour before the strike deadline.

This incredible experience enhanced my ability to read people. Watching two dozen men and women fight for the financial well being of employees and retirees in the heat of negotiations for twenty hours straight — because they truly cared about people — was awe-inspiring. I was even more impressed immediately after we reached an agreement, when the toughest negotiators went to sleep on couches in the conference room. These individuals did not rest until they had succeeded at doing the job they were trusted to do.

Neither did Roy Roberts. I was elated that we had gotten the deal done. Our agreement kept the company within the financial parameters that would allow us to move the business forward. My bosses at Lear Siegler were thrilled at the outcome, and I was lauded throughout the community in ways that elevated my stature as a successful businessman.

After that, I excelled as Labor Relations Manager. I won every arbitration -- except for one. That time, I disregarded the advice of my wise and experienced executive secretary, who had worked for local attorney Floyd Skinner. That was the last time I ignored her guidance.

Pentagon Sales Coup as Lear Marketing Manager

Next, Lear promoted me to the position of Marketing Manager. This was a sophisticated part of the operation, which involved contracts negotiation. Three weeks into the job, my assignment was to convince the Pentagon to purchase the 2156 Indicator, which was installed in airplanes to measure altitude. Determined to make the sale, I phoned the appropriate person at the Pentagon. Her dialect and tone revealed that she was African American.

"You must be new at Lear," she said.

"I'm new in this job," I answered.

"How's it going?"

"It's very difficult," I said. "I have to make this sale to save my job."

I elaborated on the difficulties of being the first African American in every position that I had taken in the company, and how arduous it felt to pitch a complex product that was rarely purchased. As a result, this sister chose to look out for a young brother and took the time to discuss with me the specifications of the product. Eventually, we negotiated a purchase agreement for the Pentagon to buy the 2156 Indicator.

My bosses were extremely impressed with my quick, lucrative sale, and everyone in the marketing department was surprised that I was successful. That experience highlights a common theme in my career: I always wanted the toughest job, because it provided the greatest return on investment of my time and energy.

My success impressed executives at the Steelcase office furniture company. I was called at work by the Steelcase personnel department about a potential meeting with the company's president. I returned the call later from home, and set a meeting date.

At that meeting, the Steelcase president and his team told me: "Mr. Roberts, we'd like to make you Vice President of Production Inventory Control. You would work at our global headquarters in Grand Rapids."

I would be the only African American in upper management, earning an excellent salary, benefits and upward mobility. I accepted, but I immediately reflected on how good Lear had been to me and my family. After intense contemplation, I withdrew my acceptance of the position at Steelcase.

New Family Dynamics

My loyalty paid off, because I was earning more money and excelling faster than I ever imagined. I wanted to celebrate this with the ultimate symbol of success: a spectacular home. That was the American Dream, and I wanted that for my family.

At the same time, the public school system embarked on a controversial plan to integrate the public schools. This set off a dramatic demographic shift in the early1970s.

"When our local elementary school suddenly experienced a huge influx of black students," Robin recalls, "we had no less than twelve houses all go up for sale on our street. By fourth grade, when I was nine years old in 1969, our local elementary school was almost all black."

Ruby and I were disturbed that class sizes suddenly swelled to the point that teachers could no longer provide a nurturing educational environment.

"The classrooms were so crowded," Robin remembers, "they were teaching kids in the gym, in the cafeteria and even in the hallway. We weren't learning anything. Teachers were complaining. It was chaotic."

Ruby and I sent the kids to St. Stephen Catholic School in affluent East Grand Rapids. The mostly Caucasian student body included several other black students. I remember being shocked at the number of people who could afford to pay tuition. Our plan was that the children would attend private school until they reached high school. Then, to ensure that they interfaced with people from all walks of life, they would attend public high school.

Sending three children to private school – on top of tuition that I was paying for myself and Ruby — was a smart investment. On another positive note, Ruby's parents purchased a home across the street from us; their proximity was great for the kids. Plus, our new black neighbors hosted a fun block party that summer. Yet changing times inspired me to list our house for sale, and have a new home built in East Grand Rapids. Building our own residence and moving into an unfamiliar community amounted to breaking new ground on two different levels.

"While we were having a house built," Robin remembers, "we'd go out on Saturdays and Sundays and look at it. We'd walk through it, and Ricky, Ronald and I would pick out our bedrooms. We were so excited!"

Building a house motivated me to work even harder. I remained convinced that Ruby would tolerate my long hours at Lear and in the community because my success was advancing our family. But I was wrong: Ruby and I ultimately agreed to divorce.

"You keep the house," I insisted. To minimize costs, we chose to use the same lawyer, Alfonso Lewis, a noted attorney and entrepreneur. But as we waited for our court date, one of her uncles talked Ruby into using his college buddy -- who was an attorney and a known drunk. As expected, when we arrived in court in early 1971, we were before Judge John T. Letts. As we proceeded with the divorce, my lawyer was taking them to the cleaners.

"Your honor, my client would like to approach the bench," my attorney said.

Judge Letts agreed. I approached with the lawyers.

"Judge," I said, "please tell me what you're getting ready to give her."

The judge read his intentions for the property settlement. Then I took a sheet of paper from my pocket and said, "This is what I want to give her." I read my list. It was considerably more than what the judge was going to give her. Judge Letts convinced the two lawyers to modify the settlement in Ruby's favor.

"Decreed!" the judge announced, pounding his gavel on the bench. "Mr. Roberts, I want to see you in my chambers."

I joined him with my lawyer.

I was moved when I saw that Judge Letts was crying!

"I've been on the bench for twelve years," he said, "and I've never seen anybody do this. I'm convinced you did the right thing. You're going to find the right person who will dance to your music and you will never look back."

"Daddy, Don't Leave!"

Divorce made me feel like a failure, and I hated everything about it.

"Daddy, don't leave!" cried eleven-year-old Robin, sitting in the passenger seat of my car. "Don't get divorced!" This scene played out many nights in the driveway. Eight-year-old Ronald and twelve-year-old Ricky were equally upset, because the divorce came as a shock to the children.

"I had never heard our parents argue," Robin recalls. "Ever. They sat us down and said, 'We're getting a divorce.'"

We would not be moving into the new house, and we took our home off the market, because Ruby would remain there with the children. Ruby and I had joint custody, and I rented a nearby condo.

"For the first couple of years after the divorce," Robin recalls, "we saw Daddy every day because he would pick all of us up in the morning. He would take me and my brothers to St. Stephens, then take our mother to her modeling jobs, or to her job at Gantos (women's clothing store), and to her college classes."

This schedule gave me a strong presence in our children's lives. At the same time, Ruby did not drive, and I was happy to help her attend Grand Rapids Junior College.

"During parent-teacher conference," Robin recalls, "Daddy would get out of work, regardless of his job, and go to the school to meet with our teachers."

But during the early 1970s, my ever-multiplying professional and civic duties precluded me from continuing this routine. Robin never revealed the painful challenges that she endured, until she was well into adulthood. Now, in hindsight, I wish that Ruby and I had invested the time and energy into strategizing how we would raise the kids as co-parents. Robin remained very close to me, but if Ricky didn't like his mother's rules, he'd come and stay with me. If Ronald felt my restrictions were too harsh, he'd retreat to Ruby's house. We allowed that, and it was a mistake. Ronald ultimately spent the most time with Ruby because his dog was at her house.

Meanwhile, Ruby earned a master's degree in education from WMU, secured a good teaching position, and was active with the children's educations.

She remained graceful and considerate as I ascended the corporate ladder and steadily earned higher salaries. She never returned to court to demand more money.

"Every year for Daddy's birthday, Father's Day and Christmas," Robin recalls, "our mother got him a gift for us kids to wrap and give to him with a card that we all signed. It would have been so sad to be fourteen or fifteen when you don't have money, and it's your dad's birthday, and you don't even have a card to give him."

Likewise, Robin says that she never heard Ruby speak ill of me, nor I of her.

What Doesn't Kill You Makes You Stronger

The German philosopher *Friedrich Nietzsche* once said, "That which does not kill us makes us stronger." My divorce made me stronger in terms of developing a higher degree of sensitivity to myself and to the responsibility that each spouse has for nurturing the marriage. I began to share this wisdom with young newlyweds, explaining that, "You are derelict if you fail to put forth the effort to make it work."

Meanwhile, I refused to allow divorce to tarnish my professional reputation or block my ambition. I wanted to look successful at all times, so I purchased a large, luxury car, despite the financial difficulties of supporting two separate households. The car alerted the world that Roy Roberts was aiming for the top.

In 1971, I was ecstatic when General Motors made history by becoming the first major corporation to appoint an African American to its board of directors. I was impressed by GM's bold choice: Reverend Leon Sullivan was an influential civil rights activist and pastor of Philadelphia's Zion Baptist Church, which would become one of America's largest congregations. He led a self-help movement for black economic empowerment and founded the Opportunities Industrialization Centers, which helped people learn life skills and find employment. The IOC would become so successful that it would spawn affiliates around the world.

As the months and years progressed, my admiration deepened for Reverend Sullivan. He courageously used his powerful position on the General Motors Board of Directors to advocate that companies — including GM — relinquish business operations in apartheid South Africa. He outlined his strategy in the Sullivan Principles, a blueprint for companies to curtail commerce until South Africa abolished its racist system.

Like me, Reverend Sullivan had been born in the segregated South, and was raised by a single parent in abject poverty. He was driven by a passion for helping people, which inspired powerful individuals such as New York Congressman Adam Clayton Powell, Jr., to help him ascend to a position where he could make widespread change. I hoped one day to meet this great man.

Meanwhile, Lear promoted me to Staff Assistant to the President, which enabled me to write speeches, compile financial reports and travel to company headquarters in California.

On one such trip, I learned a valuable lesson: never drink and party the night before a presentation. En route, I met three people who were staying at my hotel. They invited me for cocktails and dancing and, being a single man, I had a great time. But I paid the price. The next morning I was so hung-over, I gave the worst presentation of my life. Never again! I promised myself I would never drink in excess or stay up late when I needed to work the next morning.

Meanwhile, it was exciting to play an important role in a company that, by 1970, had 56 divisions in 17 countries. These divisions included avionics, real estate, commercial products and power equipment. These endeavors earned more than $600 million in profits at the time.

I also taught classes at nearby Aquinas College, Grand Valley State University and later, Michigan State University. Throngs of students attended my liberal arts courses on labor relations, collective bargaining and contemporary minority issues.

Despite the steady progress I was making, persistent racism fueled my ambition to make a difference. Once, I was standing near the desk of the assistant to the vice president of manufacturing when the phone rang. It was 6:30 p.m., and because he had left for the day, I answered.

"Hello," a man said. "I'm with one of the Southern technology companies."

"How may I help you?" I asked.

"These niggers down here are trying to charge us with discrimination!" the man said angrily as he launched into a racist rant. "We heard y'all had some of the same problems up there. How'd you take care of it?"

"It's simple," I responded. "I took care of it."

"Well who are you?" he asked.

"I'm Roy Roberts."

At that moment, the vice president of manufacturing, who was my boss at the time, approached, and I handed him the phone. After listening to the caller's vitriol, my boss demanded, "Do you know who you're talking to?"

When he learned I was black, the caller apologized for six months!

A "Pacesetter" in Business Attire Early on

Robin recently showed me a magazine published in 1973, when I was the 34-year-old Labor Relations Manager at Lear Siegler. The Grand Rapids *Accent* magazine featured me among a dozen men (I was the only African American) in a cover story called The Accent Gallery of Pacesetters in Business and Fashion.

"These busy executives and professionals all have one thing in common," it said, "an appreciation of the importance of clothes and fashion awareness to the pursuit of a successful career in today's business world." One photo shows me wearing an ultra-1970s dark gray and crimson plaid suit, matching wide, paisley tie and crimson shirt; and sporting a bright plum-colored suit with wide lapels and a large honeycomb pattern. "It picks me up to look well," I said in the article. "I function better when I know I am well dressed and ready for anything the day may bring. I feel it's very important that a man's wardrobe is well coordinated and if I find that the proper accessories are not at hand I won't wear the suit until they are."

Little has changed when it comes to my clothing philosophy. Nor has the media's recognition of my style. Detroit's upscale HOUR magazine named me on its 2011 Best-Dressed List. My photo appears inside the glossy cover; I'm wearing a brown Brioni suit, leather lace-up shoes, a crisp white shirt and a purple-striped silk tie.

"I have to dress for the kids, for the teachers, for the school system," I say under a heading for my Trademark Style. "I like dressy clothes that play on the edge, but not too far, mixing textures and patterns. But I never let the clothes outshine me."

Words of a Divorce Judge Prove Prophetic

During the early 1970s, I had the honor and privilege of becoming the first African American to serve on a hospital board of directors in Grand Rapids. I relished the irony that Blodgett Hospital had invited me to become a member of its board. Back in 1958, this hospital had sent me that letter notifying me of the $300 down payment that was required for Ricky's birth. Now, I felt proud that I had advanced so far from an unemployed teenaged father to an educated businessman who was respected in both corporate circles and in the community.

One day about eighteen months after the divorce, I was leaving a board meeting at Blodgett Hospital. As I stepped out of the conference room, I bumped into a nurse.

It was Maureen Robinson! I had not seen her in thirteen years, since she had gone off to nursing school and married a guy who had once played sports against me.

"Roy," she said playfully, "you're the last person I wanted to see."

"That's bullshit," I teased. "You were looking for me!"

Maureen and I chatted, updating each other about our lives since high school.

"I'm a nurse here in the hospital nursery, working with premature babies," she said. After high school, she had come to Grand Rapids to attend nursing school. Married for almost five years, she divorced and returned to Muskegon to work at a hospital and attend Junior College. The position at Blodgett Hospital ultimately brought her back to Grand Rapids.

"I was strongly against getting re-married," Maureen remembers. "I didn't want to be bothered. My feeling was, I can be by myself and be perfectly content. Then my doctor asked me one day, 'Maureen, are you dating?' and I said, 'I am not ever going to sign another document to get married again.' The doctor tried to convince me that I deserved to have a wonderful man in my life, and that marriage can be very happy when you find the right person. That's when I saw Roy."

Maureen's independence and success were ultra-impressive. While she owned a Buick and was renting a condominium, she had amassed significant savings in a John Hancock account that was offered to nurses at the hospital.

"After my divorce," Maureen explained as we began to spend time together as friends, "I worked at this hospital and they were signing people up for a John Hancock savings program. At that time, nurses did not have retirement savings programs; we would have to rely on Social Security. The hospital director said, 'Maureen, you're making a lot of money, and you don't spend a lot. Why don't you consider joining John Hancock?' I did, and they began to automatically withdraw a certain amount from every paycheck. As a result, I saved a lot of money."

This reminded me that Maureen had always been my ideal lady because of her value system and her moral compass. She was internally driven to achieve, unswayed by trends or the need to impress others. On top of that, she knew all about me and I knew all about her. We had no secrets.

After dating for two years, I asked Maureen to spend the rest of her life with me. She was fully aware that my ambition would require long hours and hard work. We made it a major priority to be a team, and expressed our mutual desire to never divorce again; we were both truly committed "'til death do us part." Maureen and I agreed that open communication and consideration of each other's needs and preferences would ensure our marital success.

For the wedding, we asked our friends, Johnny and Bobbi Butler, to stand up with us before Reverend W. Abney at Bethel Church.

"We're coming!" announced my friend Bob Brown, who was the Director of the Michigan Department of Corrections. He and his wife Joy had heard news of our impending nuptials. "We have to see this. We'll be the proof that you got married."

They attended our small ceremony on December 7, 1974, and the day was perfect.

"I never wanted a big wedding," recalls Maureen, who still has the beige, polyester dress that she wore while I sported my sharpest suit.

We celebrated by going to dinner. Then Maureen and I flew to California for several days to visit my brother Bob and his wife Bobbi, who had attended nursing school with Maureen.

"Roy, be careful when you get here," Bob warned. "There's a lot of dope and illegal firearms coming in from Mexico." Sure enough, as I was driving on the busy 405 Freeway, another driver sped down an entrance ramp and struck our rental car.

"My neck is stiff," Maureen said as I pulled over.

While tending to her, I glimpsed the rear-view mirror. The other driver, who appeared Mexican, had pulled up behind us and was approaching our vehicle on foot. His hand was in his coat pocket.

"He's got a gun," I warned Maureen.

"You okay?" he asked with a Spanish accent.

"We're okay," I said.

"You no call police." He pulled a wad of twenty-dollar bills from his pocket, then nodded at our dented car. "Take this," he said, handing me the cash. "You get it fixed."

"OK, we'll get it fixed," I said.

I'm convinced that was a dangerous situation. I did not call the police. In fact, I needed the money. And I always say in jest that I earned money on our honeymoon.

At the time of our wedding, Maureen and I were each renting apartments; hers was larger.

"Why don't we buy a house," Maureen said.

At the time, my salary from Lear was largely committed to paying child support and resolving debts that remained from my first marriage.

"Buying a house is a great idea," I said. "But I don't have any money. So you go get your money out of the bank and I'll show you how to do it."

Thanks to Maureen's savings, we purchased a nice brick home on Franklin Street in Grand Rapids. With almost 2,000 square feet of living space, it had three bedrooms, upstairs laundry and a fireplace. Because the builder had constructed the home for his wife, it had marble trim around the windows, a heated towel rack in the bathroom and a quiet air conditioner during an era when units were typically bulky and loud.

Meanwhile, Maureen took a teaching position in the nursing program at Grand Rapids Junior College. Three years later, she became the administrative supervisor for nurses in the health services program in the local school district. At the same time, the state of Michigan passed a law mandating one semester of health education for students from kindergarten through twelfth grade. Maureen was selected to develop that curriculum with experts from the University of Michigan and the state of Michigan. She did this for seven years.

Meanwhile, my own teaching would ultimately enable me to become Special Assistant to the President of Aquinas College, where Maureen would later serve on the board of trustees.

Home life with Maureen was harmonious and joyous, and it provided a solid foundation that enabled me to go out into the world and excel on every level.

When Ricky, Robin and Ronald visited for dinner or stayed with us, Maureen never tried to take their mother's place or win them over with special favors. She nurtured a genuinely warm atmosphere in our home that made the kids feel they were welcome anytime.

All the while, our marriage prompted me to remember what Judge Letts had said in his chambers after granting my divorce:

"You're going to find the right person who will dance to your music and you will never look back."

His words were prophetic. Because Maureen is that person.

Family Friction: Placing Papa in Assisted Living

During one holiday season during the mid 1970s, I gathered my brothers and sisters together to discuss how to address our father's failing health.

"I'm beginning to question whether Papa is capable of living on his own anymore," I told Bob, Gene, Minnie Ruth, Ludine and Retha Mae as we gathered in the family room of the home that Maureen and I had purchased.

Tang was also with us. While my older brother was skilled at making a lot of money by hustling numbers, my siblings did not perceive him as being the smartest of the bunch.

"Papa is reaching an age where his health requires him to have assistance," I continued. "What do you think we ought to do?"

"Hey," Tang said, "we probably ought to look at getting him into an assisted living place."

The room exploded. Retha Mae, the tough one who always had a lot of things to say, led the chorus of outrage.

"What the hell are you talking about?" she shouted. "You're not going to put my father in an assisted living place!"

Tang stared her down and declared, "Shit, sister! You're the last one who should talk! No way will he spend one day with you!"

Finally, I calmed everyone down, and the conversation focused on finding the best option for our father. Gene took the initiative to find a nice assisted living home in Muskegon. We moved Papa in, and were quite pleased with the care he received. Ironically, we are now considering that same place for Gene, whose health is failing.

Meanwhile, I would visit Papa periodically. He always had a great sense of humor — and an eye for the ladies. One Sunday, Maureen and I were visiting and I was talking to a nurse about my father's health.

"Look at that old boy over there," the nurse said, nodding at Papa and a woman nearby. "He's trying to hit on that woman!"

Interestingly, he quickly became acclimated to that being his home. If we took him out for dinner with the kids, it would only take a few hours for him to declare, "I'm ready to go home."

When My Resume was Rejected by General Motors

As my career flourished at Lear Siegler, my competitive spirit inspired a strong desire to join the world's number one manufacturing company. I viewed the world headquarters in Detroit's 15-story GM Building as the zenith of corporate America, and indeed the automobile industry around the world.

Do I have what it takes to get there?

I wanted to find out. So I devised a plan to get my foot in the door, closer to home, because General Motors had three divisions and two plants in Grand Rapids.

Ambition surged within me as I prepared my resume, then drove to the Metal Fabrication Plant on Thirty-Sixth Street.

"Good morning," I told the receptionist. I wore one of my sharpest business suits, while exuding confidence and an upbeat demeanor.

"My name is Roy Roberts," I said, gripping my resumé in an envelope, "and I'd like to speak with the personnel manager, so I can submit my resume."

It had been nearly twenty years since I had applied for a job at Kelvinator's. During that time, my stellar track record at Lear had demonstrated that I was a valuable asset to the company; certainly General Motors would recognize my charisma and talent — and hire me right away.

"We're not accepting applications." The receptionist's terse tone was like a pin popping a balloon; my confidence deflated just as quickly. In addition, my work experience had taught me that companies typically accepted resumes, even during periods when they were not hiring, to keep on file and review when jobs opened up.

I had endured my share of disappointment throughout my life, so I took this one in stride. I considered it a dream deferred, not abandoned.

So I continued to apply myself 110 percent at Lear, as well as in the community. As the best known and most powerful African American businessperson in town, I was determined to continue to excel in every way.

SIX

Joining General Motors Corporation

Three months after General Motors refused to accept my resume, I received a phone call from the General Manager of GM's Diesel Equipment Division in Grand Rapids.

"Roy," said Davis Donnelly, "we've got Reverend Leon Sullivan coming to town to give the keynote speech for OIC at their annual meeting here in Grand Rapids."

As NAACP President, I was impressed with how Dr. Sullivan's Opportunities Industrialization Centers of America had a Grand Rapids location that trained blacks with his "self help" philosophy to find employment and build economic power through entrepreneurship.

Aware that Mr. Donnelly was president of the OIC's Board, I asked, "How can I help you?"

"Well Roy, since you're a well-known and highly respected leader in town," the manager said, "we'd like you to introduce Reverend Sullivan."

I was elated! I was called to this momentous task because I had the most prominent job of any African American in the city. Neither Steelcase nor General Motors had any high-ranking black managers or executives.

"I would be honored to introduce Reverend Sullivan," I responded.

In 1971, I had heard Reverend Sullivan speak when he received the NAACP's highest honor, The Spingarn Medal. For more than an hour, no one in the crowd moved as he delivered one of the most riveting speeches I've ever heard. Now, the honor of introducing this great man inspired me to set a goal for myself: *Roy, you do a good job of introducing this person, and you do it right, and you do it with integrity.*

When the night arrived, I was thrilled to meet Reverend Sullivan. Standing six-feet, five inches tall, he was as handsome, elegant and charismatic as I had imagined he would be. All evening, I had the privilege of sitting with him and the general manager of GM's Diesel Equipment Division, who was also a very stately man.

The three of us had incredible conversations about everything under the sun. This included fascinating insights that Mr. Donnelly shared about General Motors that I had read in the newspapers. At the time, Oldsmobile sales were soaring, because critics and customers loved the Rocket V8 engine. In fact, the top-selling car in North America was The Cutlass series.

"The Olds V8 is so popular," Davis Donnelly said, "production is working at breakneck speed to keep up with the demand."

A short time later, when I introduced Reverend Sullivan, I explained how he had attended a segregated high school in West Virginia, before going to West Virginia State College on a basketball and football scholarship. But when he injured his foot, thus ending his athletic scholarship, he worked in a steel mill to pay for college. Concurrently, he became a member of the Tau Chapter of *Kappa Alpha Psi* Fraternity. Of course I touched on how he had founded the OIC, and was working with corporations on how to participate in South African commerce under apartheid. I also shared that he had received the NAACP's highest honor, the Spingarn Award.

I was really pleased with my introduction, which set the stage for Reverend Sullivan's booming voice and powerful message to captivate the hundreds of people attending the banquet. His oratory skills as a Baptist minister were in full effect as he started out low, and continued to build in intensity and volume.

Reverend Sullivan spoke at length about his historic appointment to the GM Board, and why he was so passionately committed to convincing companies to use economic sanctions against South Africa to crush apartheid. He also shared a poignant anecdote about when he was a boy in Charleston, West Virginia in 1934, and a white man refused to serve him a Coca-Cola because he was black. That spurred him into a life of civil rights activism.

For more than an hour, he delivered an ultra-impressive speech about Affirmative Action and race relations. His spellbinding eloquence cast a silent stillness over the crowd, as he electrified the room and the people in it. The crescendo concluding Reverend Sullivan's speech roused a thunderous standing ovation. When the night was over, I was euphoric, telling myself, "Roy, *you* got to introduce the man!"

Meanwhile, unbeknownst to me, Reverend Sullivan went to the General Motors World Headquarters in Detroit, and told Chairman and Chief Executive Officer Roger B. Smith: "I met a young man. If you don't go and recruit him, you're not serious about wanting to integrate this company."

Allow me to emphasize that I was not aware of this conversation. Fast-forward six years later, to 1983. I was in the executive dining room at GM headquarters debating important issues, one-on-one with Roger Smith. I made an emphatic comment, which prompted Roger to say, "You know, Sullivan said you'd do that. He's the person who recommended that I recruit you."

I was stunned! Reverend Sullivan's endorsement underscored the power of one person to transform another's life. I vowed to use my ever-increasing influence to continue to elevate black professionals who would follow in my footsteps. in any sphere where I had the clout to make a difference.

Now let's rewind back to 1977 when I still worked at Lear Siegler, and Reverend Sullivan had recommended me to Roger Smith. Shortly thereafter, I received another call from Davis Donnelly, the General Manager at Diesel Equipment Division, who said, "Roy, they want to meet you in Detroit."

When I arrived at General Motors' world headquarters, I was interviewed by one executive vice president after another. Reverend Sullivan was on hand, offering what simply felt like moral support. The attention flabbergasted me. With a great degree of naïveté, I marveled, "Boy, this is how they hire people!" I later learned that this attention was highly unusual, because the edict to hire Roy Roberts had come from the chairman himself. Then I heard the words that brought my dream to reality: "Roy, we'd like to hire you. We'd like you to go with the Diesel Equipment Division in Grand Rapids as a Manager in Training."

This was the perfect position for me to get acclimated to General Motors, and for the company to assess my abilities, so that I could be placed into future positions accordingly. During the course of this, as with every important decision in my life, I consulted with my wife. I needed assurance that Maureen, who was still working as a nurse and had never lived outside western Michigan, would support such a lifestyle.

"You know," I said, "working for General Motors could mean moving out of state or even to another country. Part of paying your dues to rise to the top of GM could require an assignment in a foreign country. What do you think about that?"

Maureen smiled, and without hesitation said, "Roy, if you want to do it, you ought to do it. We'll chase your career. I'll go anywhere GM will move you. Anywhere except Flint, Michigan." We shared a laugh; Flint was a blue-collar factory town whose similarity to Muskegon had zero appeal for her. That playful comment aside, Maureen's willingness to move with my corporate assignments could not have pleased me more, because this was the first test of our commitment to use open communication and consideration to ensure that we operated as a team while striving for our unified success.

"We think about how it's going to affect the marriage," Maureen says now. "You're being considerate of the other person. If you're introducing something that might cause a lot of stress, you have to find out how the other person feels about it, and then decide."

Therefore, as we contemplated the offer for me to join General Motors, Maureen's blessing meant everything. I accepted the position in the presence of executives as well as Reverend Leon Sullivan, who was very pleased.

"Now the next time I come," he told the executives, "I want you to have two, not one." Then he squeezed my hand without saying anything. He just squeezed it, while radiating immense pride, and I knew that I now had a great counselor in my corner.

However, while this experience, and talk of foreign assignments may have sounded glamorous, the reality of my new job was anything but.

Beer, Bowling and Culture Shock

"Culture shock" best describes my experience in 1977 when I joined General Motors as a salaried employee-in-training at the Diesel Equipment Division in Grand Rapids. Leaving the executive lifestyle at Lear Siegler to work my way up through the ranks at GM required dramatic changes on several levels.

First, I took a pay cut. Second, unlike my traditional business hours at Lear from 8 a.m. until 5 p.m., I now worked the second shift, which began at three o'clock in the afternoon and ended at 11 p.m.

Third, I left a white-collar atmosphere where my peers had attended college and cultivated social graces and professional polish. I had become accustomed to these standards in the workplace, as well as in the upper echelon social circles in Grand Rapids. Now, at General Motors, I found myself in a quintessentially blue-collar environment. I hasten to add that these men were doing quite well, earning a middle-class lifestyle for their families, thanks to good salaries, benefits and bonuses.

However, leaving the luxury of corporate offices with windows, to spend my afternoons and evenings in a noisy, greasy, fluorescent-lit factory, further contributed to my culture shock. While I knew that the insights gleaned at this level could ultimately fuel my ascension up the company ranks, it was not an easy adjustment.

First and foremost, I was excruciatingly aware that if I strode into the plant with a superior attitude about my education, my profession and social status in the community, these factory workers would eat me alive. They would resent me, and I would never rise to the top as a result.

Like prisons, plants have powerful and unique modes of communication. Some of the world's languages are rooted in Latin, but automobile plant communications are based on the old saying: "actions speak louder than words." Conformity to plant culture was the key to success. For example, if you were a rookie or a first line supervisor, and you wanted to work faster than other people, you wouldn't do that very long.

"Hey, college boy," someone would taunt. "You think you're better than us?"

Worse, they would arrange for your car to mysteriously get damaged. This inspired conformity. You would not make them look bad by producing a lot more than they did. The line workers were smart as hell. If you learned to relate to them and talk to them in an appropriate way, it would take you far. But until you learned that language and understood the nuances of the workers' behavior, you could miss crucial information.

I began my first job at General Motors with an acute understanding of this. I wholeheartedly endorsed the old adage that advises, "Sometimes you have to go along, to get along." Never as a follower, but as an observer.

Now 38 years old, I was well-practiced at tapping into my lifelong ability to become extremely sensitive to my environment, and adjust my behavior accordingly. Having grown up amongst working-class blacks – including my father – in Muskegon and Muskegon Heights, my memory contained a ready repertoire of what behaviors would or would not be acceptable in my new environment. This was not being fake, or disingenuous, or brown-nosing. This was simply being adept at succeeding in any circumstances. It required effacing the ego, and humbly seeking learning opportunities at every turn.

I was assigned to work with a wise, older gentleman named Jim Hulsebus. A high school graduate who had served in the U.S. Navy, he was a very worldly guy, but not formally educated. However, Jim was extremely knowledgeable about the automobile business, and he became an excellent teacher.

Jim showed me everything he knew, and I really enjoyed being with him. It was exciting to learn, and I quickly surmised that the fastest way to navigate upward from the plant floor would be to become a plant manager. As we toured the plant, I reveled in the challenge of mastering every detail in the process of building carburetors and engine systems. In fact, Diesel Equipment Division was the world's biggest manufacturer of valve lifters – parts that are central to the engine of a car.

"Roy, if you remember one word from all of this," Jim said, "it's quality. We need it, every step of the way. Can't cut corners with quality to save time or money. Anybody who cuts quality is asking for big problems down the line."

Unfortunately, GM was learning a tough lesson on this, and a public relations nightmare was playing out in the media and in court. Customers had filed a class action lawsuit after it was revealed that GM had installed Chevrolet 350 engines into the ultra-popular Oldsmobile Cutlass and Cutlass Supreme. The company did this because production could not keep pace with demand for the Rocket V8 engines that had made those the number-one selling vehicles in North America. The problem was exposed when customers took the cars in for maintenance, and new parts for the Rocket V8 engine did not fit. I watched this debacle unfold in the media, and listened to people around me in the company talk about it.

My observations underscored the importance of Jim's advice: put QUALITY above production speed and profits. Otherwise, it would always backfire and cost the company more in lawsuits and loss of customer base than the expense of doing it right the first time around.

Another exciting learning experience was being privy to internal communications at General Motors, which showcased how the company educated its employees from within. The General Motors Institute in Flint provided college classes and degrees that enabled employees to advance within the corporation.

GM also offered the highly coveted Executive Development Program at Harvard Business School and the General Motors Advanced International General Management Program in Switzerland. Company newsletters profiled the fortunate few who were selected from the global employee base of nearly one million people. Selection for those programs signaled that company leadership had anointed one as a future leader of GM. Attaining such ranks, at the moment, seemed a distant, if impossible, fantasy from my lowly position in the plant, because fully acclimating to my new learning environment meant "networking" with my blue-collar colleagues outside of work. Here again, snubbing the opportunity for inclusion would be career suicide. I would be ostracized as a snob amongst the very people whom I hoped to lead one day.

"Hey Roy," they said, "come join our bowling league. We play in the mornings before work. You can drink some beer with us and have a good time."

I complied, but I absolutely hated it. First, I was not a good bowler. Number two, I didn't want to drink beer at eight o'clock in the morning. And three, they misspelled my name on my bowling shirt. (I still have the bowling ball I used back then. To this day, Maureen teases me about being in the bowling league).

During warmer weather, the guys invited me to play golf. Although I had tried golf at Lear, my poor performance made it a miserable experience. The first course I ever played was Indian Trails Golf Course in Grand Rapids. It was the only public course in town, and was visible from busy Twenty-Eighth Street. Motivated to improve my game through practice, I played often. I also had to dress well on the course, and I invested in a handsome set of clubs. This prompted my colleagues to joke, "Here comes Roy Roberts with some five-hundred-dollar clubs and his fifty-cents game!"

Unfortunately, the sight of black men on a golf course roused more than one racist response. Once, a group of white guys in a car drove past and yelled:

"Hey, who's watching the ghetto?"

My struggles with beer, bowling and golf made for a trying time. But my philosophy was, "If you're going to be part of the team, you have to be part of the team."

A Harmonious Home Life

Maureen and I purchased a larger house in Grand Rapids, after our accountant suggested that we would fare better at tax time if we invested more money into property ownership. We had 3,000 square-feet of living space, and the kids would visit frequently.

Ricky would often call and ask to stay with us for awhile, and I would pick him up. Robin spent the summer between her junior and senior years in high school with us. During the school year, Ricky and Robin ran track. My daughter did not talk much about it, so when I attended a track meet, I was overjoyed to see that she was an absolute star! I was so proud to watch Ricky graduate from high school in 1977. Robin collected her diploma one year later, and Ronald completed school three years after that.

In the interim, it was an honor to welcome my exemplary son-in-law, Roger Huff, into the Roberts family. His courtship of Robin began the old-fashioned way, with him living around the corner from Ruby and the kids. After a friend introduced them, Roger — five years older than Robin — waited a year until she turned sixteen before he asked her on a date. All the while, he impressed Ruby, her parents and me.

Roger was a student, working full time in a co-op program at General Motors, where he had started at age seventeen. (Ironically, in later years, people would assume that I had been instrumental in securing Roger's employment at GM, when he had actually been at the company long before me).

Robin and Roger married on December 7, 1979 — the same date that Maureen and I had married — and had two sons, Rory and Roger Junior, in quick succession.

Kappa Alpha Psi Fraternity

During my early years with General Motors, I joined the alumni chapter of Kappa Alpha Psi Fraternity, Incorporated. This fulfilled a goal that I had set as a student at Western Michigan University.

Pledging a graduate chapter in 1978 still involved a degree of hazing. One winter night, my "line brothers" and I were forced to sled bare-bottomed down a hill, weighted down with fifty pounds of ice. We were also blindfolded and driven into the woods, then released and told to find our way home. Fortunately, I had taped a dime to my shoe, so I called Maureen and she picked us up! We made it back to town before our Kappa brothers, and it was big fun.

After that, it was exciting to become one of thousands of Kappas in hundreds of chapters across the nation and around the world. Today the fraternity has 105,000 members in more than 800 undergraduate and alumni chapters in every state, as well as chapters in Africa, the *Caribbean*, Asia and Europe.

For me, membership has provided many opportunities to network with black professional men. Not only did I develop and nurture many important relationships in western Michigan, but I would ultimately be invited to speak on two different occasions at the annual national convention, known as the Kappa Conclave. In addition, Maureen and I enjoyed attending many social functions hosted by the Kappas.

Also during my early years with General Motors in Grand Rapids, I was invited to join an exclusive black men's social fraternity called the Boulé. With only about 5,000 members, Sigma Pi Phi differs from other fraternities because induction into the Boulé — which means "a council of noblemen" — occurs after members have already earned their degrees and accomplished something in life.

I was introduced to the Boulé when Federal Judge Ben Gibson moved to the city from Lansing. He approached a number of prominent black professional men, myself included, about forming a Boulé chapter. With our enthusiastic agreement, Judge Gibson obtained permission from the Lansing Boulé to sponsor a Grand Rapids Sigma Pi Phi chapter. We assembled a group of leading black men — including doctors and lawyers — and created a chapter that became a source of pride and enjoyment for each of us.

Like many of the social clubs I had enjoyed in the past, the Boulé reinforced a feeling that I was part of "the talented tenth." NAACP co-founder and Harlem Renaissance scholar W.E.B. DuBois used that term to quantify the percentage of black men who became educated and used their stature to elevate the other 90 percent of the race. I was extremely proud to consider myself as such a person.

Planning for Product Change

My automotive career began to accelerate early on when GM's Diesel Equipment Division decided to build the most advanced fuel systems plant in the United States.

This would make GM a leader in the industry trend to replace carburetors with fuel injection systems. That required a factory to produce the new, modern fuel systems. To explore how to make this happen, management selected a high potential employee from every department of the division.

"Roy, you're a new thinker," management said. "We want you to join the brainstorming session for how we go about building this new plant."

On the first day, I joined eight people who had been selected.

"Who's in charge?" I asked in the conference room.

"Nobody's in charge," the group responded. "They didn't put anybody in charge."

"Then I must be in charge." I took over, and we teamed up to do an excellent job on our assignment. For research, we traveled to plants across the United States to study operations and labor situations. In the south, we studied successful strategies that General Motors was using. We also examined the company's relationship with the UAW, and tried to identify ways to skirt the union. We immediately recognized that would be catastrophic.

With our findings, I led the team in reporting back to the council, the general manager and his staff. They agreed to build the plant in Coopersville, Michigan, which is halfway between Muskegon and Grand Rapids. Then I recommended Dave Stephanovich to manage that plant, and he did an incredible job. The new plant did, indeed, become one of the most advanced fuel system plants in the country.

This was a pioneering triumph for GM, and a real breakthrough for Roy Roberts. I returned to work in different operations in the division, being promoted in quick succession to Supervisor, then General Supervisor. In 1981, I was elevated to Director of Quality Assurance for GM's Grand Rapids Plant #1. Shortly thereafter, I was promoted to Plant Manager, responsible for two plants under one roof. In short order, two more plants were added to my responsibility.

Then Diesel Equipment Division merged with Rochester Products Division. Headquartered in Rochester, New York, it was composed of more than ten thousand employees in 14 or 15 plants. I was put in charge of half of those plants.

While I was the first African American in every position, I made certain that I was never the last. My increasing prominence enabled me to recommend and hire blacks on every level. ; I was proud to facilitate a triple-win situation for African Americans, General Motors and Roy Roberts.

Success Strategy: Reinventing Roy

While I was positively aggressive in pursuing opportunities for advancement, I was smart enough to know that I didn't know everything, so I would constantly critique my performance. When I moved into a new job in General Motors, I would ask myself a series of questions and answer them myself.

"Who are my peers? And who's the best?"

"Frank's the best."

"Why is Frank the best?"

"He's a self-starter, self-motivated, polished. Always finishes his work, does an outstanding job, and does more than he's asked to do."

I would write all this down, making sure to keep the evaluation positive. Rather than write, "Frank gets ahead because he's a brown-noser," I would write, "Frank excels because he makes his bosses look good in everything he does." With my list complete, I would study it and see clearly why Frank was the best.

Then I would declare, "Roy, in six months, you're going to beat Frank at everything he's doing." Next, I would identify everything about myself that I would have to improve to succeed at that goal. This process enabled me to constantly reinvent Roy — learning, improving and growing in that process. As a result, I outperformed all the competition.

I took this process to another level during an annual retreat. Every summer, I would get a convertible from General Motors and drive alone to the picturesque, resort town of Traverse City in northern Michigan. I would stay at a hotel with views of Grand Traverse Bay, which connects to Lake Michigan.

During this solitary retreat, I would reflect on my performance during the prior year. I would strategize how I could improve my performance, and I would set personal and professional goals for the coming year. Then I would grade myself on each of the above points.

"Are you pleased with that?" I would ask myself. "Or could you have done better?" If the answer were no, I would vow to apply more discipline to improving where necessary. In addition, if I gave a speech – whether inside the company or in the community – and I believed it was well-received, I would always ask, "What could I have done better?"

This extremely helpful process was rooted in what would become an oft-repeated Roy-ism: "If you want the reward, you've got to be willing to take the journey with hard work and discipline."

My quick succession of promotions and high visibility prompted many people to ask, "Roy, what's the silver bullet? How did you get here so fast?"

"There is no silver bullet!" I would reply. "There are no shortcuts!" Then I would explain that my success resulted from an accumulation of excellent performance, discipline and ambition. This message often went unheard, because so many people want the rewards — the big salaries, the corporate perks and the prestige — without investing the time and effort.

Nothing can substitute for hard work. It's like exercise. You have to do your own sit-ups if you want to see the results.

Selected for Harvard

During the early 1980s, when I was running plants for Rochester Products Division, I was in Rochester, New York, for a divisional corporate meeting. I was staying at a hotel, two rooms down from my boss, who oversaw all manufacturing for the division. I had always suspected that he was envious of my quick ascent and the attention that my continuously stellar performance was attracting from the corporate offices.

"Roy," my boss said, "stop by my room after you come in from dinner tonight."

I did as he requested. "Guess what happened," he challenged, as I stepped inside.

"What?"

"Dammit, Roy!" He snatched several pieces of letter-sized paper from the table and waved them at me. "GM selected you to go to Harvard," he said, referring to the Harvard Executive Development Program held at the prestigious Ivy League university each year for students from all over the world. It is a powerful program with a powerful message, because each participating individual is recommended to the General Motors Board of Directors as "an executive in transition" -- singled out for promotion within a year after completing the fifteen-week course.

"I've always wanted to go to Harvard!" my boss continued. "I've been an engineer for so many years, and I always dreamed of being chosen for this!"

118

Being hand-picked to attend this program was one of the highest honors that GM could bestow upon an employee. Each year, only two people — a maximum of four people — were chosen from 950,000 employees around the world. The arduous selection process involved Human Resources, the chairman and his executive committee.

I was thrilled, but didn't show it to my irate boss as I asked, "What the hell am I going to do about this? I didn't ask for this. Why don't you take this paperwork and go to Harvard? I'll stay here and I'll be happy."

"I can't do that!" he snapped. "Roy, you know I can't do that."

Delightful Addition to the Family: Adopting Katrina

A short time before this, Maureen had expressed the desire to adopt a child. Having been a nurse for premature babies for eighteen years, she preferred a child who was five or six years old. I agreed, but quite honestly, I had no intentions of adopting a child, and I was convinced that we would not find a child.

"I found the perfect child for you," our social worker said, telling us that the girl was born on February 15, 1973, and was eight-and-a-half years old. She lived with foster parents — a hardworking, salt-of-the-earth couple. The father worked at a GM plant in Lansing, while the mother stayed home to care for the foster children.

Maureen and I drove through a snowstorm, sixty miles east to the state capital, to meet Katrina and the social worker at a McDonald's restaurant. Inside, we were delighted to meet this cute little girl. Her hair was braided, and she was munching on animal crackers. Katrina was extremely well-mannered, articulate and smart, because the social workers had exposed her to museums and other educational outings.

Sitting beside her, I pointed to her snack. "Can I have one of these?"

She daintily gave me one animal cracker. Maureen and I were smitten!

"Start the paperwork," I told the social worker after just ten minutes.

Our daughter Katrina at age 9, soon after Maureen and I adopted her.

We brought Katrina to visit our home for the Thanksgiving weekend, and we had a wonderful time. After that, I went to Harvard University in Cambridge, Massachusetts. My single recess from the program was for the Christmas holiday. Katrina joined us then, and never left. The adoption was finalized the following year.

"Boy, she's the luckiest girl in the world," people often commented.

My consistent retort has been: "We're all lucky!" And I mean that. You get as much as you give, and Katrina has been a wonderful addition to our family.

Roy Roberts Attends Harvard University

It was November of 1981, and I had just left my wife and newly adopted daughter to attend the sixteen-week Harvard course.

120

Maureen, along with the other spouses, would join me for the final week of the program. My 150 accomplished classmates awed me! And the global scope of our class opened my eyes to new cultures and life experiences that I had never encountered.

I was delighted to befriend Sam Mollavenso, a bread company executive who was the first African to earn an MBA in South Africa during apartheid. One classmate was the son of the Ann Landers of Australia; another Australian guy's father had cornered the market on hatbands. The Aussies were so smart, they could drink Foster's beer all night and still earn A's.

One day, we watched Harvard play football against Yale. As we returned to our suite, a lively discussion educated our foreign friends about American football. Sadni Nakamori, the vice chairman of the Industrial Bank of Japan, was taking it all in. He was heading up the stairs when he abruptly turned and asked, "Roy, what is 'som-ma-bitch?'" I still laugh about spending the next three hours explaining the meaning of "son of a bitch."

I received the ultimate compliment when my dignified, sophisticated peers selected me as class leader! Meanwhile, General Motors provided me with a new car every two or three weeks. Boy, did I have fun zipping around Boston in 1982 Corvettes, Cadillacs and Oldsmobiles. Many days after lunch, Sam Mollavenso and I would cruise around, and he would tell me about his work with the anti-apartheid movement in South Africa and New England.

All the while, I processed our classroom lessons through a lens of real-life situations that I had and could potentially experience at General Motors. It was interesting to debate these ideas with classmate J.T. Battenberg, a rising star at GM who would one day be my boss, and later become president and chairman of Delphi Corporation. J.T. was in the Executive Development Program, while I was in the Professional Manager Development Program.

Throughout the course, I was profoundly impacted by a professor from Spain and his lesson about how an executive must cultivate a healthy balance between one's personal and professional lives struck a chord in me.

"You must quantify the time and the quality that you invest into each of these important areas of your life," the professor said. "Ask yourself the following questions about the most significant areas of your life." :

"How much effort do you put into your work? How much energy do you put into your work? How much effort do you put into your family? How much energy do you put into your family? How much effort do you put into your marriage? How much energy do you put into your marriage?"

His lecture about balance and time management inspired me to make that a top priority with Maureen, Katrina, and my three grown children. I vowed to incorporate his questions into my annual self-analysis and exert unwavering discipline in their application on a day-to-day basis.

Another professor taught me how to study and emulate models of success, by using business directories that compiled pertinent information about leaders in the corporate world.

"You can use these directories," the professor said, "to pull up an executive and learn everything about him or her. You can ascertain their religion, political party, whether they're married or divorced, and what positions they held as stepping stones to the top."

This exercise was valuable for strategizing how to excel up the company ladder.

"If you look at a corporation," the professor said, "and nine of the top executives attended a particular university, or seven people in leadership attend the same church or belong to the same civic organization, then this provides insight into the corporate culture. Is the top leadership primarily Republican? Or do they tend to make political contributions to the Democratic Party?"

The professor recommended that this type of research be incorporated into job searches as well as strategies for advancement within a company.

"Once you have this information," he continued, "you can decide whether that company is a good fit for you, and whether they would perceive you as a good fit for them. Then you can tailor your responses during a job interview accordingly."

This was pure genius! It added a new dimension to my lifelong belief and ability in the importance of being sensitive to my environment, and adjusting my behavior to thrive. Now, in a classroom at one of the world's most revered educational institutions, I reflected on my childhood in the black neighborhood, observing pimps, prostitutes, working folks and professionals like Sticks Green. I appreciated these "street smarts," which had equipped me with skills that have been crucial for my success in business.

The reality of racism did not discourage me; it encouraged me to prove it was wrong. While I was at Harvard, a magazine reporter asked GM President F. James McDonald: "Will an African American ever become a vice president of General Motors?"

"No, not in this lifetime," he responded.

I had news for Jim McDonald and anyone else who endorsed his racist viewpoint: An African American would, indeed, become a vice president at General Motors. Like many of my black peers, I carried that magazine around in my attaché case as a motivator.

Confrontation with a Jealous Boss

On my first day back to work after completing the program at Harvard, I attended a staff meeting led by the same boss who had been so furious about my selection. It's important to note that a representative from corporate headquarters was present at this meeting.

As my boss proceeded through the agenda, his self-aggrandizement became a vicious verbal attack on me. I had done nothing wrong; my boss was attempting to prove that he was still the boss by putting Harvard-trained Roy Roberts in his place.

Though I was stunned by my boss' verbal abuse, I did not respond publicly. However, I vowed to ensure that he would never verbally abuse me or anyone who looked like me — ever. Therefore, I asked my boss to meet with me the next morning at six-thirty. He agreed.

"Maureen," I said that night at home. "I've always fed you, right?"

"Right," she answered.

"I've always provided."

"Yes."

"Tomorrow night when I come home, I might not have a job. Don't worry. If that happens, I'll have another job. Don't worry, I'll feed you. Count on it."

The next morning in my boss' office, he spoke on several topics, then added with a nasty tone, "By the way, I had to manage your plants while you were gone." With that, he assumed the meeting was over. "Oh great," he said in an upbeat way, as if the prior day's verbal abuse had never occurred. "Now I can go out and do what I want to do this morning."

"No, wait a minute," I said. "I asked for this meeting, and I have some things I'd like to talk about."

I pulled off my watch and dangled it in front of him.

"Do you know what this is?" I asked.

"A watch."

"It's a good watch," I said. "It's an expensive watch. It's a Rolex. When you hear it tick, you talk. Until then, I'm talking."

I then proceeded to lambaste him for his verbal attacks on me.

"Roy—" he protested.

"Did you hear my watch tick?"

"No."

"I'm still talking!"

When I finished, he almost cried.

Concurrent with this, the representative from corporate headquarters who had witnessed my boss' outburst returned to Detroit and told the chairman what had transpired. From that day on, my boss remained in that same position. He was never promoted at General Motors. While he was technically smart, his behavior was blatantly wrong, and he paid the price.

124

SEVEN

Pioneering Eastward and Upward

A short time after attending Harvard, I was promoted to Eastern Operations Manager for the Rochester Products Division of General Motors. I became responsible for six component plants that manufactured cruise control systems, carburetors and emissions control devices.

As with every job during my career, it was historic: I was the first African American ever elevated to this position. This promotion required me to move our family to Rochester, New York. We purchased a nice home in the affluent suburb of Pittsford, which sits on the banks of the Erie Canal.

As Maureen had agreed prior to my employment with General Motors, she was completely amenable to relocating. This was extremely important; I had witnessed many failed marriages because one mate did not want to move to another city, state or country when his or her spouse received a new corporate assignment. On the contrary, Maureen and I soon discovered that moving was one of the best things that could have happened to us. In a new town, you can only rely on your mate, so you grow closer together.

While Katrina acclimated well in grade school, Maureen was hired as the supervisor of nurses in the Health Services Department in the East Irondequoit Central School District. I was proud that, in a small school district dominated by Italian men with traditional values about women, Maureen negotiated an attractive salary for herself.

Meanwhile, I worked long hours running the plants, usually arriving at 6 a.m. and staying until 4 p.m. or 5 p.m., when the second shift was underway. I ascertained early on that a plant manager's presence inspired an atmosphere of industriousness, good morale and quality work amongst the employees. When the boss showed that he or she cared passionately about the workers and the product, morale remained high, along with productivity and quality. At the same time, I worked overtime to impress my subordinates and bosses. This sometimes involved a degree of bravado and bluffing, but it always brought stunning results.

This was especially true during our annual budget meetings. Every time my boss would come for a financial review to kick off a year, we'd argue for hours on what my financial needs were for the plant. He'd want to take cuts and remove funding in various areas, but I would counter with strong arguments to keep as much as possible.

"Bullshit!" he'd say, handing me a sheet that detailed the financial parameters for the year. "That's it. Those are the numbers, Roberts. This is your budget for the plant. End of conversation."

The next time he returned for a review, I would hand him the exact same sheet and say, "This is where we ended up. This is what you said I have to do, and here are the numbers."

It was thrilling to show the boss that no matter what annual budget he gave me, I would deliver impressive results. This was the reality of business. I never saw a budget that hadn't been slashed somewhere. Likewise, I never saw a budget that killed me. You can always make it work. How? Every time I agreed to a budget with my boss, he would hardly have left the building before I would call a meeting for my entire staff.

"The boss is such an incredible guy," I would tell them, to keep morale high. "He really went easy on us with this budget, and we're going to make this work as a team."

If I were working on a 10 percent improvement, I would simply dole out the responsibility.

"I need 12 percent from you," I would tell one manager. "And I need 12 percent from you," I would inform another manager. Then, when I combined everyone's numbers, our results would easily meet our requirements. The numbers told a story, and reflected my management style that enabled everyone to shine for the success of the team. That was my secret to orchestrating impressive numbers for my boss.

This annual dynamic would, in later years, become especially dramatic with one boss in particular — J.T. Battenberg, who would ultimately become president and chairman of Delphi Corporation. Always well-dressed and well-groomed, J.T. would stride into the plant and throw his coat over his shoulder.

"How are you doing, Roy?"

"Good, J.T."

"How are Maureen and Katrina?"

"Doing fine. How's your family?"

"Good. Everybody's doing fine." Then he'd cut right to it: "Roy, if the numbers are right, this is going to be a good day. If not, you're going to have one helluva day!"

Now it was time to talk business. The bottom line was the numbers. Period. And Roy Roberts always had good numbers. I made those numbers tap dance! It was a game, a good game, and I loved it!

This leads to another crucial tenet of my triumph in business: My job is to make my boss look good. This has a "trickle up" effect. When I delivered optimum numbers to my boss, he could take those to his bosses. This made him look good, and as a result, he appreciated me more.

At the same time, this accelerated both of our upward mobility in the company. Upper management was confident in promoting my boss, because they knew I could replace him. And since I had hired smart people and groomed them to take my place one day, they subsequently were elevated when I vacated my position.

This may contradict some conventional thinking, but it actually put pressure on managers to grow their staff. As a result, it benefited the entire company by creating a smarter workforce.

Bringing the Boule to Rochester

While work was progressing well in Rochester, I wanted to build a stronger social network. After living there for about 18 months, I took action, by exploring the possibility of forming a Boulé chapter in Rochester.

"Sorry, Roy," warned a black professional colleague. "You can't do that here. All the guys are ultra-professional, and they like to do things very low key."

I ignored that advice. I compiled a list of prominent African American men in the area, and invited them to a meeting at our home. About two dozen men attended, and I served the best food with an extensive open bar.

My guest of honor was an accomplished gentleman from Buffalo, New York. He was a Tuskegee Airman and longtime Boulé member who would provide a first-hand, highly credible account of how each man could benefit from Boulé membership. Also in attendance that Sunday afternoon were executives from Bausch & Lomb, Xerox and GM.

As I led the meeting, I walked everyone through what it would mean to form a Boulé chapter in Rochester. A spirited discussion ensued for three hours, with many questions posed and answered by the esteemed Boulé member from Buffalo.

"Roy," someone asked. "How do we cover the cost of this meeting?"

"It's simple," I retorted. "It's my cost. This is the way the Boulé does it."

That got people's attention. Six weeks later, I called a follow-up meeting. After reiterating the same points from the first gathering, I announced, "Now it's time for a call to action."

"Maybe everybody shouldn't belong to the Boulé," said a patent attorney from Bausch & Lomb, who was a very strong-willed guy.

"Maybe you're right," I said. "Maybe you shouldn't belong."

He became very quiet.

"How much does it cost?" someone asked.

"Most chapters charge one thousand dollars annually," I said. "But I've heard so much about this body and how accomplished you are, we're going to go for five thousand dollars each, annually. By the way, here's my five."

I placed a check on the table. A hush came over the room. No one left. Everyone joined. I hasten to add that the Bausch & Lomb attorney became an outstanding member of Sigma Pi Phi.

As president – or Sire Archon – of our group, I led our chapter to success. We hosted unforgettably fun and elegant social events. These gatherings enabled us to network and nurture relationships that celebrated our common bond as black men who were blazing bold trails in corporate America.

It's important to emphasize that I never joined the Boulé or other social groups to further myself professionally. My motivation was actually quite the opposite. I had an acute understanding that my power in the corporate world emanated from my people. If you lack influence and respect among your own people, then the men and women of another race who sit in the corporate structure will not respect you; they won't think you're bringing anything special to the table.

As a result, I was valued at the corporate table because I was trusted and admired by the larger black community. Every business magazine had a write-up about Roy Roberts to showcase his performance and his success. That impressed my peers in the business world.

This is a very powerful piece of the success puzzle. Your social standing interrelates with your business stature in ways that can either hurt you or help you.

Another Historic First: Joining a Non-GM Corporate Board

During this period, the regional chairman of a large bank invited me to serve on a regional board of directors that reigned over several eastern states. This made me the first non-chairman of General Motors to receive such a prestigious invitation.

"I would be honored to serve," I told the chairman. "However, I'm obliged to request clearance from my corporate headquarters first."

I applied for approval at General Motors. The answer was "No." So I petitioned the help of a dear friend, Nettie Seabrooks. She ran the General Motors library and was extremely influential with Chairman Roger Smith.

"Mr. Smith," she said, lobbying on my behalf, "it makes good business sense to allow Roy Roberts to sit on the Chase board. He's a rising star, and the recognition would be extraordinary for GM if Roy were to serve as our representative for the state of New York."

The chairman granted approval, as did GM's board of directors.

With that, I became the first employee other than the chairman to be approved by the GM board to join the board of another corporation.

This opportunity provided incredible publicity, and it was a tremendous compliment. My belief was that Chase Bank would only bestow this honor to a community person with high visibility, high stature and high credibility. The nine-member board was composed of bright, competent people. I became one of these capable individuals, and I worked hard to prove it each time I attended quarterly meetings.

At the same time, my friendship with Nettie Seabrooks flourished. She moved into public relations, and her staff would travel to New York to help me execute some of my responsibilities as a key executive. Our friendship highlights the importance of "strategic partnerships." Building and nurturing authentic relationships has always been key to my success, because I approach them from a win-win perspective. I want to give as much as I get, or more, so that each of us benefits.

In this instance, Nettie Seabrooks exemplified that, because I was able to reciprocate her advocacy when she would later take prominent positions that included serving as Detroit's first female Deputy Mayor, Chief of Staff and Chief Operating Officer during Mayor Dennis Archer's administration.

Career Track Takes a Turn to Switzerland

During my tenure in Rochester, General Motors bestowed another incredible honor that affirmed that, once again, the corporation was grooming me for increasing responsibilities. I was selected for the General Motors Advanced International General Management Program in Vevey, Switzerland. That picturesque town is where milk chocolate was invented in 1875, and Vevey remains the world headquarters of Nestlé, which is famous for chocolate and other foods.

During the late spring of 1984, I traveled to this French-speaking town on Lake Geneva and stayed in a resort with breath-taking views of snow-capped mountains. For five weeks of intensive study, I joined a student body that was composed entirely of General Motors employees from around the world. We studied a global trade curriculum that was specially formulated for GM by Harvard University and the London School of Economics.

Our goal was to explore issues, formulate strategies, and learn how to manage globally. Very few people from the United States attended; I was the only person in General Motors selected to attend both the Harvard and Switzerland programs. In class, we teamed up to conceive programs and devise business strategies, then presented them to panels of executives who visited our class from around the globe.

Early on, it appeared that my German classmates were rigid thinkers, with an air of superiority about their business practices. These bright individuals painstakingly prepared a presentation for a panel of senior German executives from Stuttgart. My German classmates got eaten alive! It was shocking to watch the executives condemn the presentation. It was unlike anything I'd ever seen in the United States. Outside of class, we played tennis and toured vineyards that produced exquisite wines. One evening, while standing around a fireplace in the resort, my classmates and I were enjoying champagne before dinner.

"I'm embarrassed," I admitted. "All of you speak five or six languages, while I speak English and a little German."

131

"We didn't learn these languages for the fun of it," they said. "We had to learn the language to communicate with our trading partners."

When the program concluded, Maureen and I toured the French Riviera, including Monaco, Nice and Cannes. It was unreal!

Breaking the Corporate Mold with a Bold Strategy

The immeasurable knowledge that I acquired at Harvard University and in Switzerland enhanced my daily performance at work.

Very importantly, my professors and classmates taught me to think strategically with boldness, courage and innovation. This dramatically transformed my annual self-critique and goal-setting session. New ideas were popping in my mind like firecrackers. I felt emboldened by the accomplishments that I had witnessed amongst my peers.

Now, as I retreated to a hotel to contemplate my past, present and future, I felt the urgent need to brainstorm a new strategy. To *go* where no black man had gone before, I needed to *do* what no person had done before at General Motors. What action could I take that was big and bold, unparalleled and unprecedented?

Always acutely conscious of trends and economic conditions in America and the automobile industry, I analyzed the big picture of General Motors. Profits were beginning to rebound after the recessions of the late 1970s and early 1980s. But the entire auto industry was suffering a public relations nightmare in the wake of defective vehicles and financial problems. However, Chrysler's plan to unveil the first minivans in 1984 sparked excitement in the industry. Meanwhile, it was rumored that GM Chairman Roger Smith wanted to cut 100,000 jobs by 1986. Fears about plant closings always loomed. These were dramatically changing times for the immediate and distant future of General Motors.

At such a critical juncture, I needed to be daring; not hesitant or overly cautious. How could Roy Roberts stay ahead of trends and propose ideas that would help steer the company toward prosperity and expansion? My next step needed to provide positive publicity and profits for the corporation I wanted to apply my experience, expertise and ambition to launch the next phase of my career in an audacious new way.

But where? How?

I discussed my options with two friends who were highly respected professionals on upward trajectories at General Motors. Outstanding attorney Roderick D. Gillum was a senior member of GM's legal staff. He would hold many prominent positions at the company, including Secretary to the GM Board of Directors, and ultimately vice president of Corporate Responsibility and Diversity. Lewis Campbell was general manager of the Flint Automotive Group and would become vice president of GMC Truck and later chairman and CEO of Textron, then chairman of Navistar International Corporation. (I was proud to be a reference for Lewis to the Textron Board of Directors.)

During the summer of 1985, as the three of us talked about what lay ahead, Lewis noted: "The Tarrytown Plant in New York is vying for a new product. But the president of Tarrytown's local union won't negotiate a competitive labor agreement."

"Anybody who can make that happen," Rod added, "can also succeed at getting that new product, which would guarantee that the plant will stay open and thrive."

"I can make that happen," I said confidently.

We concluded that my next move should be to become manager of the North Tarrytown assembly plant, which was located in Westchester County, one of the wealthiest counties in America. With a rich history — and epic problems — it was a five-hour drive southeast of Rochester, and thirty minutes north of New York City. Accessing its ninety-acres acres of lush forestland on the Hudson River required driving through the picturesque Rockefeller Foundation property, where oil tycoon John D. Rockefeller's mansion, *Kykuit*, is a U.S. National Historic Landmark.

Ironically and unbeknownst to me at the time, Tarrytown provided a fascinating intersection of my father's early life history and my current aspirations. You may recall that Papa was 13 years old when he fled racism and poverty in Arkansas. He went to Texas and found work as a cook's helper at the Standard Oil Company. Around that same time, founder John D. Rockefeller was building his mansion in Tarrytown. Concurrently, the North Tarrytown plant opened in 1900, manufacturing cars called Walker Steamers, and the town grew.

Before that, Washington Irving described Tarrytown in his short story, *The Legend of Sleepy Hollow* in 1820. Then, at the end of the Civil War, Tarrytown was a stop on the Underground Railroad, which enabled blacks to escape slavery in the South.

Despite this rich history, the Tarrytown plant had laid off nearly half its workforce in 1982. It was faring so poorly that the night shift was eliminated for thirty-one months. On top of that, Tarrytown was expensive to run. As GM's oldest factory, its electricity bills were high, and because it lacked a train line, shipping by truck cost GM $70 per vehicle, which added up to a huge expense.

Still, I wanted the job. My desire to manage this plant was a radical notion -- for a reason that is not apparent to the average person.

A sacred truth in the automobile industry was that a distinct boundary existed between leadership on the component side and the assembly side of the organization. Managers were not transferred or promoted across that boundary. You were either on the component side — manufacturing doors, windows, fuel systems, ignition systems and every other part of a vehicle; or you were on the assembly side — using those components to build cars on the assembly line.

The boundary between component plants and assembly plants was sacrosanct and religiously protected within GM and every other car manufacturer. Moving a person from a component plant to an assembly plant was unheard of. People with component backgrounds had been elevated to higher levels of responsibility, but not to directly manage an assembly plant. This caste system placed assembly plants at the top. They were the company darlings, because they created the vehicles that impressed customers in the marketplace.

I wanted to break this barrier by becoming the first component plant manager to take over an assembly plant. I let it be known that I wanted to take on the Tarrytown challenge. Lewis, Rod and other top executives who believed in me had positive things to say about the possibilities, as they interacted with other senior executives at GM. Everything came together and I got the appointment by the end of the summer.

EIGHT

Teamwork Saves the North Tarrytown Plant

In September of 1985, I headed to Tarrytown, feeling good that we had pulled a coup. The plant felt like a mini United Nations, because its 5,000 employees represented races and ethnicities from around the world. They made good money, but Westchester County was so expensive, employees could not afford to live there. Most commuted from more affordable communities in New York and New Jersey.

At the same time, employees remained anxious in the wake of the plant's recent history with layoffs and the nightshift shutdown. Negotiations with the UAW for employee contracts loomed on the horizon, and boosting morale and prosperity were paramount to the entire factory's success. I literally shook hands with every employee, and would later hand-write a Christmas card to each of them.

My goal was to make Tarrytown a shining star. But I soon discovered that I was flirting with catastrophe. First, within my first two weeks on the job, two mysterious fires broke out in the plant. The fires seemed to convey an ominous message about the fate of the plant.

Second, I was realizing that my job would be far more difficult than anticipated, because I was unfamiliar with the nuts and bolts operations of an auto assembly plant. Apparently my inexperience was obvious, because one afternoon, the number three man in the plant came to my office, unannounced, and closed the door.

"Mr. Roberts," said Reggie Harris. "We've checked you out, and you're alright. You're a good guy." He was African American — a sharp dresser, with rings on every finger. His demeanor and way of speaking indicated street smarts.

"Boss," Reggie said. "You don't know a damn thing about building a car, do you?"

My tone was sort of pleading as I said, "No, no, I don't know how to build a car!"

"We're going to teach you," Reggie said, as he demonstrated his unusual habit of pressing his forearms against his hips to pull up his pants.

"I've been here thirty years," he continued, "and my father worked here thirty years. We never thought we'd see a black man become a plant manager."

Reggie radiated pride, and I savored the moment.

"I was going to retire this August," he said, "but I'm going to stay around a bit longer to help you. And I'm going get two fellows that I'm close with, and we're going to teach you how to build a car, and how an assembly plant runs."

I was speechless with gratitude.

"Mr. Roberts, if it's okay with you, we want this to be a secret," Reggie said. "We'll bring you in on Sundays. We'll put the right guards on duty, because they see everything, know everything, and tell everything."

For the next three weeks, Reggie and his two colleagues proceeded to engage Roy Roberts in a crash course of Auto Assembly 101.

"You start with raw material coming in the trucks," Reggie said. "Raw material is fed into the body shop where the body is formed. It's the undergirding of the automobile. You've got to make sure that piece is right. It's like building a home. You have to get the foundation right."

Next, Reggie schooled me on how to act the part of a knowledgeable assembly plant manager.

"When you walk in Monday," he said, "you're going to ask the superintendent in the body shop, 'How's your quality?' Then he's going to walk you over to A, B, and C and tell you this, this and this."

I nodded as he described the hierarchy of people I should question, along with what questions to ask. Reggie told me what to anticipate as correct answers to those questions, so I could respond and interact in an intelligent, informed manner.

Next, they walked me through the trim and the whole operation. They showed me how vehicles were painted, how components were added, and how vehicles were tested before they left the plant. Our paint shop was obsolete. It needed an overhaul to adhere to the standards of the federal Clean Air Act. And we needed to install high-tech equipment to apply an upgraded paint finish that would be more durable and dust-free. I immediately added the implementation of a state-of-the-art paint shop to my growing "to do" list.

Meanwhile, Reggie and his buddies trained me to walk into any department, from the body shop through final assembly, and say, "Explain to me what you're doing." They gave me the knowledge to engage in conversations with workers so that I sounded like I had been running assembly plants for decades. With each interaction, I absorbed more knowledge. Very importantly, as I was getting smarter and digging deeper, I was building relationships with people on every level, and impressing them as a boss who cared about them and the products we were building.

Meanwhile, unbeknownst to me, Reggie and the guys put the word out that if Tarrytown had another fire, somebody was going to die. Perhaps it was coincidental, but we didn't have any more mysterious fires in that plant.

After three weeks of intensive learning, I knew all the pinch points, and all the factors that could drive quality for our products. What Reggie and his colleagues did for me was simply unbelievable. It was a blessing that I will forever cherish.

My Foundation for Excelling at Work: A Glorious Home Life

Outside of work, my personal life was glorious. At first, Maureen and Katrina stayed in Michigan while I became acclimated to my new job. It was a common practice for wives and families to relocate only after the executive had settled into his new job. In the beginning, I had to hit the ground running, which meant committing long hours and weekends to the job. When Maureen and Katrina did join me, we purchased a gorgeous house on a hill overlooking a pond in the hamlet of Chappaqua, New York.

Just a twenty-minute drive northeast from Tarrytown, Chappaqua epitomized a small New England town, with its quaint downtown merchant area and a plethora of historic buildings. The town's name reflects its Native American heritage and natural serenity, because it comes from the *Algonquian* word for "the rustling land." It was true. Sometimes the only sound outside our home was the breeze rustling the treetops. Chappaqua felt like paradise! Oh, how far I had come from Muskegon.

With fewer than ten thousand residents, Chappaqua was an epicenter of wealth in Westchester County. We lived adjacent to the 27-acre estate of renowned Manhattan heart surgeon and Boulé member Dr. John Hutchinson. With fifty rooms and an apple orchard, this was his family's *second* home. Today, Chappaqua is home to former U.S. President Bill Clinton, former U.S. Secretary of State Hilary Rodham Clinton, and New York Governor Mario Cuomo.

The Chappaqua Central School District was one of the best in America. As a student, Katrina was making friends, taking piano lessons and studying French in school.

"I want to spend next summer in Europe," she announced after a few weeks at school. "All my friends have been summering in Europe since they were little."

Maureen and I delighted in providing a nurturing home for Katrina, and Robin, Ricky and Ronald sometimes visited.

In addition, our home provided a strong foundation for me to work long hours and exert myself to maximum potential. After arriving at my office by 6 a.m., I would make the rounds to speak one-on-one with hourly workers on the plant floor as well as managers in the offices. I always praised their impressive work ethic and dedication. I wanted to demonstrate my appreciation for every person who was working hard to assemble cars that included the

Buick Century and Pontiac 6000. It was important that my presence and interaction communicated to everyone: "Roy Roberts cares about quality and making this plant successful, and you should, too."

I got along well with my Italian-American secretary, who was an absolute delight. She often invited Maureen and Katrina and me for dinner with her family. She served home-cooked, multi-course meals that included all the best Italian dishes. The first time we were invited, her husband devoured a huge portion of the first course, a heavy meat and pasta combination. Being a gracious guest, I followed his example. But when course after course of hearty dishes were served, I noticed that her husband was no longer eating. Again, to be a polite guest, I sampled each dish. But I became so full, I was sure that my stomach would explode.

"They Want Me to Shut Down Tarrytown!"

About three months into my tenure at Tarrytown, as I was feeling increasingly confident and comfortable with my ability to run an assembly plant, a number of factors convinced me that I had been set up to fail. I was struck by a sobering realization:

General Motors did not send me here to run this plant. They sent me here to shut it down!

The truth was that GM management always played it safe by conforming to how things had always been done in the past. That meant operating by the numbers -- and Tarrytown's profit-and-loss sheets were hemorrhaging red ink. The writing was emblazoned on the wall; my blind ambition had prevented me from seeing it.

However, rather than being discouraged by this revelation, I was emboldened to transform Tarrytown into a success story for General Motors. It would take a miracle, but I was determined to make one happen.

"The most successful business strategies always involve teamwork," my professors at Harvard had said. "Coalitions. Campaigns. Forming strategic partnerships with key individuals in both the

141

public and private sectors, as well as solving problems with multifaceted solutions."

With that in mind, I devised a three-part strategy to unite the power of management, labor and government. For part one, I teamed up with the oldest reigning president of a UAW local in the United States. Ray Calore was savvy, respected and popular, as evidenced by his being elected president of UAW Local 664 by 450,000 people. An easy-going Italian family man, Ray was a strategic thinker who was always three moves ahead of everyone else.

"Ray, they're going to shut this plant down," I told him. "As far as management is concerned, Tarrytown is on life support, and they think it's too far gone for whatever CPR we might attempt."

"No," Ray said, shaking his head. "I've been working here since 1939 when I started on the assembly line. We have to keep this plant alive."

I nodded. "We can force GM to keep it open, if we make a few things happen."

My experience at Lear Siegler with Owen Bieber — now UAW President — had taught me that union negotiations had the power to make or break a company.

"Ray," I said, "we can do three things, concurrently, to keep Tarrytown going. First, we need a new paint shop. Ours is so obsolete, it's about to violate the new federal guidelines. Second, we have to negotiate a labor agreement to match or exceed the most competitive one in GM."

"Let's do it," Ray agreed. Our relationship was new, yet our mutual respect for each other suggested that we would make a formidable team. I was forty-six; he was sixty-six. We shared a passion for helping people — and for ensuring General Motors' success.

"A top-notch labor agreement will earn us the leverage to achieve part three of my strategy," I continued.

General Motors' share of U.S. passenger car and light truck sales were heading for a downward slide, and Ford sales were inching ahead of GM. To counteract this, GM was making momentous changes to maintain its global dominance. It was dramatically reorganizing the corporate structure while brutally cutting costs. Very importantly, the company intended to revv sales, according to the internal grapevine, by making massive investments in plants to facilitate the manufacturing of five new products over the next eighteen months. This information helped me formulate a strategy to save Tarrytown.

"Ray," I said. "We need to talk GM into giving us a new product. Right now, we're one plant too many -- making the same cars as two other plants."

"I agree," Ray said. "Rolling out a new vehicle would be our salvation."

After we committed to this three-part strategy, Ray and I met with the UAW bargaining committee and GM's Tarrytown management team.

"We're trying to save this plant and five thousand jobs," I told the group. "The only way we can do that is to negotiate the most competitive labor agreement in General Motors. We have to match it and beat it, with quality and cost."

Engaging Every Employee to Boost Our Competitive Edge

Next, I engaged Tarrytown employees on every level of our campaign to save the plant. Massive layoffs and the nightshift shutdown in recent years had crushed their morale. Now, my goal was to excite these men and women about the plant's future, by seeing themselves as part of a big, important picture on a global scale. To do this, Ray Calore and I hosted a series of meetings with employees on every shift.

"It's time to shift into a new gear," I told the groups. "And it's time for all of you to get involved in sharing your ideas and visions for how we can make Tarrytown stand out as a plant that General Motors ranks as one of its best."

Then I announced that to do that, we were designating a room in the middle of the plant as the Competition Center. Each employee would be required to make two presentations that examined our competition on every level.

"You can make displays with pictures, words, statistics, ideas," I said. "Anything you want. As you create them, I want you to ask, 'Who are we competing with? What are their strengths and weaknesses? What are their top-selling vehicles? Why? What are their known strategies?' Find out everything you can about these competitors, and ask, 'How can we do better? How do we compare in terms of quality, cost and relationships with customers?'"

As I looked around the room at our eager faces, I asked, "What do we think about every day? What do we need to do better to keep our jobs?" Then I explained that their displays would cover two walls in our Competition Center, so that tour groups from the community and corporate headquarters could witness the excitement and creative ideas that Tarrytown employees were bringing to the company.

At the time, it felt that I was engineering this on the fly, but I came to realize that this endeavor was a culmination of my personal annual review, as well as the team presentations that I had experienced at Harvard and in Switzerland. The stakes were high. As I've said before, plant culture is very unique. People like to do what they've always done, the way they've always done it. How would they respond to my idea?

They loved it! I was stunned as our employees created beautiful displays with photographs, charts and proposals full of new ideas. Their presentations were enthusiastic and imaginative. The union also loved it, because we were involving everyone at every level in our campaign to save the plant. Interestingly, as we focused on GM's global competitiveness, our employees began to compete with each other to determine who could produce the best possible displays.

Keep in mind, this had never been done. The middle of an automobile plant is sacred territory, and the focus is 100 percent on building a quarter of a million cars every year. But our Competition Center was infusing the plant with new energy. Our people actually had their chests stuck out with pride over the ideas and presentations they had shared. As the initiator of this endeavor, I was fully invested in the plant's fight for survival. I was determined that our efforts result in nothing less than victory.

Seeking Support from Albany and the Community

My strategy to save the North Tarrytown plant required me to create a coalition of local and state leaders that included New York Governor Mario Cuomo. His office enthusiastically granted my request for a meeting because I was General Motors' key executive in the state of New York. As such, I represented every GM employee at every office and plant in the Empire State. And my oversight included philanthropy and other important community endeavors that involved General Motors.

These were exciting times! Managing a billion-dollar operation away from General Motors headquarters endowed me with tremendous clout and respect as I met with the governor's chief of staff and economic development team.

"Bringing the state on board to play an instrumental role to save the plant," I told them, "would protect five thousand jobs and the economic well-being of the surrounding community. Since the plant lacks rail access, General Motors is forced to pay a $70 truck penalty per vehicle. That, on top of the high electricity bill, is sounding the death knell for Tarrytown. Can you build railroad bridges north of Tarrytown and south of Tarrytown, so we can ship by train?"

The team agreed to relay my request to Governor Cuomo. "With his approval," they promised, "we'll do the research and ask the state of New York for clearance to construct new rail lines. We'll also explore other ways that we can help."

After that, I had many occasions to interface with Governor Cuomo, who became a strong ally for the survival of the Tarrytown plant. I had also established a powerful relationship with the United Way, by serving as chair of its annual fund drive and raising impressive funds. In addition, my coalition-building strategy inspired me to invite the Tarrytown school board and the city council to the plant for tours that included riding a train that wound through the factory.

"This is your plant," I told them. "We're the biggest employer in town, and we want you to challenge us all the time to be the best we can be."

A highlight on the tour was a stop in the employees' Competitiveness Center, where hourly and salaried workers alike gave presentations about our efforts to surpass our competitors. Our visitors were amazed! And our employees were thrilled to showcase their knowledge and ideas about how we were striving to beat other automakers with quality products and pricing. This was unprecedented! Our job was to build cars, so investing time on a Competitiveness Center could have drawn criticism as counterproductive. Quite the contrary -- it drew praise because our employees were motivated by the desire to perform better and to feel that their work maximized the company's success.

After the tour, we served refreshments. Then, as word spread about the tours, we began to receive requests from community groups that wanted to witness the exciting inner-workings of our auto assembly plant. Even General Motors executives asked to visit! When vice presidents and members of the Board of Directors were in Manhattan for meetings, they would travel up to Tarrytown for a tour.

The campaign was setting me up for a power play: if GM instructed me to close Tarrytown, I would call on these supporters to lobby for its survival.

Manhattan Boule: New Friendships and a Greater Social Network

As I worked fervently to save the Tarrytown plant, I wanted to expand my social network with the Boulé, which had chapters in Westchester County, Brooklyn and Manhattan. I joined the Manhattan chapter because its members included individuals whom I had admired for many years. Indeed, I enjoyed acquaintances with world tennis champion Arthur Ashe, Manhattan Borough President and future New York City Mayor David Dinkins, and Kenneth Chenault, an American Express executive who would become its CEO and chairman.

Having been a Boulé member in good standing in Rochester, I was not subjected to the harsh evaluation that new members

146

endured. In fact, I had the privilege of automatic membership in the Manhattan Boulé. This provided me with two especially unforgettable experiences.

First, we partnered with the Westchester County Boulé chapter to host a spectacular, black tie Christmas party. Five hundred people attended this dinner-dance gala in Windows on the World, which comprised the entire 106th and 107th floors of the World Trade Center in Lower Manhattan. The glittering crowd was the who's who of African American intelligentsia and celebrity, while the lavish atmosphere defied description. The entire evening was one of those life experiences that Maureen and I agreed you simply had to see to believe.

The second Boulé experience that I will never forget involved a business meeting that occurred around the time of the Christmas party. The Treasurer's report involved calling out the name of anyone who was delinquent in paying his dues. For instance, if they had said, "Roy Roberts, you're delinquent by X amount," then everyone would joke, "Roy, Maureen, we'll take up a collection for you!" No one wanted to be the poor soul to suffer such humiliation. Believe me, an experience like that convinced you to pay your Boulé dues before you paid your mortgage!

Thankfully, I developed lasting relationships in New York that I continue to cherish today. One year, when the bi-annual Boule convention was held in New York, Dr. John Hutchinson hosted the most magnificent barbecue for 4,000 people at his estate in Chappaqua. Today it's a joy to reconnect with many of these individuals at our conventions around the country.

A Hush of Astonishment Came Over the Room

Meanwhile, Ray Calore and I continued our diligent work to save the Tarrytown plant. About three months after we had conveyed our need for a superior labor contract to the UAW and management negotiators, I received a phone call from my Director of Labor Relations.

"Mr. Roberts, we have a tentative labor agreement," he said. "Can you please join us in the dining room?"

When Ray and I arrived, both parties were assembled. They presented a stack of transparencies that was six inches thick! Back then, before computers and PowerPoint, we did presentations by displaying 8 ½" x 11" clear slides called "flimsies" on an overhead projector.

"This is the labor agreement," the labor relations director said, as he began to summarize each section of the huge document.

"Wait a minute," I said, addressing the negotiating teams for GM and the UAW. "Let me understand. What was the challenge I gave you?"

They repeated it to me.

"Now tell me," I said, "did you achieve that objective?"

"Yes, we did," they said.

"Give me the signature page," I ordered.

They gave it to me.

I immediately signed it.

A hush of astonishment overcame the room. Everyone was in shock, because I approved the labor agreement without reading a single word in it! The truth was, I didn't want to see anything proposed in that labor agreement because I couldn't change a damn thing. The bottom line was that they had achieved our goal.

The UAW was ecstatic, and that spelled relief for everyone in the executive offices at GM headquarters in Detroit. Ray and I were praised as saviors for reaching an amicable agreement that met the goals of management and the union.

Saved by the Minivan

However, our work was not done. We still needed to convince GM to allocate a new product to our plant.

"I want to come down and see the new van," I said during an informal phone call to GM's vice president for product development.

GM's code name for its new, fiberglass-body minivan was the APV200. This vehicle, I decided, would be the saving grace of the North Tarrytown plant.

Why? The new minivan was built on the same front-wheel drive chassis as the Buick Century and Pontiac 6000 models that we were already building at Tarrytown. Plus, I was convinced that minivans were not just a trendy product for the automotive industry. The popularity of the Chrysler minivan had proven that this type of transportation was here to stay. Consumers were raving about these spacious vehicles that were as easy to drive and park as a car.

"We need this van at Tarrytown," I told our product development V.P. We simply had to have it. And after our corporate leaders deliberated -- considering the competitive labor agreement, our leverage and cooperation with state government, and the bold new spirit of unity and determination throughout the plant – we got it!

Our three-part strategy to save Tarrytown was so successful, that General Motors agreed not only to keep Tarrytown open, but also to invest $250 million in new product allocation and a new, state-of-the-art paint shop. In addition, my efforts to garner support from Governor Cuomo and the surrounding community resulted in even more advantages that improved efficiency and reduced costs at the plant.

Notably, the $170 million that GM provided to build our new paint shop brought it into compliance with the federal Clean Air Act. Its many high-tech features included fifty robots that would spare workers from inhaling paint fumes.

Expanding our transportation capabilities was paramount to the many cost-cutting measures. Specifically, my work with the governor's economic development team resulted in raising bridges on the Metro North Hudson commuter rail line. This facilitated train transport of our vehicles, which eliminated the huge expense of the $70 truck penalty per vehicle! That was a major improvement on the price of a product.

To reduce the factory's high electric bill, we collaborated with a nearby nuclear power plant to slash one million dollars from the plant's annual energy costs. Another savings resulted from lowering the property tax assessment in nearby municipalities.

All of the above combined to breathe new life into the North Tarrytown plant. Momentous and unprecedented, my successful strategy showed GM leadership that Roy Roberts had the boldness and vision to make magic happen for the world's number one automaker.

High-Profile Media Day Celebrates Innovation and Collaboration

To celebrate Tarrytown as a crown jewel for General Motors, I orchestrated a media extravaganza to proclaim to the world that GM's North Tarrytown plant was making a dramatic comeback by manufacturing a new product: the APV 200 fiberglass minivan.

This was significant because Tarrytown would become one of only five plants to roll out new products, with the goal of helping GM recoup its status from Ford as the number-one automaker. This good news on February 3, 1987, was all the more dramatic against an economic backdrop that saw GM's share of U.S. passenger car and light truck sales dip nearly 5 percent over the prior year. That reality had cast a gloomy cloud over management and labor alike, because poor sales resulted in lay-offs and plant closings.

"We're participating in a lot of meetings that are not as joyous as this one," said UAW Vice President Donald Ephlin. (Sadly, GM would close five plants within a year of that statement, with more plants designated for closure during the late 1980s. This bad news made the good news at Tarrytown all the more dramatic.)

That somber reality made our Media Day at Tarrytown shimmer with optimism and excitement. Governor Cuomo arrived via helicopter, landing on the Tarrytown grounds to join the chorus of praise for our momentous turnaround.

I emceed a lavish ceremony in the plant's Big Room with more than one hundred media professionals, alongside dozens of labor officials, management leaders, government dignitaries and assembly line workers. Excitement was palpable in the Tarrytown plant as Ray Calore and I were lauded by our 5,000 employees for securing their financial futures. Leaders from GM, the UAW and Governor Cuomo all congratulated our success. GM President F. James McDonald was the highest-ranking corporate person to attend; his presence added special significance for me. My attaché case still contained the magazine quoting his doubts about an African American becoming a GM vice president.

Back in Detroit, our triumph gave General Motors something to brag about. "You make us proud, Roy," Chairman Smith said. Likewise, everyone at the UAW Solidarity House went wild with celebration.

"This is the way we're supposed to run plants!" I was told repeatedly.

Newspaper, radio and TV reports dominated the local and national news, because saving the plant and getting a new product was a huge business and economic story.

"I Didn't Do It Alone" --
Roy Roberts + Ray Calore = $250 Million Victory

Saving Tarrytown inspired accolades that included a phone call from an executive at the Gannett newspaper chain who said: "Roy, we want to give you our Business Leader of the Year award."

Past recipients of this prestigious honor included leaders of corporate behemoths in Westchester County, including: two chairmen of IBM, the chairman of PepsiCo, and the chairman of General Foods.

"I can't accept that award," I said. "I didn't save Tarrytown by myself. I did it with the president of the union, Ray Calore."

Ray and I were elated to become co-recipients of the 1988 Gannett Westchester Newspapers Business Leadership Award.

The newspaper chain devoted its January 17, 1988, Commerce and Industry Section to a SPECIAL BUSINESS REPORT cover story with the headline: THE MEN WHO SAVED TARRYTOWN. The cover showed color photographs of Ray and me. A spread of stories chronicled our plant-saving saga, with an angle toward the future. The coverage included many photographs of the two of us – the innovative, coalition-building new plant manager, and the veteran, forward-thinking, and very popular president of Local 664. In addition, there were plenty of "beauty shots" of the new minivan that would roll off the Tarrytown assembly line in February of 1989.

"It's an extremely important product because it's going into a segment of the business where we do not currently have a product," I was quoted as saying. "The foreign and domestic competitors have done extremely well in that niche. The product we're going to produce will surpass anything that's in the marketplace."

I spoke on the marketplace demand for this vehicle, and that I would personally purchase one. "It's an exciting product. The Tarrytown plant will be the only plant building the product. It will be kind of like looking at the free enterprise system. All you have to do is build a quality product and it's going to sell."

Ray and I received the award at a banquet on February 23, 1988, at the Rye Town Hilton in Rye Brook, New York. I reveled in this celebration, because our triumph at Tarrytown convinced me that bold innovation, hard work and teamwork would continue to provide more opportunities to make positive, powerful contributions to the success of General Motors.

NINE

Roy Roberts, Vice President of General Motors Corporation

In the midst of the excitement over what our team had accomplished, I received a phone call from Elmer W. Johnson, GM's executive vice president for operating staffs and a member of the Board of Directors. Prior to his appointment by Chairman Smith, Elmer had run the prominent Chicago law firm of Kirkland Ellis. It was widely believed that Roger Smith had recruited Elmer Johnson as his successor. Though no date was set, this changing of the guard would be a radical shift. Elmer was a tough, outspoken guy who had publicly declared that to fix General Motors, he needed to change its corporate culture. I privately endorsed his strategy to sweep traditionalists from the fourteenth floor, to make room for innovation, progress and profits. As he began to eliminate those whom he decreed as ineffective or resistant to his vision, and replaced them by hiring and promoting his people into key positions, many high-ranking executives were terrified. Though I had never met Elmer Johnson, I admired his reputation as a fearless firebrand.

"How can I help you, Mr. Johnson?" I asked eagerly when he called my office at the Tarrytown plant.

"Roy, I've heard so many good things about what you're achieving there," he said. "I'd like to pay you a visit and see for myself. I'll be in Manhattan for the Board of Directors meeting, so I'd like to come to Tarrytown a few days before that."

"It would be my honor to personally give you a tour," I said. "Your visit will coincide with our Quality Meeting, and I think you might glean some important insights from attending that as well."

"It's a deal," Elmer said.

I also invited him to our home with his support team for the shareholders meeting: Rod Gillum, Lewis Campbell, and Attorney Edmond J. Dilworth, Jr., Group Counsel to the Chevrolet Pontiac Canada Group of GM, and a member of GM's national labor negotiating team. Maureen provided the utmost hospitality with drinks and hors d'oeuvres, while Katrina delighted our visitors by conversing in French and playing our baby grand piano.

Then I took them to my favorite restaurant, which I had bought out for the entire evening. The ambiance was elegant and intimate, because it seated only thirty-five people and was situated inside a picturesque house overlooking the Hudson River. As the five of us proceeded to dine on succulent duck entrées, we engaged in a spirited discussion about all of the factors that drive success at GM.

"Making your people feel like they're an important part of the process," I said, "is the key foundation for successfully managing a plant or a department or any other body of individuals."

Meanwhile, the waiter continuously replenished my guests' wine glasses. I nursed my drink. It would be wrong to over-imbibe around senior officers in the corporation.

"The corporation's success hinges on making people believe they're more than the willing worker," I said, "but that they're impacting the place where they work. You'll see that tomorrow in our Competitiveness Center."

I also emphasized another secret to my success. "When you run plants, you have to arrive early. You have to be with the people. When they see that I care about them and the product, hat makes them care, too. The result is quality, and that drives business."

After dessert, I announced that I needed to practice what I preach by going home for a good night's sleep, to get to work early. But by the time I drove them all back to their hotel, Elmer was feeling no pain.

"I'm going to pick you up at six o'clock tomorrow morning," I said, fearing he might be hung over. "Be ready."

Sure enough, when I pulled up to the hotel, Elmer looked like he'd been hit by a truck! I started filling him up with coffee and aspirin; he perked up. When we arrived at the Tarrytown plant, I gave them a tour, during which hourly and salaried employees greeted me with joyous words and gestures.

"I am amazed at how people respond to you," Elmer remarked. "They respect you like a boss, but also look at you with reverence in their eyes. I have never seen anything like this in my life!"

Next we proceeded to the Quality Meeting in the Big Room, where the stage held large displays of our vehicles. Representatives from each department read off quality scores.

"We're extremely honored today," I told the gathering of about seventy people, "to host Elmer Johnson, executive vice president of General Motors. He's heard so much good news about Tarrytown, he wanted to visit us and bring his team."

I introduced them. After much applause, I spoke about how our quality scores reflected the plant's upward trajectory on every level.

"Thanks to you," I said, "we are the biggest success story in General Motors right now. Now it's up to each of us to take the privilege of GM's investment of $250 million in our plant, and show that we deserve it and that we're glad they did it. How do we do that? By building the best damn cars and minivans that have ever rolled off an assembly line at General Motors Corporation!"

Everyone went wild!

"We're always going to be successful!" I declared. "We've got our quality right and our cost right, better than anybody in the world!"

An explosion of cheers inspired an expression of awe on Elmer Johnson's face that was worth its weight in gold.

I invited Elmer to speak. He took the podium.

"I am so impressed with Tarrytown!" he exclaimed. "I have never witnessed anything like your team spirit and enthusiasm!" Elmer raved about our Competitiveness Center and our commitment to quality.

"I am so pleased that Roy Roberts is offering his leadership here," he said, "and that all of you are rallying around his impressive management style. You're getting your quality scores up. You're making your labor relationships right. And you're making your people relationships right. I have to say, Tarrytown under Roy Roberts' leadership is an exemplary operation that is making General Motors very proud!"

I was grateful that this high-ranking executive praised me in front of people from every level of the plant. In addition, I was pleased that a local newspaper reporter was attending the meeting. The next day, a flattering write-up about Elmer's visit to the North Tarrytown plant would add another great dimension to Elmer's trip.

At the conclusion of the meeting, I privately told Elmer that I deeply appreciated his encouraging comments.

"Roy," Elmer said. "I am awestruck by this experience. The employees' admiration speaks volumes about how you are a caring and compassionate leader who truly makes your employees feel valued and celebrated."

"Thank you," I said, nearly speechless that Elmer had recognized this core value in my management style.

"Roy, what would you do if we asked you to take over HR?"

"Well," I responded with a matter-of-fact tone, "I'd find out what the Strategic Plan is for the short-term and the long-term. I'd study it, then develop a five-year, Human Resources strategy that would complement the Strategic Plan. Then I'd do everything possible to implement that plan." Quite honestly, I thought he was talking about me potentially taking over a regional vice president's job.

"Roy, I'm talking about the personnel job for the entire General Motors Corporation."

"Hell, I'd do the same thing!" I exclaimed.

"Great answer," Elmer said. "As I expected."

156

Excitement pulsed through me. That was a huge job! It was open because the individual who had held that post had been let go. Now, a very capable African American executive, Bill Brooks, was serving as acting vice president of Personnel Administration and Development.

That Elmer had posed this hypothetical question suggested that he and the powers that be at General Motors were considering me for this position. With the Board of Directors' approval, this title would make me the second African American in the history of General Motors to become a vice president. Otis Smith was the first; he had retired in 1984 as vice president and General Counsel.

Sure enough, a few days after our meeting, Elmer called to say: "Roy, I want you to become our Vice President of Personnel Administration and Development."

I was ecstatic! This was the biggest personnel job in the world, with 950,000 employees in thirty-seven countries. The offer felt surreal. This promotion would enable me to catapult over several layers of management positions that were typically requisite rungs on a plant manager's corporate climb. I was forty-seven years old, and confident that the only way I would ever need to ever need to leave such a high post at the world's largest corporation would be to turn sixty-five — GM's mandatory retirement age.

At the time, I was conscious of the prevalent mindset in the African American community: *You get a job and you keep it for life. Attain and maintain financial security by playing it safe.* No, not Roy Roberts. Risk excites me! Therefore, I maintained the conviction that I would thrive under any circumstances, and prosper as a result. I would not stay in any job — even at the zenith of General Motors Corporation — unless it excited me, challenged me and provided opportunities to impact the company's people and profits.

An Ally in the Boardroom Blocks a Detractor

As I approached the fifty-story General Motors office tower in New York City, I was overwhelmed with the feeling that I had come a

157

very long way from the projects of Muskegon Heights, Michigan. With its expansive plaza and sleek white stone façade, the GM building, at 767 Fifth Ave., dominated a full block between Fifth Avenue and Madison Avenue, from Fifty-Eighth Street to Fifty-Ninth Street, and faced the famed Plaza Hotel. The building housed FAO Schwartz, the famous toy store featured in *Big*, the 1988 movie starring Tom Hanks.

"Roy, this is your big day," Elmer Johnson said as we strode past a gleaming display of Corvettes and Cadillacs in the lobby. As we ascended to the twenty-fifth floor and approached the rosewood-paneled boardroom, I was euphoric, yet anxious. "Roy, you wait here while we vote," Elmer said. "I'm going to come out of there and tell you some good news."

Elmer stepped into the legendary conference room, followed by a stream of high-powered executives, including Chairman Roger Smith. I was in awe! If I had ever wanted to play with the big boys, this was it! My fate with the company was in their hands. Behind the closed doors of the conference room, they would vote on whether I should be appointed as GM's vice president of Personnel Development and Administration. That would establish me as the highest-ranking African American in the world's largest corporation!

In the hallway, I was approached by Ross Perot, who was waging a verbal battle with GM over how its management team was running the company. The Texas billionaire struck up a conversation with me, and the president of his company, Mort Meyerson, joined us.

"Roy," a GM lawyer said, motioning for me to walk with him. "There's a call for you in the bank of phones down this way."

"Excuse me, gentlemen," I said, walking away with the lawyer, who had been keeping an eye on Perot and Meyerson in the hallway.

"Get away from those guys!" the attorney admonished. "They have brought the Board of Directors to a standstill." He explained that Ross Perot was a demagogue who was airing GM's dirty laundry by talking publicly about what he believed was going wrong inside the company. The lawyer relayed that the directors inside the meeting had berated Ross by saying, "You're no smarter than the rest of us!"

Inside the boardroom, the vote on my appointment sparked high drama. Elmer Johnson would later recount how GM's vice president of Communications passed a hand-written note to Roger Smith that said: "You can't take a plant manager and make him a vice president of General Motors."

Roger appeared perplexed as he glanced at the paper, then silently looked at the communications vice president. The chairman handed the note to Elmer, sitting to his right. Elmer read the note, looked at the chairman, and wrote on that same note:

"If you don't name Roy Roberts as vice president of Personnel Administration and Development today, announce that I just quit!"

Elmer handed that note back to Chairman Smith.

"Roy Roberts, congratulations!" Elmer exclaimed a short time later in the hallway. "The Board of Directors of General Motors Corporation has officially appointed you as Vice President of Personnel Administration and Development!"

Rod Gillum would later inform me that Reverend Leon Sullivan had asked his fellow board members for the special privilege of making the motion to appoint me. I would come to understand that this great man who had asked Chairman Smith to hire me, and who had monitored my progress over the years, experienced great fulfillment through my accomplishments. I represented what he wanted to accomplish at General Motors.

I was ushered into a press conference to announce my appointment that same day in a large lobby of GM's New York tower. I was in awe! The global media asked questions, and many tried to attribute my selection to race. To downplay this idea, I responded, "The white-collar work force at General Motors is composed of 13.7 percent minorities. I view my appointment as the corporation's continuing and admirable efforts to create and sustain a balanced work force."

With a cadence that has been compared in the national media to that of a country preacher, I explained that the key to marketplace success in an increasingly diverse world depended on hiring people of color in influential positions.

"When the people running the company reflect the full spectrum of the population," I said, "we can best target our marketing and product base to appeal to people from every race, culture and walk of life. Companies that fail to make this a major tenet of their business model will lose market share faster than a Corvette can go from zero to sixty."

Another reporter asked me to reflect on the highly unusual move to elevate a plant manager to a vice president. I echoed something that Donald F. Ephlin, the UAW vice president who interfaced with GM, would later proclaim in the national media: that my background on the shop floor would bring an immense sensitivity to the dynamics of the fourteenth floor of General Motors.

In keeping with that, I told the reporter, "I think Martin Luther King, Jr., said it best: 'Quite often you can't lead where you don't go and don't know.'"

After the press conference, Elmer said, "Roy, we need you to come to Detroit next week, so you can talk to the HR staff at headquarters and get to work."

A Mysterious Secretary Appears on My First Day

A few hours after the Board approved my appointment, my predecessor called and said, "Roy, I'm not upset because you got the job. You didn't fire me. Elmer Johnson did. He and I just didn't hit it off. You and I have been friends over the years, so I'm calling because I want to help make sure you're successful. If you have the time, I'd like to give you some guidance for the job."

"Great," I said. "I'd love it."

Sunday morning, he called me at home in Chappaqua. For three hours, he offered advice, guidance and warnings about strategy, people and different functional areas.

"Roy, you have an executive assistant who is outstanding," he said. "Confidentiality is her middle name. She's Asian American, petite and absolutely brilliant. She's incredibly loyal and will protect you to the Nth degree. You want to keep her. She will do great work for you."

I appreciated his counsel, which I kept at the forefront of my mind on Monday morning when I reported to corporate headquarters in Detroit. Human Resources personnel whisked me through the huge hallways for a whirlwind day that began with a breakfast gathering in my honor. Because I was the second black vice president in GM's history, and because I would impact the entire organization, everybody wanted to see me and talk to me. The day didn't offer enough hours to accommodate that, so I spent time with my boss, who escorted me into a large room with about sixty Human Resources staff members. My boss introduced me and invited me to give a short speech that roused applause and congratulations.

After a few minutes of chatting with people I knew, I was taken upstairs to my fourteenth-floor office. A wide hallway on the floor separated facing rows of executive offices. I noticed that in front of each vice president's office was the desk of his executive secretary, and I looked forward to meeting the outstanding woman that my predecessor had described. But the person at the desk outside my office was not Asian American. She was middle-aged and Caucasian, with silver-blond hair. I stayed calm and cordial, but I was deeply disturbed. My instincts told me that the mysterious disappearance of the Asian American secretary was part of a ploy to hinder my performance.

I entered my office, which was lined with shelves displaying books about the history of General Motors. At my desk, I tried to review paperwork, but I was too agitated. I had to rectify this situation immediately.

Across from me was the office of Alfred Warren, vice president of labor. Outside his office sat his executive assistant, who was African American. With my back to the mysterious lady with white hair, I approached Mr. Warren's secretary and spoke in a tone that only she could hear:

"You don't know me. I'm Roy Roberts. I'm new, and I was told that there was a great lady in my office, and I need you to answer a question for me. It's critically important."

"Yes, sir."

"Is the lady sitting behind me at that desk as good and efficient as the lady who was there last week?"

"No, sir, Mr. Roberts, and everybody on the fourteenth floor is wondering what you're going to do about it."

"Thank you very much." I turned and walked down the hall to speak with Joan Rodney, who oversaw issues pertaining to the building. She recommended that I call Joanne Stark, who handled personnel matters.

"Joanne," I said on the phone. "The secretary who's in my office now, I want her out by noon. I want the executive assistant who was in my office last week *back* in my office."

I was told that my predecessor's secretary had been moved to a general typing pool.

Thankfully, the Asian American woman returned by noon. She immediately impressed me as being as phenomenal as my predecessor had indicated. She helped me immeasurably, because she knew the building, the history and the people. I treasured our relationship, because she knew what was spoken and what was unspoken. As one of the finest executive secretaries I have ever known, she was instrumental to my success in managing the three-tiered department that governed personnel development, salary administration and benefits for white-collar employees. My department was also responsible for establishing corporate personnel policies and procedures for the hiring, retention and training of salaried employees.

Each day, I arrived at six o'clock to attend breakfast meetings, prepare my agenda for thirteen-hour days, and consult with some of the 250 people on my Human Resources staff, which included several African Americans. We had the strongest human resources group in the history of General Motors. Since then, each person has moved on and made great achievements.

Beyond Human Resources, the following African American executives were in place when I became a vice president – and were greatly respected: Haven Cockerham, Barry Morris, Elmer Jackson, Phil Saunders, Barbara Mahone, and Bill Brooks. Shortly after my appointment, Bill was promoted to vice president of Community Affairs, becoming the third African American vice president at General Motors.

First Assignment from The Chairman Establishes "Right-Size Roberts"

I was eager to get to work, so it was with great excitement that I met with Chairman Roger Smith for my first assignments. At some point, I would have to trim the bloat from GM's $3 billion annual health care costs. For now, the company was embarking on a massive campaign to cut costs by streamlining and re-organizing from top to bottom.

"We need to get about forty thousand people out of this organization," he said. "Roberts, you head that up."

It was clear that Chairman Smith and everyone else believed that it was my job to orchestrate the exodus of these white-collar employees. None would be laid off. However, they would be enticed to leave with generous buy-outs and early retirement packages – some being offered twenty months' pay for employees who had at least fourteen years of seniority.

After getting rid of non-essential employees through retirement and attrition, the remaining 108,000 white-collar workers who remained would no longer receive automatic pay raises. Instead, they would get on-the-spot bonuses and salary increases linked to performance. It was important that merit raises were earned, I told *The Wall Street Journal* for an article on January 26, 1988.

My philosophy was rooted in some of the facts that I had gleaned in our Competitiveness Centers at Tarrytown. Specifically, that 600 different automobiles were being presented for sale in America. General Motors was operating in an extremely competitive marketplace, in a constant battle for profits against Ford, Chrysler and foreign automakers. Our market share had plunged from 40.9 percent in 1986 to 37.3 percent in 1987. Likewise, earnings dropped from $3.9 billion on $96 billion in sales in 1985 to $2.9 billion on sales of $102 billion in 1986. With our new plan, GM expected to save $500 million by the end of 1988 and slash expenses by $10 billion by 1990.

The bottom line was that Roy Roberts' job was to force people out of General Motors. If I may interject a bit of context here, it's important to note that throughout the history of General Motors, Human Resources was never lauded as a crown jewel of the corporation. It was not treated with pride or respect. I don't know why, except that HR employees were not considered central to the business.

As a result, my experience convinced me that the corporation leaned on the Human Resources department to do the nasty work, which included terminating individuals and large numbers of employees. Knowing this, I intended to make sure that we functioned in a way that inspired corporate leadership and employees alike to perceive us as total professionals who were adding value to General Motors.

Therefore, upon receipt of my first assignment, I devised a strategy to deflect and disperse its negative impact. I did something that had never been done; I turned the tables on all the group executives, right up front. My strategy was bold, yet simple. I used the same tactic that had been so successful in making the numbers tap dance for annual budget reviews with plant bosses. To do this, I scheduled individual conversations with every group vice president. Then I allocated *to each of them* the responsibility of downsizing their individual staffs.

"Each of you has a percentage of the people," I told them, "and I want you to put together a plan to get the people out."

At the next chairman's meeting, Roger Smith asked, "Roberts, how are you doing with your plan for the reduction of forty thousand employees?"

I turned to the Group Executives, and addressed every one of them individually: "Okay, Bill, why don't you tell me about your plan to get rid of your 10 percent."

People were shocked!

I diffused their resistance to my plan by saying, "They're not my people. They're your people. I can't say who'll leave your organization. You've got to make that decision."

GM was not alone in reducing its workforce. Ford was in the process of downsizing its staff by one-third, resulting in a more dominant presence in the marketplace. At the same time, our foreign competitors — Toyota, Honda and Nissan — were encroaching on our territory by operating assembly plants in the United States. What really revved GM to get lean and strong to grow our market share was the opening of the Mazda Motor Corporation's new assembly plant in the Detroit suburb of Flat Rock.

Meanwhile, the local and national media highlighted General Motors' multi-pronged strategy to downsize. *Black Enterprise* magazine featured me on the cover in December of 1987 with the headline: "Roy Roberts' Mission: To Build A More Competitive Workforce at GM." The cover showed me smiling and wearing a business suit, leaning against a Cadillac.

Inside, the six-page spread featured a photograph of me standing on West Grand Boulevard with the General Motors Building in the background. The headline said, "Can Roy Roberts Rebuild the GM Machine?" The smaller, sub-headline said: "Cutting 40,000 salaried workers is no easy task, but GM's vice president is determined to complete his one-year mission."

The excellent article by Kevin D. Thompson questioned how blacks would fare in the downsizing. *Black Enterprise* had named GM in 1985 as one of the top 25 companies for African Americans to work. Now, I assured him that the percentage of black managers had been increasing for three years.

"In 1985, 4,304, or 8.9 percent, of GM's 47,380 managers were black, a slight increase from 4,092, or 8 percent, in 1984," the article said. "Although the number of black managers fell in 1986 to 4,187, the percentage increased to 9.3 percent as the total number of GM managers declined to 44,672."

The article also highlighted that African American blue-collar workers would lose jobs as GM closed 11 plants before 1991. "In 1985, blacks comprised 18.3 percent, or 84,014, of the 431,199 hourly workers," the magazine reported. "Last year, the number of black assembly-line workers dropped to 77,003."

Over the next year, we successfully swept about forty-two thousand people from the system. In retrospect, it probably should have been ninety thousand.

In the midst of this, on February 29, 1988, *The New York Times* published an extensive story by John Holusha about me under the headline, "G.M.'s Specialist in Job Shake-Ups."

During that process, a *Wall Street Journal* reporter interviewed me in front of GM headquarters while we were standing in the middle of West Grand Boulevard.

"Mr. Roberts," the reporter said. "You're going to be known as a hatchet man to all these people out here."

My response: "I don't understand that. I'm simply trying to 'right-size' the human resources of this corporation to match the demand in the marketplace."

The term "right-size" caught on and was used all over the world. *Inc.* magazine attributed the founding of that term to me, and called me "Right-Size Roberts." That nickname stuck in certain circles, and I thought it was very apropos.

"Detroit Embraced Roy Very Quickly"

Maureen and I wanted to buy a home in The Palmer Woods Historic District, where stately mansions built by auto barons rise on winding, tree-lined streets. By the late 1980s, property values for enormous homes in the city of Detroit were quite low. (Detroit's real estate values improved in the 1990s but dropped significantly during the Great Recession of the late 2000s). We found a beautiful house that cost $167,000. We also wanted to purchase the adjacent lot for $10,000. However, I needed to reinvest one million dollars or pay capital gains taxes. This prevented us from purchasing a home in Detroit.

Instead, Maureen and I bought a spectacular house in the affluent suburb of Birmingham. It had an impressive, sixty-foot gallery, as well as a tennis court and a swimming pool. The home was in an area where, years ago, blacks and Jews had united to help each other purchase property.

The local public high school had an excellent academic reputation, but its student body had only one African American student. Maureen and I wanted Katrina to see successful, intelligent African Americans, both amongst her peers and their parents.

We enrolled her in the Detroit Country Day School in nearby Bloomfield Hills. The prestigious private school provided our daughter with a rigorous, college preparatory, liberal arts education. Her classmates included future University of Michigan Fab Five basketball phenomenon and NBA All-Star Chris Webber, as well as the sons of Dennis Archer, my former classmate at Western Michigan University who would become Detroit's mayor. Katrina thrived and developed great writing skills.

Meanwhile, my work kept me so busy that leisure activity was restricted to weekend golf and tennis with friends.

At the same time, I was welcomed into the upper echelon of Detroit's black bourgeoisie, which continues to boast impressive numbers of doctors, lawyers, judges and entrepreneurs. It was an honor that these accomplished individuals invited me to participate in the Southfield chapter of Kappa Alpha Psi, and the Detroit chapters of The Boulé, The Rogues and The Guardsmen.

"Detroit embraced Roy very quickly," says my son-in-law, Roger Huff, who was Superintendent of Manufacturing at GM's Hydramatic Division at the time. "Part of it was because of his position at General Motors, and the other part was because of just him. He is very confident in his ability to meet people and make them very comfortable. That's what sold the Detroit community on Roy. He's very people-centered and very smart. People genuinely like him."

Roger and Robin, who owned a day-care center in Ann Arbor, moved to the Metropolitan Detroit area one year before we did. The close proximity was a blessing because it enabled Maureen and me to spend a lot of time with them, and we became very close.

Robin and Roger attended the black-tie charity preview event that precedes the North American International Auto Show each January. Tickets cost $350 per person to mingle with celebrities, dignitaries, business leaders and the who's who of the Big Three and global auto industry. It's a fabulous affair where tuxedoed men and beautifully gowned women sip champagne and stroll around gleaming vehicle displays inside the enormous Cobo Center. Automakers from around the world throw lavish receptions, and the global media feasts on every new tidbit of information about new cars and the companies that manufacture them. Many consider this to be the Motor City's most high profile social and business event of the year.

"During the late '80s," Roger recalls, "we attended the Charity Preview for the first time as guests of Roy and Maureen. He seemingly knew everyone, and everyone knew him! Others approached because they recognized him as someone they wanted to meet. We couldn't walk ten feet without people stopping us. To me, that was pretty dramatic to see the presence he had within his role at GM and the presence of the community, in such a short time."

"Robin and I have been with Roy and Maureen at many social occasions," Roger says, "and we're always amazed at how, when Roy walks in the room, the room changes. He has a presence with the business community and the social community; folks just gravitate to him. It's really dramatic to witness."

When Roger and Robin accompanied us to social events hosted by The Boulé and The Guardsmen, "It was quite clear that those members looked to him as a leader amongst leaders," Roger says.

My association with these social groups in Detroit has blessed me with too many special memories to recount. The Guardsmen, in particular, stand out. Chapters of The Guardsmen across America alternate hosting three annual social events, which can be held in any location in the world. The planning and execution of these events is wildly competitive, as each chapter attempts to outshine the prior year's hosts. One year, the Los Angeles chapter was bedazzling members from across the country with a spectacular itinerary that included golf at the exclusive LaCosta Country Club.

When a white gentlemen who was not with our group became curious about the well-dressed African American men on the putting green, he approached and asked, "Where are all of you from?"

One of our Guardsmen, my dear friend and noted Detroit attorney Wilson Copeland, answered, "We're here with The Guardsmen."

"What do you guard?" the gentleman asked.

"Not a damn thing!" Wilson retorted.

That was the truth, and we still laugh about it today.

My robust social agenda on weekends was a saving grace to temper the stress and high-pressure atmosphere of my work each week.

"I don't know if there were two other people in General Motors who outworked him," Roger recalls. "We saw him coming home on weekdays with two briefcases full of work. And this was after working long hours during the day. For example, if he had a meeting the next day at six or seven o'clock in the morning, he was tenacious at preparation."

This is the trait that set me apart from most people at General Motors. I'd come home late at night with those two attaché cases, and my goal was to get through them to prepare for the next day. On the weekend, I'd try to reconcile what had happened during the previous week, while getting ready for the next week. I was reading reports, and preparing responses to questions that might arise from my bosses. All the while, I was making sure that everything I was doing synchronized with the goals of the corporation.

"Few people saw the preparation aspect of Roy's work," Roger says. "But they saw the results. When you're tenacious about preparation, you'll have more confidence. You'll know the answers to every angle of an issue when people come at you with hard questions. Then, the Q & A becomes the fun part of a presentation. Roy was always ready. You wouldn't see him sweating too much."

Perks of the Job: World Travel, a Platform to Speak

My job as vice president of Personnel Administration and Development required me to travel around the world. Overseeing a global staff of 950,000 employees involved visiting their offices abroad to ensure organization, accountability and policy structure.

This was exciting, albeit overwhelming sometimes, as I adjusted to times zones, foreign languages and cultures. It was clear to Maureen that I was thoroughly enjoying my work.

"Why don't you go with me?" I said. "The next trip is starting in Paris, then we're going to see the GM plant in Zaragoza, Spain. After that, we're going to London to visit our offices and see *The Phantom of the Opera.*"

Maureen joined me for a whirlwind trip. By the time we reached London, we were drained.

"I'm not going to the theatre tonight," I said.

"Roy, you have to go. They worked hard to get you the tickets, and Andrew Lloyd Webber will be there."

I attended, and Maureen didn't have to keep me awake. The show, in its second week, was unbelievable!

Frequent speaking engagements included the American Newspaper Publishers Association's annual convention in Honolulu, Hawaii. At the time, African Americans, Asians, Native Americans and people of Hispanic descent composed only 7 percent of newsroom staffs, which put the media at an inherent disadvantage. In many instances, they would miss important stories -- and often lacked the perspective to cover certain issues in a sensitive manner.

"Like it or not," I said in comments to the publishers that were printed in *The New York Times* on April 27, 1988, "companies that fail to make the connection between a minority work force and the bottom line will be companies that lose the competitive race, and you can take that to the bank."

Two other speaking engagements were memorable because they involved both Chairman Smith and myself. First, I asked Roger Smith to accompany me to Florida A&M University to address freshmen in the School of Business and Industry, ranked as one of the best in the United States. The founding dean of the business school, Sybil Collins Mobley, introduced us to a large gathering of professionally attired students in a business boardroom with a Wall Street style electronic ticker tape streaming around the walls with the latest stock quotations.

After Roger's presentation, the students at this historically black university in Tallahassee, Florida, politely and intelligently asked questions.

"Chairman Smith," a student asked, "why did you form Saturn and build a new company, rather than use the facilities that GM already had?"

I was stunned. A significant number of people inside GM wondered exactly that. The unpublicized answer was that he was the boss and he did it his way. Of course Roger Smith answered the student's question with the diplomatic, appropriate explanation that had been frequently recounted in media analysis.

"Roy!" Roger exclaimed after we left. "I thought you said we'd be speaking to freshmen!"

"They are freshmen," I answered. "They're just bright as hell!"

Roger was so impressed that General Motors donated the first million dollars to the business school at Florida Agricultural and Mechanical University. Campus visitors see "General Motors Corporation" on a prominently displayed plaque that showcases the school's major donors.

GM has always been a benevolent company that believed in the communities where it does business. GM has continuously supported the NAACP, the UNCF, the National Urban League and many other endeavors impacting the African American and Hispanic communities. (Even during GM's darkest hours before filing for bankruptcy in 2009, it never cut contributions to those organizations).

My second memorable speaking event occurred closer to home, when I asked Roger to address hundreds of college interns at the conclusion of their summer jobs at General Motors. The undergraduate and graduate students from across America and Canada were gathered in a ballroom in the St. Regis Hotel across the street from GM headquarters when Chairman Smith arrived to give the luncheon address.

He did a respectable job of talking about how General Motors would tackle its many challenges. What followed was a Q&A session that I will remember for as long as I live. A young lady who had just completed her first year at Harvard stepped to the microphone and asked, "Mr. Smith, what kind of people is General Motors looking to hire?"

"We want self starters who are self-motivated people who can be creative and innovative," he responded. "And we want to pay them well."

"Why do you want to hire the brightest, most motivated people," she asked, "and bring them into a stifling environment where they're forced to do what you want them to do? The message they receive essentially is, 'Don't innovate. Don't create.' That's the opposite of what you just said."

Roger's complexion turned ruddy.

Once again, he put the best possible spin on his answer to an assertive young student's provocative challenge. Her words were shocking, but I was pleasantly surprised that she had the intellect and the courage to ask the chairman of the largest corporation in the world such a provocative question. The young lady had asked the most poignant question that anyone could raise, but insiders lacked the courage to ask it. The truth was, she had just summarized GM's corporate culture with keen accuracy. The question she asked remains relevant today for many corporations.

Yearning for "Tough Work" of Manufacturing

It bode well for GM to have a black person as head of Human Resources, because it was defending a $100 million class action lawsuit by a group of black employees who accused the corporation of racial discrimination in its employee appraisal process.

As I assessed the many benefits that GM was enjoying with me in this job, I began to wonder, *What incentive would the corporation have to promote me from this position where my performance was benefiting them so dramatically?*

None. I began to feel that I was the token black guy who became a vice president and was really good news for General Motors and big news in the auto industry. As such, I loathed the idea of being a one-trick pony.

"What is my true value in General Motors?" I demanded of myself. My goal was to use my talent and passion to maximize my contributions to help the corporation. Yet, as I worked diligently to do that in the pampered environment of my executive office, I yearned for the hands-on work that I had experienced in manufacturing. That was tough work, measured by harsh standards that included productivity and quality. By comparison, I didn't love staff work per se, because I never perceived it as hard, tough work. I believed it would be easy for critics to make excuses for my success by saying it came easily in my "soft" job.

I realized that my heart had always been in manufacturing and operations, and I wanted to return to that rigorous and rugged environment.

Leaving GM: Daring to Do What No One Had Ever Done

It was 1988, about a year into the job, and the winds of change, I believed, were blowing in the wrong direction. The man who had catapulted me up many levels of management to this position — Elmer Johnson — had fallen from grace with Chairman Smith.

The most palpable turning point occurred after Elmer, who was a music lover with a passion for jazz, appeared on the cover of *The Detroit Free Press Sunday Magazine* — playing a saxophone.

This was the kiss of death for his career at General Motors! He was shunned and lambasted throughout the corporation. The consensus was that he had violated the conservative, white-collar image that General Motors wanted its executives — and especially a potential chairman — to project.

"That's not the GM way!" they exclaimed as scathing criticism crackled in private conversations throughout the company. "He shouldn't be doing that!"

As a result, people united to oust him. Elmer believed that his chances for becoming chairman were over, and that his efforts to revamp the company from his current position would fail. He resigned from General Motors and returned to Chicago in June of 1988.

This underscored my discontent. A short time later, a headhunter who had followed my career approached me and recommended that I consider a position that would ultimately enable me to run Navistar International Corporation. The Chicago-based company, formerly known as International Harvester Corporation, manufactured and marketed medium- and heavy-duty trucks, as well as mid-range diesel engines. At that time, Navistar was becoming a leading manufacturer of bus chassis that were especially popular for school buses.

"Roy," the headhunter said, "they want to bring you in with the goal of making you chairman and CEO. You would start as vice president and general manager of Truck Operations, presiding over engineering, manufacturing and marketing for Navistar's line of medium- and heavy-duty trucks. That's a four-billion dollar operation."

That appealed to me.

The headhunter introduced me to Navistar Chairman/President Neil Springer, and his boss, Jim Cotting, chairman of the holding company. Extensive discussions about my role at Navistar enabled us to negotiate a deal that included a handsome salary and stock in the company.

Contrary to popular belief, it didn't require much discussion or persuasion for me to embrace this opportunity. My decision was somewhat motivated by emotion; my dissatisfaction with my position at GM incited tremendous excitement about the chance to potentially take the helm of an entire, albeit much smaller, corporation.

At the same time, Navistar appealed to my enthusiasm for being in operations, building things and making things happen. And it would enable me to be measured by the harsh standards that are integral to manufacturing and operations.

With 18,000 employees, Navistar was not a major company, but its $4 billion in annual sales were impressive, and its truck division was the leader in North America. I believed that my work there would demonstrate conclusively that I was an effective, innovative leader under the toughest circumstances.

With Maureen's consent, I accepted the position. Then I arranged a meeting with GM Chairman Roger Smith.

"Roger," I said, "I've accepted a position at Navistar."

He was absolutely stunned and really upset.

To my knowledge, no officer had never quit General Motors to go to another company. An executive who had achieved the prestige and honor of making it to the fourteenth floor of the world's largest manufacturing company simply did not abandon the security, privilege and financial rewards that such a position afforded.

Given the praise my work had received in the press, my departure would be detrimental to the company's image if the only African American vice president had the gall to quit such a coveted, high-profile post. Clearly, it would be in General Motors' best interest to keep me on board to prevent the inevitable news analysis and worse, negative perceptions from African American customers who might conclude that I had been mistreated or forced out.

"Look," Roger said. "We'll make you chairman of GM de Mexico. That would give you great operating experience."

"I can't do that," I retorted. "It's a matter of integrity. If you had something for me last week, and you didn't give it to me, you cheated me. If you have something for me today because you think I have a gun to your head, that's not fair. I can't accept that, either. This is a principled relationship."

As head of HR, I knew all too well that when an executive told General Motors he was leaving, he would be out at noon. His car, his keys and identification badge would be confiscated, and he would be escorted to the door, with no invitation to return. Ever. In a radical departure from protocol, GM kept me around for almost a month. I was somewhat sequestered as the chairman and others tried to dissuade me from leaving.

"I made a commitment to another company," I said. "As a matter of integrity, I have to follow through on that commitment."

In retrospect, I was probably making a major mistake in terms of how fast or how far I could have gone in General Motors at the time. As indicated by Roger's suggestion that I lead GM de Mexico, I was on a fast track and could have easily returned to operations in a top-notch position. However, in terms of ethics, I felt it was the right thing to do. Yet, I made certain that my departure from General Motors was diplomatic, so that I never burned bridges. Never, never, never.

Quitting GM, Going To Navistar Makes Global Headlines

My departure from General Motors made national and international headlines. On August 1, 1988, Navistar International Corporation named me as its Vice President and General Manager for Truck Operations.

It was exciting to report to the corporate headquarters at 401 North Michigan Avenue in Chicago's bustling *Michigan-Wacker Historic District*. Next door was the neo-gothic Tribune Tower, which houses *The Chicago Tribune* and the Tribune Company. The Chicago River flows through the area of high rise office buildings and restaurants, which created a very cosmopolitan setting.

During my first day on the job, however, I discovered that the company was in absolute turmoil. I made this alarming discovery as I began to oversee Navistar's assembly plants in Springfield, Illinois and Chatham, Ontario, along with a technical center in Fort Wayne, Indiana. The people running manufacturing were not especially skilled or experienced in manufacturing. Sales were stagnant. The "order board" that displayed orders for trucks had a lot of "water" — orders that people didn't want, so they would cancel them at the last minute. This caused financial loss.

Simply put, Navistar was in terrible shape, financially and operationally. The company was teetering on the verge of bankruptcy.

We were afraid to continue manufacturing school buses because one or two lawsuits — which are surefire losers when involving school buses and children — would crush the company financially. We considered selling off that operation, but we held off for awhile.

Another problem at Navistar was that the paint booths were painting each other rather than vehicles, because the sprayers were mis-aimed. The vice president of manufacturing was unable to repair the paint shop, so I took on the challenge. Rectifying that problem required a significant amount of my attention. The company also needed a new vice president of engineering. Recruiting to fill that position also consumed my time. We hired an African American fellow from Chrysler, who did an admirable job.

Meanwhile, as I evaluated the dynamics of several plants, I realized that the abundance of hard-working people were hindered by a lack of both technology and strong leadership.

"Roy, I need you to create a strategy to turn operations around," the chairman said.

In the midst of this, board members came to meet me. I met with the staff. The chairman took me into the financial markets to demonstrate that he had someone of substance who could really make a difference in his operations and transform the company into an efficient, money-making powerhouse.

This was a major undertaking. My team lacked the understanding of the importance of creating an outstanding strategic plan. As we embarked on this mission, they struggled to get it done at the level that I preferred. Meanwhile, I hosted a series of meetings to excite people about transforming the company. Once, I gave a speech that I thought was powerful and persuasive.

"Mr. Roberts," said a colleague who owned a Navistar dealership in Florida. "You're not listening to the right radio station."

"Tell me more," I said.

"Until you tell me what's in it for me," he said, "I'm not going to pay too much attention. You've got to play Station WIIFM. That stands for 'What's In It For Me'?"

That inspired an epiphany: the best way to motivate the staff into working hard to make major improvements in the company would be to implement a reward structure. Performance-based bonuses, promotions, and other perks would be awarded to people who demonstrated that they could drive change the fastest.

Meanwhile, Navistar's top leadership was confident that I could tackle the big, tough issues and make the company succeed. But I knew it would be a long, difficult journey hindered by many roadblocks.

"I'm Not Moving to Chicago!"

As with all of my transfers, I had moved to Chicago in advance of my family. I made a down payment on the perfect home in the new Wynstone Golf Club development created by golf champion Jack Nicklaus and a builder. Located in the village of Barrington, thirty-two miles northwest of Chicago, it boasted nature preserves and one of America's wealthiest zip codes.

"I'm not moving to Chicago!" Katrina announced when I went home to Birmingham one weekend. "I'm going to stay at Country Day to finish high school."

For two years, I had been preaching in my Human Resources position at General Motors that "We're not in the business of breaking up families," when individuals were tapped for promotions and transfers in other states and countries. "We're doing everything we can to keep families together," I said frequently.

Now I had failed to practice what I preached -- by not consulting with my daughter about uprooting her from a school community where she was thriving, and transplanting her in a place where she knew no one. Maureen and I decided that Katrina's tenth-grade education was of utmost importance, so she joined four boarding students who lived with teachers on the Detroit Country Day School campus. It was a great situation that provided the academic and social stability that she needed.

Meanwhile, Maureen and I loved our home in Barrington. I enjoyed the convenience of playing golf, while Maureen was improving her game. We both delighted in the club's first class amenities that included an excellent restaurant.

Company Politics Complicate Duties at Navistar

At Navistar, company politics and protocols were tricky business, because it had two chairmen. I officially reported to Chairman/President Neil Springer, who reported to the chairman of the holding company, Jim Cotting.

At Lear and General Motors, I had become accustomed to operating within and respecting a distinct chain of command. This ensured clear communications and assignments. However, at Navistar, this hierarchy was convoluted because Jim Cotting would sidestep my boss and speak directly to me. This hindered the transparency and straightforward work-style that I felt was the best way to operate in the corporate structure. It also gave the appearance of secrecy and conspiracy, which made me very uncomfortable.

As a result, Neil Springer was always suspicious that I was there to take his place. He was right. No one had told me up front that I would take his position, but I had no doubt that if a company were in financial trouble, it was ludicrous to pay two chairmen. One would have to go.

Neither was an effective leader. Neil Springer was an outgoing, boisterous guy who talked a good game, but failed to perform on the field. He was not a technical superstar, but he was not a bad guy. Jim Cotting was a bright, honest, wonderful guy, but he lacked a good understanding of the operating business. I could not lean on him for help.

This left me in an untenable position. When I expressed frustration to the headhunter who had brought me on board, he said: "Why don't you go to the board of directors and tell them and the chairman of the holding company that you want Neil Springer out of here and that you want his job. Tell them to put him out."

This cutthroat idea was foreign to me. It felt disloyal, because the people above me were not bad people. Instead, we were all caught in a negative, circumstantial situation. The bottom line was that the headhunter's suggestion violated my ethical code of conduct. I had never ousted someone that way to get the next job. I could not pull the trigger on Neil Springer. Nor could I ask the board and take him out. While there is no doubt in my mind that

I was hired to take over, it was their responsibility to clear my path.

Meanwhile, my strategy to turn the company around began to show profits. But the relationship between the two chairmen was becoming increasingly fractured. Now nearly 18 months into the job, I realized that this was not the best place for me, but I would make the most of it.

A Top Honor: The George Bush American Success Award

Despite my disillusionment at Navistar, my public image continued to shine. I was awarded one of the highest honors of my life.

On the warm, sunny morning of September 11, 1989, Maureen joined me in the Rose Garden at the White House in Washington, D.C. as President George H.W. Bush bestowed upon me the George Bush American Success Award.

"Building a world-class work force, then, must be a national priority," President Bush said at 11:07 a.m. in remarks that are published on the website of the George Bush Presidential Library and Museum.

"Improving America's capacity to educate and train workers is critical to the future of this country. And that's why today we're presenting to you — not all of you, some of you — the American Success Awards. You have become American success stories through your involvement in vocational-technical education, and you're building a better America every day. Each of you has lived the American dream, and each one of you deserves our congratulations and thanks for your work in vocational - technical education. God bless you all, and thank you all for coming today."

I was overwhelmed with joy to receive the award — a beautiful, 16-inch crystal vase that's hand-carved by a California artist with the American flag. I treasure this lovely piece that's displayed in a lighted trophy case in our living room, with other awards.

I was in the company of nine other accomplished recipients who included: Kraft Vice President Dorothy Holland; space shuttle commander Gen. Joseph H. Engle; fashion designer Norma Kamali; and George Strait, the Country Music Association's Male Vocalist of the Year in 1986.

I was selected for this award after working with the Barbara Bush Foundation for Family Literacy. I had worked at her home when George Bush was vice president. She wanted me to be recognized for the work I did in literacy issues with young people and for my lifetime achievements.

Jet, the African American news and society magazine that has been a staple in black homes for decades, published a story in its November 27, 1989, edition stating that I was "among 10 outstanding persons" to receive the George Bush American Success Award.

In addition, the Bush administration extended the extremely flattering invitation for me to serve as Undersecretary of Education. Given the intense pace of my corporate work, I declined.

Maureen and I with President George H. W. Bush, who presented me with the George Bush American Success Award at the White House in 1989.

An Invitation to Return to GM

In the midst of my discontent at Navistar, I was invited to speak about leadership at the annual Automotive News World Congress in Detroit. Hosted by Crain's Automotive, this event in January of 1990 attracted 700 international power players in the auto industry to convene and discuss the important issues of the day. Keith Crain, chairman of Crain Communications, Inc., which publishes Automotive News, emceed the event with his number two guy.

Inside a ballroom at the prestigious St. Regis Hotel — across the street from the GM Headquarters — I delivered a poignant speech about leadership. I stressed the importance of challenging people and managing them to achieve their greatest potential. My message drew a rousing applause. At its conclusion, Keith Crain posed audience questions collected on note cards. One of the first questions was:

"Roy, it seems like people here generally agree with your approach to leadership and management. Therefore, it raises the question, 'What do think about the leadership across the street at GM?'"

"Keith," I retorted, "I don't believe you asked me that! The guy across the street has 950,000 employees. I've got about 18,000 employees who pray every day that I make the right decision and do the right thing. Who am I to ever criticize or critique the guy across the street? He's got more employees than all of us in this room! So that's not even a good question."

One half hour later, as I mingled with the audience, four men from General Motors whisked me into the hallway. With a somewhat anxious demeanor, they said, "Roger Smith wants to talk to you at the Detroit Athletic Club."

I obliged, meeting the chairman at the city's most prestigious, private social and athletic club. There, Roger got right to the point:

"Roy, when are you gonna leave that little chicken-shit company and come back home?"

"I can't come back," I said. "You're getting ready to retire. If I come back now, my rear end is out in the wind. I'm afraid I might get shot at pretty harshly by some people, because nobody's ever left and come back to General Motors, -- especially an officer."

"Roy, we'll put together a meeting next week," Roger said. "You come in and I'll bring some people together and we'll talk about what coming back might look like for you. I'll bring the chairman-elect."

I was instructed to schedule the meeting off-site, to prevent GM secretaries from spreading the news on the grapevine.

At the meeting the following week, Chairman-Elect Robert Stempel was not there. Instead, Chairman Smith brought President- Elect Lloyd Reuss, who was serving as President of North America; J.T. Battenberg, vice-president of Buick-Oldsmobile-Cadillac Luxury Division, and one other person.

As I entered this meeting, I was acutely conscious of the unique and unprecedented dynamics of my situation. No officer of General Motors Corporation had ever quit such a coveted position. Therefore, to do that — and be *invited back* to the company — was simply extraordinary. That I had been the company's highest-ranking African American, and that my promotion and subsequent departure had made global headlines, intensified the drama.

This inspired me to posture myself in a way that would earn the respect of General Motors' employees and the community at large. I was certain that if I took a "soft" or "sugary" staff job, I would be derided as a prima donna. Instead, I preferred a meaningful, difficult job that would enable me to prove myself as an innovative, hands-on and steadfast leader for the people at General Motors. A job with broad manufacturing responsibilities would afford the opportunity to do that with panache.

With all this in mind, I eagerly listened to Chairman Smith and the others as they presented five jobs as new possibilities for me. Three of them carried the title of vice president.

"Roy," Roger said, "we'd also like you to consider taking over Cadillac."

Bingo! That was a top manufacturing/engineering job. Cadillac was enjoying a nearly fifty-year winning streak as America's best-selling luxury car. The Cadillac brand was synonymous with prestige and classiness; that appealed to me.

As Manufacturing and Engineering Manager of the Cadillac Motor Car Division, I would oversee the final assembly plant in Hamtramck, the Reatta craft center in Lansing, component operations in Detroit, as well as stamping operations in Grand Blanc. All of this would require my oversight for component and final assembly of the Buick Riviera and Reatta, the Oldsmobile Toronado, and the Cadillac Eldorado, Seville and Allante. Although this position ranked below vice president on the corporate hierarchy, I believed it was a powerful opportunity to contribute to the success of General Motors.

I was convinced that taking on that challenge at Cadillac, which was probably the toughest job around, would do more to get me back into good graces at General Motors than any other job at the corporation. There were two new products coming out. The toughest thing you can do in manufacturing is introduce a new product, and GM was launching two bookend products: the Seville and the Eldorado, low-end and high-end. I wanted to do the job primarily for that reason. If I were successful with those two products, I would have significant influence on the well-being of Cadillac in the marketplace going forward.

TEN

The Cadillac Man
Inspires Pride and Praise

I returned to General Motors knowing how to operate an entire company, and I could not wait to sink my teeth into the rigors of manufacturing at Cadillac. My new job officially began on Sunday, April 1, 1990, but I was not due to report to work until Monday, so I used the weekend to do a "dry run." My plan was to drive to the Cadillac assembly plant and explore the facility, so that when I reported to my first day of work the next day, I would do so with familiarity and confidence.

However, as I drove through a tough, west-side Detroit neighborhood, I could not find the Cadillac corporate headquarters, which also housed the engineering center and a plant. This was well before cell phones and GPS, so I stopped for directions at a dingy little store in a run-down neighborhood. Inside, behind the counter, sat a big lady who looked spaced out. A pistol lay on the back counter.

Oh Lord, I thought, *I'd better buy something.*

"Ma'am," I said, placing a pack of chewing gum on the counter. "You think the workers are over at the Cadillac plant today?"

"Why do you want to know?" she asked.

"I want to know because I'm the new General Manager. I'm going to run it."

She laughed so hard, she almost fell on the floor. "You're gonna run it!? You son of a bitch! You can't even find it!"

I backed up, never looking away from her. Then, when I got to the door, I said, "When I find the son of a bitch, I'm gonna run it!" I ran out the door. I eventually found the plant, and I still laugh today about that encounter.

Unfortunately, the woman's negative attitude was prophetic of some initial responses I received at my new job. The entire Cadillac team was suspicious of my return to GM. One significant dynamic that inspired their feelings was that Cadillac people always felt that they were special. The status of their luxury product in the marketplace fueled an almost snobbish, superior attitude toward other divisions and the entire auto industry. They were steeped in clubbish pride and did not welcome outsiders who might disrupt their culture. In addition, some of the resistance that I encountered was tinged with racism.

Ironically, one of my most vicious critics was an African American woman who oversaw strategic planning. Three weeks into my new position, I encountered her in the executive garage.

"Roy Roberts," she snarled, "you have no business coming back! All you did was take a big position when somebody black could have had that job! I am so pissed off at you!"

I was stunned. She was small in stature and extremely smart, but fuming mad.

"I'm pissed off at Roger Smith, too!" she snapped. "And if I ever see him, I'll give him a piece of my mind, too!"

As I walked away from her to get in my car, I turned back and said, "Rosetta, you shouldn't talk like that."

My refusal to react to her vitriol angered her even more. I drove off and never paid her any attention.

Other critics, however, had a field day when I accompanied GM leadership to Washington, D.C., to accept the prestigious Malcolm Baldridge Award. Cadillac remains the first and only automobile manufacturer and brand to win this extremely competitive honor. It was a thrill to join Cadillac General Manager John Grettenberger and President Lloyd Reuss to accept the award on behalf of Cadillac's ten thousand employees, its UAW partners, and more than 1,600 Cadillac dealers.

President George W. Bush presented our team with a crystal trophy on December 13, 1990, at the U.S. Department of Commerce, which sponsored the award. It was created by Congress to promote national awareness for producing quality products and services.

This award was big news! Our public relations person set up a major press conference, and asked me to play a significant part in the interview that would be broadcast live in General Motors facilities in Detroit and around the world.

I was uncomfortably aware that speaking about the award would give the appearance that I was taking credit for it, when in fact, I could not. The application process had been nearly complete when I joined Cadillac. However, it was my duty to serve as a "filler" or "stocking stuffer" for the broadcast. It would have been inappropriate to concern the General Manager with such a task; I was the logical choice.

Unfortunately, my detractors were upset. Their criticism intensified my "walking on eggshells" efforts to avoid doing anything to confirm their suspicions that I was there to take over and ruin their playpen.

"Roy, are you here to take my place?" asked my boss, John Grettenberger, vice president of Cadillac Luxury Division. He was well-liked and respected both within the company and on a national level in the automotive industry.

"No," I answered. "I'm here to work for you and to do the job that you want done. And if I were going to be moving into your job, you would know faster than I would."

Meanwhile, my new post provided the manufacturing rigors that I desired. This was an exciting and challenging assignment, because we were launching two new products: the 1991 Eldorado and Seville.

As with all of my jobs, I made a daily effort to interact with everyone from the plant floors to the fourteenth floor of the

General Motors Headquarters. Just as I had done at Tarrytown, I walked the assembly line, observing, asking questions, and getting to know the men and women who were building the most prestigious, expensive automobiles sold by an American company.

All the while, the rumor mill continued to fuel my boss' suspicion. "Roy," he asked one day when he called me into his office. "You takin' over here at Cadillac?"

I laughed. "Why are you asking me? You're the boss!"

I finessed this uncomfortable dynamic by doing my best to make the boss look good. While attending staff meetings and working around the facilities, I made certain never to subordinate him. I did not want to look like the smartest guy in the room all the time. Coming off as smarter than the boss would alienate him and backfire if he turned jealous or resentful. Therefore, I was careful to pick and choose the best times to participate.

Another awkward experience occurred when my boss's boss visited to assess our program. This man verbally attacked a female engineer whom we had invited to help us solve some problems.

"Time out," I said. We took a break, and I told the executive, "That young lady didn't cause these problems. She's here to help us solve these problems. And if you don't apologize, this goddamn meeting is over, and I mean it."

We returned to the meeting and he offered enough of an apology to relieve her angst that had resulted from his criticism. Navigating relationships with sensitivity and respect is a crucial aspect of success in corporate America.

In that position, I built such great relationships with people on every level in the company – as well as in the national media and in the public at large – that I was dubbed "The Cadillac Man."

My Success Inspires African American Pride

It's important to note the significance of my role at Cadillac through the eyes of African American employees and the community. A large percentage of the plant employees were black, and they had always worked for white foremen and plant managers. Now, upon meeting me and embracing my compassionate leadership style, they echoed Reggie Harris in Tarrytown.

"We never dreamed we'd ever see a black plant manager," they told me, "much less an African American over all of manufacturing for Cadillac."

The pride glowing on their faces and in their eyes filled my heart in a way that I cannot express with words. I was their hero, their role model, their symbol of hope that African Americans could break barriers and prove our abilities as professionals and as corporate leaders.

This stature imbued me with tremendous responsibility. It was imperative that I conducted myself in a very professional manner and that I simultaneously remained approachable by everyone. No one ever tried to take advantage of that. Instead, the employees were supportive of my position and my role. Likewise, I made it a top priority to make sure that individuals were treated equally and that qualified minorities were promoted.

My unprecedented, highly publicized departure and return to General Motors elevated me to a somewhat heroic status amongst many African Americans across the United States. The perception was that I had been anointed not once, but twice, by the world's most prominent corporation. First, during my meteoric rise over eleven years, then by the company wooing me back just eighteen months after I left. It merits repeating that no other African American had achieved a position as high as mine at General Motors — only to quit and take another prestigious job — and then be recruited back. All of this was unparalleled, unprecedented, and pioneering.

This is not a braggadocious statement.

Business Week magazine wrote on March 4, 1996, that Roy Roberts "stunned industry insiders by leaving GM for Navistar International Corp.—then making an unlikely return that revived his career."

This illustrates that I had been given the ultimate professional compliment. And it demonstrated that when you're good at what you do, you are valued and trusted with important responsibilities. This was an especially important message for young African Americans: Don't burn bridges.

My high profile and widespread acclaim garnered many awards and accolades that I proudly added to a honorary doctorate of law I had received from Grand Valley State University in 1988 and an honorary doctorate of humane letters from Florida A& M University in 1989. I was particularly proud to receive the "Candle in the Dark" Award from Morehouse College in February of 1992. This award is given during the historically black college's annual Founder's Week gala that raises money for scholarships. Candle Award recipients are not Morehouse graduates, but have achieved excellence in their fields.

As I received the "Candle in Business" honor, actor Louis Gossett, Jr., received the "Candle in Arts and Entertainment," Morehouse professor and future Education President Robert H. Brisbane received the "Candle in Education," and Chicago Reverend George H. Clements won the "Candle in Religion." This black-tie event was spectacular. As hundreds of formally attired people watched, a Morehouse business student escorted me across the stage to receive the award under spotlights reminiscent of the Academy Awards. When asked to speak in the chapel the following day, I discussed my career, then took questions from parents and students.

"Mr. Roberts," asked one young man, "why would GM recruit you back when they could've hired anybody in the world?"

"Son," I said, "you're going to learn a lot in this august situation. I'm going to teach you one thing. They hired me back because I'm damn good! They did what's in their best interest, and I did what's in my best interest. I went back. They always do what's in their best interest."

Parents shot to their feet, clapping. I will forever cherish the pride glowing on their faces.

Maureen and I were so touched by that experience, we began to mentor young men whom we met there and in Detroit. The gentleman who walked me across the stage to receive the award became a lawyer in New York and has kept in touch with us for decades. Back in Detroit, I quasi-adopted one young fellow from a Detroit ghetto because his mother could not financially take care of her four children.

In addition, Maureen and I invited college students to stay with us while they worked summer jobs in GM's Legal Department. We would sit around the dinner table and discuss anything a family would talk about. While these young men were enabling us to share our good fortune to help others, we were exposing them to information and experiences that would advance them in the world.

In fact, after they became lawyers, one young man worked for the White House while another was hired by General Motors. As many of them continue to keep in touch with us, it has been a tremendous source of joy for both myself and Maureen to help them.

"You're Going To Love Your Commute!"

About halfway through our launch of the new 1991 Eldorado and Seville, I was promoted to Manufacturing Manager of General Motors Corporation's North American Operations Flint Automotive Division.

This would require me to work in Flint, Michigan, a blue-collar factory town similar to Muskegon. You may recall that when Maureen and I first discussed the potential transfers that typically distinguished a General Motors career, she agreed to follow me anywhere — except to Flint, Michigan.

This preference was especially acute after we purchased a gorgeous, 12,000 square foot home in the affluent suburb of Bloomfield Hills, located about twenty-five miles north of Detroit. When Maureen and I and Katrina originally looked at the French Provincial home, it was half-finished. We decided to purchase it and put the finishing touches on it. Among its many features, the home has a dramatic, double staircase in the entranceway, spacious rooms with vaulted ceilings, a ballroom, a wine cellar, a fitness room, a state-of the-art kitchen, and two wings containing bed-room suites.

One day, as we were settling into our home, Maureen called me at work. This was extremely unusual; she rarely interfered with my work or phoned the office.

"Roy, you need to come home tonight after work," she said. "They finished installing the draperies, and they're just gorgeous. You've got to see them."

"Okay, I'll be home."

She was absolutely right; the draperies were elegant and strik-ing.

"Maureen, guess what?" I said as she stood on a ladder with her back to me while adjusting the drapes.

"What?"

"I got promoted again."

"You did! What are you going to do?"

"I'm going to head up the Flint Automotive Group."

Maureen didn't even turn around to look at me as she said, "You're going to love your commute!"

We still laugh about that today. It was not even a question of whether Maureen would move to Flint with me. The forty-five-minute drive up I-75 created no need to move. And I did, in fact, love my commute.

Just as I loved my new job at Buick City, a 235-acre site north of Flint. The sprawling complex included one major building that housed the car assembly plant. Several other buildings were empty or officially closed.

Navigating personalities and power plays was always a challenge that I prided myself on finessing every time.

This was especially true with my boss, Don Hackworth, General Manager of the Flint Automotive Group. He was undoubtedly one of the most powerful people at General Motors. His influence extended far beyond his title; Don was the unofficial head of manufacturing in the eyes of everyone. In fact, the president and chairman of GM would often acquiesce to Don on a lot of issues pertaining to manufacturing. Don was really sharp. He had a degree in history, but he did an incredible job at developing and producing vehicles. If left unattended, he would run every functional area of General Motors if you let him. From time to time, he did!

Don had a powerful personality. He was notorious for making executives quiver in their shoes if they failed to meet his expectations. To be perfectly blunt, he could be as mean as a junkyard dog and eat you alive! Even worse, it was like a sport with him. I saw him abuse people. He'd just beat the cowboy hell out of them. This would especially occur if he asked a question, and someone offered a bullshit response, because Don always knew the correct answer.

Don didn't abuse me. In fact, he liked me so much that he bestowed his manufacturing expertise by talking and demonstrating many aspects of the business. His instruction made me a better operations person and a better manager, and that made me appreciate him.

I think Don had taken on the assignment to make sure that I got to where the chairman wanted me to be. That was never spoken. But he treated me with much more respect and dignity than he showed others. Don would divulge personal feelings and experiences to me as we frequently made a two-hour drive to visit a fabrication plant in Kalamazoo. Powerful individuals often view sharing personal information as a sign of weakness. The fact that Don did so with me indicated a strong degree of trust and respect. As a result, I felt good about working for him.

All the while, I maintained an acute sensitivity to my environment, always adjusting my behavior accordingly. This was especially evident when I partnered with Don in a foursome to play in the Pro-Am golf tournament at the PGA Tour's Buick Open. As I was departing for the private Warwick Hills Golf and Country Club in the Flint suburb of Grand Blanc Township, I stopped in our executive garage to talk with a colleague. Don entered the garage and raked his eyes up and down my spiffy golf outfit.

"How 'ya doing, Roy?"

"Good, good."

"Look," Don said. "There's one peacock in this group, and it's not you!"

The average person might have smiled, shrugged and walked away. Not Roy Roberts. I changed my golf outfit! Don did not want me to outshine him. So I put my ego aside, knowing that it was the little things that got the big things done for you. That set the tone for an outstanding June afternoon. In fact, Don Hackworth made a 35-foot putt on the eighteenth hole, and our foursome won the Pro-Am tournament.

In the midst of my corporate activities, I also was involved in civic endeavors around Flint. It was especially fulfilling to participate in the 100 Club, which raised money for family members of police, firefighters and other county officers who were killed in the line of duty in Genesee County.

Hiding Cars at Buick City Provokes the Wrath of Roy Roberts

Meanwhile, back at work, I was fortunate that my colleagues helped ensure that I remained on top of my game as head of the Flint Automotive Group.

"Roy," asked a friend who worked in Worldwide Global Facilities. "Do you know where our people are hiding vehicles in buildings around Buick City?"

"No." I drove around the complex and discovered a disgraceful number of rejected products that were stuck in abandoned buildings on many floors!

I called a meeting with Tim Lee, Buick City's plant manager, who ultimately became worldwide manufacturing manager. I told him my strategy for resolving this problem that would make one helluva bad headline if discovered. Then I rented a bus, and had it parked out of sight outside the plant. Next, I assembled the first and second shifts.

"Normally," I told the group, "when we start something new, we always start with the first shift. I'm going to start with the second shift. Come with me."

They followed me onto the bus, where I stood in the aisle, at the front, facing them. I pulled off my watch and dangled it.

"Do you know what this is?" I asked.

"A watch," someone said.

"It's a good watch," I said. "It's an expensive watch. It's a Rolex. When you hear it tick, you talk. Until then, I'm talking."

I instructed the bus driver to cruise around the premises, while I condemned the employees' deplorable behavior. All the while, we were looking at cars stuck in buildings — ostensibly hidden from me and from management.

"But Mr. Roberts," someone said with a tone of protest. "You don't understand why we—"

"Did you hear my watch tick?"

"No."

"I'm still talking!"

When I finished, the bus was silent. The fear on everyone's faces made it clear they had learned their lesson. When we returned to the plant, I said: "I don't want anybody getting off this bus to say one word to the first shift." Then I took them inside and repeated this exercise with the first shift.

Within one week, every defective product had been removed from the empty buildings. And my employees knew, they had better never to pull that trick again, because I had made it clear. That was the wrong thing to do.

Meanwhile, GM leadership was noticing that I continued to do the right thing. This was apparent late in 1992, when Don Hackworth and I were driving to Kalamazoo. He divulged that the chairman and president had asked him, "Is Roberts ready to be a vice president?"

Don said that he had told them, "Roberts is ready to be a vice president of anything you can think of in General Motors. You just have to figure out what job you want to give him. He can handle it."

My excitement was tempered by a horrendous labor strike in September of 1992. About three thousand workers at a plant in Lansing walked off the job, which idled 4,200 more workers. The eight-week strike crippled GM across America. It cost the company billions and fractured relations with the UAW. Don, who played an instrumental role in negotiations as they spiraled downward, retired after working hard to end the strike.

This was a tough time at General Motors.

Taking Over GMC Truck Division: I was Never Given a Goal

In October of 1992, the Board of Directors voted to make me a vice president — for a second time — and I was promoted to General Manager of the GMC Truck Division. The division produced premium, upscale SUVs and light trucks that included the Syclone, the world's fastest stock pickup truck. Likewise, GMC's Typhoon SUV was the high-performance version of the GMC Jimmy SUV.

Despite these superstar vehicles, GMC Truck was plagued by two major problems that I needed to fix to save the division. First, GMC Truck was an old division relegated to second-class status within GM. As one of GM's smallest divisions, it tended to receive products that Chevrolet rejected or had passed. Knowing this, customers would comparison shop at Chevrolet and GMC Truck dealerships, then haggle between the two, finally making the purchase from the dealer offering the lower price. This major problem threatened the sustainability of the GMC Truck division.

The second dilemma was that GMC Truck had antiquated systems that disconnected it from the corporation; its only link was the financial system, which tied all divisions together. A limb that is disconnected from the heartbeat ultimately gets amputated. Such a demise for GMC Truck would become a distinct possibility if dramatic changes were not made immediately.

Unfortunately, GMC Truck employees and managers were afflicted by a Rodney Dangerfield mentality and an Ichabod Crane mindset. The late comedian Rodney Dangerfield always exclaimed, "I don't get no respect!" And the fictional character Ichabod Crane in *The Legend of Sleepy Hollow* lived in constant fear. The folks at GMC Truck felt disrespected and terrified to flex their muscles to propose new ideas.

However, GM's new leadership made it clear: the status quo was a formula for bankruptcy. It was time for Roy Roberts to shake things up, in a big way. I wanted my employees to be bold, and stick their chests out with a prideful, competitive spirit to take on anybody, anywhere.

After my experience at Navistar, I stood head and shoulders above my peers in terms of knowing how to take over truck operations at General Motors. I could not identify a single person in the corporation who had the extensive truck manufacturing experience that I had gained at Navistar.

At the same time, it was a blessing that the only directive that my superiors had uttered was simply, "We want you to be vice president and head of GMC Truck." By offering no objectives, goals or expectations, they gave me carte blanche to do as I pleased! This was the corporation's modus operandi for managers who typically assumed new positions and functioned like clones of their predecessors.

During my 24-year tenure at General Motors, my marching orders were essentially "just go run it" — whether it was a plant, a department, a division or a group. Yes, I received specific assignments in each job, but I was never given strategies, goals or objectives. Not ever.

Now, the company was reeling in financial crisis, and desperate for a turnaround. In 1991, under the leadership of Roger Smith's successor, Robert Stempel, GM had lost $4.5 billion amidst his slow efforts to reorganize the company. This was the worst annual loss for an American corporation in history, and it occurred as part of the economic recession under President George Bush during the Persian Gulf War.

Concurrently, GM had announced a plan to trim staff and close twenty-one plants, including the Willow Run assembly plant in Ypsilanti, Michigan. This left 16,000 people jobless and outraged UAW President Owen Bieber.

Ford and Chrysler were also suffering; the Big Three lost a total of $7.7 billion in 1991. The national media publicized Chairman Stempel's declaration that GM was taking "aggressive action" to drive future profits. But a $24 billion loss the following year plunged General Motors to the brink of bankruptcy.

During a dramatic boardroom coup led by Procter & Gamble CEO John G. Smale, Stempel was ousted, along with his hand-picked president, Lloyd Reuss.

John G. Smale became non-executive chairman, with John F. "Jack" Smith, Jr., serving as CEO. They took the helm on November 2, 1992, just one month after I became General Manager of GMC Truck.

Smale had led Procter & Gamble into a period of tremendous growth and prosperity — emphasizing "brand management" — and he planned to do the same at GM. This atmosphere inspired me to envision a better way to run GMC Truck and the entire corporation.

At the time, Americans were falling in love with sport utility vehicles. Men liked their rugged image and towing capacity for boats and trailers. Women loved the safe-feeling elevation and the large cabin size – often with three rows of seating plus cargo space. Female buyers, however, were repelled by the word "truck," according to market research. Likewise, I thought "GMC Truck" was redundant.

So I made the bold, unilateral decision to drop that word from the name of my division. In an instant, Roy Roberts decreed that GMC Truck became, simply, GMC. A month later, a man from the Audit Department charged into my office.

"Roy!" he exclaimed, red-faced with anger. "Roy, you can't do that! You can't change the name of the division! We have to take that to the Board of Directors and the Audit Committee!"

"Hell," I answered, "I didn't know that. Why don't you change it back?" I knew good and well, he couldn't change it back, and to this day it's called GMC. When you do the right thing for the right reasons, no one can argue with you.

Another example was the executive fitness center, which was all-male until we hired a female senior vice president. The group vice presidents assembled to address complaints, but nobody made a decision. So I posted a big sign on the fitness center's door: "After 1:30 p.m., this center is for women." Nobody said a damn word. If you want to make change, you just have to do it!

Next Order of Business: Re-Engineering GMC

GMC was a diamond in the rough, and I was going to make it sparkle! I embarked on an unprecedented mission to re-engineer the GMC division, and I didn't ask permission from my boss or anyone else in the corporation. Though my strategy would cost millions of dollars, its success would save millions in perpetuity.

To do this, I hired a St. Louis consulting firm, which provided a bright, capable Indian fellow who was a great communicator. He helped me strategize how to make GMC more efficient, popular and prosperous. During the one-year consulting process, we did some of the best work that I witnessed at General Motors.

First, we streamlined the workforce by transferring about 300 people to other areas where their talents could better serve GM. The corporation praised this action, because it prevented layoffs (although some did occur).

Integral to this process was the sort of pep rally atmosphere that I created amongst the GMC staff. Just as I had reinvigorated employees at Tarrytown with the Competitiveness Center, I sparked excitement and passion amongst the GMC team by encouraging each person to be his or her best.

Emphasizing that more sales meant bigger bonuses was also a powerful incentive. It was exciting to watch enthusiasm blossom amongst my employees as they gave 110 percent to help make GMC shine.

As I have told reporters many times during my career, I never minimize the people side of the business. I learned that as an hourly worker. Every person, from the lowest paid to the highest, from the least educated to the highest, has value and plays an important role in the company's success. My job as a leader has always been to inspire that confidence within every person under my charge, and I did that with gusto at GMC.

Another facet of my strategy was to conserve resources by cultivating teamwork with another division. I worked closely with Pontiac General Manager John Middlebrook, doing joint marketing events, trainings, dealer gatherings and announcement meetings.

Our events were successful because I often thought of GMC and Pontiac as the perfect marriage of sporty cars and upscale trucks. However, every General Motors division operated autonomously and with its own distinct culture.

"As long ago as 1994," *Detroit Free Press* reporter Alan L. Adler would write on February 21, 1996, "Roberts talked about how sensible it would be to merge Pontiac — GM's performance car division — and GMC — its upscale truck business."

Meanwhile, concurrent with the cultural shifts that I was encouraging within GMC, I launched an aggressive campaign to distinguish our products. I made it known loudly and clearly on the fourteenth floor of GM Headquarters that I wanted to differentiate GMC from Chevrolet.

Any person on the street knew that grilles and nameplates were the only difference between GMC and Chevrolet trucks. Likewise, the Chevrolet/GMC line of trucks — *Silverado/Sierra, Blazer/Jimmy, Tahoe/Yukon* — were called "sister models" because they were nearly identical except for trims and prices.

Creating a distinct GMC brand was imperative to making the division stand out to lure the most coveted customer demographic: the young, middle- to upper-income individual. It was important to capture them now, during the SUV and light truck boom, to secure their loyalty – and thus company profits — for years to come.

However, my desire to differentiate GMC from Chevrolet required the approval of top-level management. As a result, an important discussion about the future of GMC headlined a big meeting that was scheduled with the corporation's top ten or twelve people. This included my boss, GM's former chief financial officer.

I was not planning to attend the meeting because I had another pressing engagement, so I was going to send my general sales manager. The day of the meeting, my boss met my general sales manager in the hallway and said, "If anybody comes in this meeting today to talk about GMC's product, there's gonna be hell to pay!"

Naturally, my guy came back to me all flustered and explained what happened. "What do I do?" he asked.

"Simple," I answered. "You stay home. I'm going to the meeting."

In a theatre-like room, the chairman and his management team sat on ascending tiers. They were all looking down at me when I explained why we needed to diversify GMC from Chevrolet, and that it was in the company's best interest to stop taking hand-off products. When I concluded, I wasn't sure if anybody was going to endorse my proposal. And no one would take my side until Chairman Jack Smith had made his preference known.

The room was quiet. I turned to the chairman and said, "Jack, think of it this way. You and your wife Lydia have two kids and they go off to college. They're really bright kids. They do well in school, finish school, and don't quite know what to do."

He cast a quizzical look down at me, as did all the officers.

"You and Lydia have a little extra money," I continued. "Would you give them each some money and have them each start a different grocery store on the same block and compete with each other?"

A ghastly hush came over the room. I didn't know where in the hell that conversation was going to take me. After what seemed like a ten-minute silence, Jack Smith said to me: "Differentiate the product!"

The meeting was over.

"You're the Next Son of a Bitch to Get Fired"

I had one more obstacle to remove before we could catapult GMC to it rightful place as a shining star in the General Motors constellation: bad advertising. The marketing divisions of Buick, GMC, Cadillac, and all the other General Motors brands were catching hell from management and the world about our advertising. It was all wrong. It failed to resonate with people.

"I'm going to do something about this," I told the chairman and president, "but I want you to stay out of it."

This was important, because ad executives were adept at aggressively cozying up to GM's chairman and president to secure long-term contracts and earn entrée into automotive events around the world. These relationships were a bonanza for advertisers, and I did not want them to try to leverage their friendships with leadership as I did what was best for the corporation:

Fire the ad agency. I went to New York with the GM manager who was the liaison to the advertising agency.

"Look," I told the advertising agency executive. "We gave you a one-year reprieve to get the advertising right. You came to us six months in and said you need three months longer. We gave you the three months."

The ad executive nodded.

"I told you, you had to get it 100 percent right. Not seventy-five. You didn't achieve that, so we have to sever the relationship."

Angst pinched the ad executive's face, but his demeanor was diplomatic: "Okay, Mr. Roberts, I understand. I want to thank you for doing business with us, Mr. Roberts."

I nodded. "Well, I need you to stick with us for the next three months while we get the other agency up to speed."

"We'll do anything you need us to do. Again, we thank you for having done business with us."

That took about four minutes. A chauffeured black car shuttled us across Manhattan to another agency.

"We want to hire you as the head of advertising for GMC," I told the CEO in his office.

"Great!" he exclaimed. "Bring out the champagne!"

"Hold on," I cautioned. "Don't do that yet."

He looked puzzled.

"You need to know," I warned, "you're the next son of a bitch to get fired if you don't do this job right. I'm dead serious. I want it done right."

This ad agency did an outstanding job! Its extremely effective advertising helped GMC flourish. In fact, the ad agency developed the tag line "professional grade" that's still used in GMC's advertising today.

Better advertisements, along with our leaner, re-energized workforce, enabled us to capitalize on the surging popularity of SUVs and light trucks.

The results were spectacular! Every year for my first three years at GMC, our division shattered all-time sales records. In 1992, we sold 359,365 units. In 1995, we sold 462,185 units. This constituted 7.1 percent of the world market for trucks and four-wheel drive vehicles. I'm telling you, we were making a lot of money!

Our success was all the more dramatic because, of all the car groups, GMC was the smallest, but the most efficient and profitable. An outsider wouldn't know that, because earnings are consolidated.

Our employees were so proud of what we had done, and how we were operating, that they stuck their chests out. I couldn't have been more excited about our success. It was during this boom that automotive industry analysts began calling me a "visionary," and media reports about GMC's success repeatedly touted me as such.

Activities Flourish Outside of Work

During this time, my activities outside of General Motors were becoming increasingly visible and prestigious. Among them was my service on the Board of Directors of Burlington Northern Santa Fe Corporation.

I was recruited while still at Navistar, and took office the same day that Robert Stempel became chairman of General Motors: August 1, 1990. At the time, the company was Santa Fe Pacific Corporation. It merged in 1993 with Burlington Northern. In 2009, it became a wholly owned subsidiary of Warren Buffet's Berkshire Hathaway Inc.

During my twenty years of service, I took quarterly trips to the company's headquarters in Fort Worth, Texas, for board meetings to make decisions that impacted North America's second-largest freight railroad system.

For eight years, I chaired the Compensation Committee, which governed compensation decisions for all salaried employees in the company. I was also on the Executive Committee for a decade. In the absence of a full board meeting, the chairman could call a meeting with the Executive Committee to make decisions.

My service on corporate boards has enabled me to interface with some of the most brilliant minds in the business world. Being on a board of directors keeps you sharp; you are always observing and learning, while putting forth your "A game." This maintains your colleagues' respect and admiration, and enables you to serve as an effective leader for that particular corporation.

At the same time, my commitment to civic and educational endeavors never waned. I was a member of the National Urban League's executive board and a member of the Morehouse School of Medicine board of trustees. I was also active with the United Negro College Fund, which raises money to help students attending the nation's 39 historically black colleges and universities.

In 1993, I served as the General Motors Chairperson for the Fifth Annual UNCF Walkathon.

"The Detroit UNCF Walkathon has earned the distinction of being the largest indoor walkathon event held in the United States," I said in a statement quoted in the media. "Over the past four years, the event has raised approximately $500,000." It was a joy to lead five thousand people — including local and national celebrities — in Detroit's five-kilometer "Walk a Mile To Save a Mind."

I was offered opportunities in politics and government as well. After Bill Clinton was elected president in November of 1992, his team invited me to serve in his administration. The story of how it transpired would create a humorous moment years later in San Francisco. I was amongst hundreds of people attending a huge financial function hosted by San Francisco Mayor Willie Brown. Civil rights attorney Vernon Jordan was a speaker. I was standing at the back of the room when Vernon entered with Willie Brown, who gave me a hug.

"I know a lot of people in this room," Vernon said on stage. "And I'm not going to mention all their names. But there's one person I must mention: Roy Roberts."

Everyone turned around and applauded.

"We leaned on Roy to serve in the Clinton Administration," Vernon said, recalling the phone conversation when he made the offer: "Roy, you're from Arkansas, he's from Arkansas. It's a natural. You really ought to serve in this administration."

"Look," I retorted. "I haven't earned enough money. I need to earn money!"

"Goodbye!" Vernon exclaimed and hung up.

The crowd went wild.

"Fabulous Five" Thrive: One of Us Becomes Mayor of Detroit

My reaction to the election of Dennis Archer as Mayor of Detroit illustrates an important aspect of becoming a truly successful person.

Unfortunately, black achievers are too often afflicted with a "scarcity mindset" that breeds competition, jealousy and envy. The attitude is that if one succeeds and makes it to the top, he or she is robbing others of the opportunity to reach those heights.

Not so with the "Fabulous Five." Dennis Archer, Marty Taylor, Bill Pickard, Ron Hall and I had all become pioneers in our respective fields. We cultivate the conviction that success for one of us is success for the entire race. While we're blazing new trails for our people to follow, we're also proving to the mainstream that African Americans are capable and valuable assets in business, politics and the civic arena.

Therefore, when Dennis became Mayor of Detroit, I was so overwhelmed with joy for him that I didn't know what to do with myself. The same feeling applied when Marty, Bill and Ron reached career milestones.

In addition, I was ecstatic that the city of Detroit was being led by someone of his caliber. His wife, Trudy DunCombe Archer, became a judge at Detroit's Thirty-Sixth District Court. And their sons, Dennis and Vincent, had graduated from Detroit Country Day School with Katrina. This was the kind of First Family that Detroit deserved. As mayor, Dennis did everything with class and decorum.

That made me feel good. I tell people all of the time: your journey to the top has no room for jealousy or envy. Run your own race and cheer for others when they win the gold in their respective fields. When you put out positivity, you get it back exponentially.

That was certainly my experience during the mid-1990s, as Maureen and I were on "A Lists" in Detroit, Chicago and New York, thanks to my involvement in The Boulé. If any organization had a fundraiser or an event, we were invited.

"Mr. Cadillac is here!" people would exclaim when we attended events across the country. "It's Mr. General Motors!"

Since Maureen and I were invited to events in the black community, the white community and the mixed community, we were selective about what to attend. If you can go to everything, you risk overexposure. Therefore, we choose events that are in our personal and professional best interest.

Among them has always been the Charity Preview for the North American International Auto Show. Likewise, every summer, the Grand Prix transformed the streets of downtown Detroit into a Formula One racetrack. This attracted race drivers from around the world, with glamorous crowds that glittered with celebrities, royalty and global media. This was exciting! Penske Transportation CEO Roger Penske was a key player in this event that brought significant revenue and positive press to the city. Maureen and I attended spectacular parties and truly enjoyed ourselves.

On the surface, it may have seemed like a storybook life. But even in social settings, I was always "on." I was extremely cognizant of the fact that my stature and responsibility within General Motors had earned me entrée into those parties and events. Therefore, I had to represent in the most dignified, respectable manner possible. One blunder, and the world would know about it. At the same time, people always wanted to "talk shop," and I obliged in an innocuous and appropriate manner. Yes, we were living the glamorous life. But I was earning every minute of it.

With Tiger Woods at Sherwood Country Club in Thousand Oaks, Calif.

Country Club Controversy: a Microcosm of My Life

In October of 1994, an ugly racial controversy exploded with international headlines after my membership application was rejected by Metro Detroit's most exclusive country club.

Its roster included automotive magnates such as Roger Penske, former GM Chairman Roger Smith, former Chrysler Chairman Lee Iacocca, and many prominent GM executives. The club's long-standing tradition had been to welcome any vice president at General Motors to become a member.

That changed when Roy Roberts came along.

What would transpire with the Bloomfield Hills Country Club became a microcosm of my life. This two-year drama illustrated the harsh elements endured by high-achieving African Americans. Though we are well-practiced at weathering the racial storms of disappointment, rejection and controversy, that doesn't make them easy or acceptable. However, it does make us stronger. I was not going to commit suicide because some white people rejected me.

207

Nor was I going to respond publicly or accuse anyone of racism. To this day, I have not spoken a word about it to the media.

"Roy, who worked with you on your strategy to remain silent about that controversy?" asked one of Michigan's top public relations professionals, years later.

"I did," I answered. "All you can do is get in trouble by saying something. You'd be just another black guy yelling racism. If you need proof, watch what happens when somebody yells racism. Look at the number of people who come out on the other side to justify what transpired. So I let them fight each other."

Now, this chapter in *My American Success Story* is my opportunity to tell the story from my perspective.

When I first became vice president of Personnel Administration and Development, several Bloomfield Hills residents said, "Roy, you ought to join Bloomfield Hills Country Club. Membership is automatically extended to anybody who becomes a vice president of General Motors."

"You guys better check to see if that's doable," I said.

At the time, the club's 450 members included one African American — Leroy C. Richie, general counsel for Chrysler Corporation. He had been admitted two years prior to my application.

My friends checked with the club's president. I knew him; he was well known and revered in Detroit. My friends reported back to me that the president had told them, "We don't need any integration in the Bloomfield Hills Country Club."

Shortly thereafter, my boss sent an invitation to attend his Christmas party at the Bloomfield Hills Country Club.

"I'm not going to be a convenient black for anybody at any time," I told him.

"Roy, what are you talking about?" he asked.

I relayed the club president's response to my friends who had inquired about me becoming a member.

"I'll sponsor your membership," my boss said. An honorable guy, he was naïve about the politics. "I'll get a fellow senior executive to co-sponsor you with me."

Traditionally, co-sponsors would host a reception to introduce their candidate to the club. My sponsors did nothing. As the vote date approached, rumors circulated amongst members that I would be rejected. I was informed that this prompted one of my sponsors to threaten the board that they had better take me, or there would be problems. Members later told me that the voting session was contentious.

I was voted down.

The media reported this all over the world, including in magazines in Paris. I received phone calls from friends and strangers around the globe.

"Mr. Roberts," one young man said, calling from New York City. "I work for Merrill Lynch in Manhattan, and my mother does domestic day work for Miss Smith in Bloomfield. They said Roy Roberts sold dope. That's why he didn't get in."

I was furious! A myriad of emotions consumed me; it was one of the worst feelings I've ever had in my life. You can never be proud when people reject you. Especially when you know that you're probably more accomplished than 80 percent of the people in that club.

At the same time, I felt sorry for my family and friends; it was as shocking for them as for me.

When you enjoy a lifetime of success, you hold your head up and do the right thing. But I questioned, "Did I do anything wrong?" Maureen and I concluded that I had been correct in telling my boss that I would not attend his Christmas party. I later learned through the grapevine that my membership was denied to punish my sponsor who had threatened the board.

Still, the prevailing belief was that the Bloomfield Hills Country Club had rejected Roy Roberts because he is African American. That ignited nationwide outrage, media analysis and backlash.

"The president and chief executive of the General Motors Corporation has resigned from the Bloomfield Hills Country Club after a black vice president of G.M. was denied membership in the club, an exclusive bastion of the auto industry's top executives," said a story by Doron P. Levin in *The New York Times* on October

23, 1994. The article said that both GM President John F. Smith Jr. and the Chief Financial Officer quit in protest.

The club denied that my membership was rejected based on race. Ironically, some media reports said that members were put off by my "glad-handing" personality. Others blamed my sponsors for not effectively campaigning amongst members to vote in favor of my membership. Others dropped out of the club, including many young people, who were valued as the future generation of its membership.

The club's single black member, however, did not relinquish his membership. The media and other critics said he should have been the first sucker to quit that club. As a result, he was so harangued by media critics that he fled from his Birmingham home and retreated to a hotel.

At the height of this, *The Detroit Free Press* called my friend and colleague Joe Anderson, whom I had met during my first stint at General Motors, when he was plant manager of the Pressed Metal and Plating Operations in the Pontiac Motor Division. Shortly after I returned to GM, Joe was appointed General Director of the Body Hardware Business Unit of the Inland Fisher Guide Division, which had 7,000 employees and revenues of $1 billion. In 1992, however, he left GM to become the president and chief executive officer of Composite Energy Management Systems, Incorporated.

"Joe, what do you think about what's happening with Roy Roberts?" a reporter asked him.

"I have no comment," Joe responded.

Interestingly, I had experienced rejection and racism in the context of my relationship with Joe and a key player in the country club controversy. Joe was an extremely talented hard worker, and I was lobbying more aggressively for his advancement than for anyone before or since.

"Let's make Joe Anderson a vice president," I said during a meeting with top leadership.

"Roy," interrupted an executive vice president, "you came along doing all this incredible stuff and we made *you* a vice president."

I interpreted that as: *One is enough.* Outraged, I called the VP's home at 6:30 p.m. His wife said he was not there, and took a message.

When he called me later, I said, "You're the most respected group executive and you essentially said to the group executives, 'Roy, one black vice president at General Motors is enough.'"

"I didn't mean it that way," he protested.

I believe that he did. Ironically, his belief that "one is enough" mirrored what was happening at the country club. They had their one, and the consensus, apparently, was that one was enough.

Club leadership soon learned that such outmoded and racist thinking was detrimental to their finances and future. People, especially young professionals, continued to drop out in protest. A lawyer who was a member told GM Vice Chairman Harry Pearce that the club was really suffering in the wake of rejecting me.

"Roy, you need to reapply," Harry said. "We have people who are going to sponsor you."

"Bullshit," I said. "I'm not putting my family through that again."

"Look, you've been pioneering all your life," Harry said. "If you don't do this, nobody will. And if you can't do this, nobody can. You're the one, Roy."

Though Harry Pearce ranks at the top of my list of the most ethical, principled and trustworthy people I have ever met, I balked.

"Harry, I already joined Orchard Hills Country Club. They rolled out the welcome mat for me. Plus, I don't want to pay for two clubs."

Harry intimated that money was not the issue and that it would be handled for me. "Roy, I believe a positive outcome could be very beneficial for you and for General Motors."

"I want to sponsor you," Roger Penske said shortly thereafter. J.T. Battenberg — chairman, CEO and president of *Delphi Corporation*, who lived in a beautiful home overlooking the club's eighth green — also offered to sponsor me.

Roger Penske called a meeting at the upscale Townsend Hotel in Birmingham. I attended, along with three longtime members of the Bloomfield Hills Country Club. My sponsors lambasted them, saying that rejecting me was racist.

"No, no, it wasn't racist," the members insisted before agreeing to encourage other members to approve my application. I reapplied for membership in 1996.

As was the tradition, my sponsors hosted a reception to introduce me to club members. Every senior executive at General Motors who was or had been a club member attended the reception at J.T.'s home. They were ultra-supportive, and I cherished the outpouring of encouragement.

The vote came later; my application was approved. Once again, international headlines generated many phone calls — congratulatory ones this time — from my friends around the world.

"GM'S TOP BLACK EXEC FINALLY JOINS THE CLUB," said a headline in *Business Week* on December 15, 1996.

"Roy Roberts, General Motors' top-ranking African American," said the article by Kathleen Kerwin and Keith Naughton, "finally has made it into the posh Bloomfield Hills Country Club outside Detroit. The club snubbed him when he first applied in 1994. But its super-secret admissions committee gave GM Veep Roberts the O.K. on Dec. 3, according to people close to the club." It also said that GM Chairman Jack Smith and the CFO would probably reactivate their memberships.

"Roberts' admission also averts the exodus of other Detroit big shots that was expected if he had been twice denied," *Business Week* reported, adding that the possible acceptance of bank executive Aubrey Lee would be the club's third African American member. He was, subsequently, admitted.

My experience with the Bloomfield Hills Country Club illustrates the importance of continuing to pioneer when it's tempting to give up. I am extremely proud that this controversy did not impede my work at General Motors; in fact, I was enjoying some of my best successes while it was occurring.

Very importantly, during nearly two decades since, I have made many wonderful memories at the Bloomfield Hills Country Club. I was part of the first African American foursome to golf there. As I played with Walt Douglas, owner of the Avis Ford dealership in Southfield, attorney Phil Saunders and one other person, people were peering out of windows and around corners to witness this unprecedented sight. When we finished the eighteenth hole, the club's general manager was standing behind a tree, pretending not to watch us. I strode over to him and exclaimed, "Can you believe this?"

"What's that, Mr. Roberts?" he asked.

"The course is still here!" I declared, then walked off.

Over the years, my family and friends have been welcomed at the club. Some people there treat me as a friend, while others never speak, just like in everyday life. Only a few people have shown disdain.

Meanwhile, I've won the Club Championship — and I won the "Old Man Par" member-member tournament. The awards are displayed in our home.

In 2013, the Bloomfield Hills Country Club bestowed on me its highest honor by asking me to make remarks and propose the Toast to the Club: the highlight of an annual club luncheon attended by hundreds of people.

The world is changing, and I am proud to say that I've made a significant contribution to helping make it happen.

ELEVEN

GM's $100 Billion Man

My transformation of GMC into a goldmine for General Motors illustrated that Roy Roberts was a bold visionary with the Midas Touch. As a result, Chairman Smale and GM's top leadership wanted to apply my successful formula to other divisions to accelerate sales and profits.

The need was urgent; GM's market share — once 50 percent during the 1970s — had slipped to 35 percent. The approaching new millennium intensified this urgency for General Motors to downsize and streamline to compete and dominate the global automobile markets. In that context, corporate leadership recognized that my GMC success strategy was a blueprint that could be replicated by:

★ downsizing and re-energizing each division's workforce;

★ improving advertising to lure new customers and build long-term loyalty; and

★ branding products as distinct and unique.

"Brand management" was a major tenet of Chairman Smale's multifaceted strategy to reclaim GM's market share dominance. The belief was that GM could attract new customers and inspire lifetime loyalty by boosting brands such as Cadillac as the ultimate luxury vehicle, Corvette as the sexiest sports car, and the Suburban as an upscale SUV. At the time, "branding" was the hot, new commercial catchword for using advertising and persuasive imagery to associate certain emotions, lifestyles and prestige with specific products.

To invigorate branding, Chairman Smale hired Ronald Zarella, who earned a reputation as a brand management guru as CEO of Bausch & Lomb. Now, as Vice President and Group Executive for GM's North American Vehicle Sales, Service and Marketing Group, Ron was tasked with rejuvenating the images of GM's eight car lines — Cadillac, GMC, Pontiac, Buick, Oldsmobile, Chevrolet, Geo and Saturn.

Meanwhile, my success with GMC made me the natural "go to" executive to oversee big, innovative changes that would spark sales and profits. As a result, in early 1996, my boss asked:

"Roy, do you think you can merge Pontiac and GMC?"

I eagerly accepted the opportunity to merge these two powerhouses, creating a common management system to eliminate inefficiencies and maximize successes. The GM Board approved the merger on February 5. No public announcement was made, but the rumor mill – in the media and corporate circles alike – churned. Then, on February 20, 1996, *The New York Times* published a story by Keith Bradsher under the headline "G.M. to Merge GMC Division With Pontiac."

The article said, "General Motors will announce that it is combining the staffs and dealer networks of the two divisions into a single marketing unit headed by Roy S. Roberts, now the general manager of the highly successful GMC truck division, company officials said today."

This was huge news! The media went wild with analysis about how the merger would produce the automotive industry's third-largest U.S. vehicle marketing division, with sales of 1,041,129 units in 1995, surpassed only by Ford and GM's Chevrolet. It would create a $210 million advertising budget by combining Pontiac's $160 million for advertising and other marketing, with GMC's $50 million.

GM's rationale for the merger was strong. Pontiac was all cars. GMC was strictly trucks and SUVs. These vehicles were becoming so popular during "the great changeover" of the mid 1990s — that it was smart for a car division to introduce them to its loyal customer base. In fact, if you had automobiles but lacked trucks, you were in trouble. Plus, SUVs typically provided a much higher profit than other vehicles, and trucks would soon outsell passenger cars.

Another benefit? Nearly 60 percent of Pontiac franchises were already sharing space with GMC dealerships. However, Pontiac dealers who had GMC franchises had to navigate separate sales, service and warranty programs for each nameplate; these duplications were wasteful and distracting for the dealers.

"If we can get some of the clutter out of the system," I said in many media interviews, "the dealers can invest their time and energy more wisely by taking care of the customer." I also liked to say, "When you blend two rich and distinctive-tasting coffee beans to brew a great cup of coffee, what results is energizing, satisfying and definitely not the same old grind."

Posing with Pontiac and GMC vehicles in 1996, after I was assigned to merge the two divisions at Pontiac-GMC general manager.

The merger would also benefit GM by: synthesizing human resources, which included sales and marketing personnel; consolidating corporate functions in one location; and targeting young buyers in the middle- and upper-income brackets.

But merging two distinct GM divisions was like mixing oil and water. Every division was entrenched in its own culture and identity that had evolved so deeply over decades that it felt tribal. Pontiac people were aficionadoes of high-powered racing and fast cars. GMC folks ate, slept and breathed trucks and sport utility vehicles.

"Roy's got a Pontiac personality," Joseph Phillippi, an auto analyst for Lehman Brothers told *Black Enterprise* for its June 1996 edition that showcased me as Executive of the Year. "Like the Grand Prix and Bonneville, he's got pizzazz."

Playfulness aside, Pontiac viewed GMC as the insignificant little brother. Pontiac's advertising budget — more than three times GMC's — was a tangible barometer of this David and Goliath pairing.

In addition, the most resistant Pontiac folks were "Joe six pack" plant people. I don't mean that in a negative way. I love manufacturing. I love the people. I love the culture. But Pontiac's Joe Six Packs didn't want "those GMC college boys" encroaching on their turf. The huge Pontiac manufacturing complex symbolized the division's identity. Their territorial superiority made the merger tantamount to declaring war. Plus, GM was phasing out military product production there; downsizing sparked fears of layoffs and intensified detractors' resistance to the merger.

Successful people know that "change is the only constant in life" and continuously reinvent themselves and their companies accordingly. Change for most people, however, is terrifying and threatening.

As I factored these issues into my strategy, I was aware that "culture will eat strategy for breakfast." Failing to change the culture would doom our strategy. Therefore, I was constantly working on culture. Rather than say anyone was wrong, I talked about how great people were and how extraordinary we all could become if we did X, Y and Z.

"We're going to outperform the competition," I'd say during frequent meetings that often felt like pep rallies, "not in terms of sales, but in terms of how the customer will perceive our products when we go to market. Wouldn't you like to be part of that?" This was an inducement for people to be better than they thought they were. I had to rally the troops to reach their full potential.

"I always said Roy should be a gospel minister," John Peterson, a GMC dealer in Bloomington, Minnesota, told *Business Week* magazine for a March 4, 1996 article. "He would have kept the churches full all the time."

My candor and charisma convinced most people that the merger was a blessing, but unfortunately, others saw it as a curse. Some of Pontiac's most vociferous naysayers found themselves removed from their jobs, and I had no compunctions about it. In fact, they made my job easier, because the merger created two HR directors, two PR people, two sales directors, etcetera, and it was my job to decide who would stay. In addition, the merger eliminated 600 sales and marketing jobs and streamlined functions of Pontiac-GMC's headquarters and zone offices, where about 1,150 people worked.

"We're creating one team from the best resources, systems and processes that both divisions have to offer," I said during a press conference at the New York Auto Show in April of 1996. I emphasized that the Pontiac and GMC brands would remain separate, each keeping its distinct identity. "Pontiacs will remain sporty, exciting cars, and GMCs will continue their evolution into the premium, upscale truck nameplate."

The New York Auto Show showcased the horsepower of the new Pontiac-GMC division and commemorated GM's sponsorship of the U.S. Olympic Team. We unveiled the gold-edition Jimmy and three Grand Am packages. These vehicles would enable customers to drive in style while celebrating Olympic excitement and pride. I capitalized on the excitement to explain that the combined divisions would enable Pontiac and GMC to benefit from each other's strengths. For example, GMC trucks would be upgraded with Pontiac's renowned, cutting-edge technology.

Similarly, Pontiac generated a ton of media attention just a few months after the merger, when we announced the new Grand Prix, which would recapture the sleek, sexy sports-coupe image that had made it legendary during the 1960s. The new Grand Prix would join three revamped, mid-sized sedans – one each from Chevrolet, Buick and Oldsmobile – aimed at showcasing the new pizzazz that GM was injecting into its favorite brands.

"You will never see us do what we did in the '80s with cookie-cutter vehicles again," I told *The Wall Street Journal* in a June 17, 1996 article by Rebecca Blumenstein. "What you see in this product is really the new General Motors." Under the headline, "Pontiac's Grand Prix Returns To Its Past to Build a New Image," the article discussed how the new Pontiac Grand Prix would be "the first fruit of GM's new emphasis on brand management, or differentiating among muddled car images."

As the merger proceeded, I likened my job responsibilities to "changing the wheels on a car while you're moving."

The merger required me to implement a "channel distribution strategy" to streamline the network of 8,500 dealers by eliminating 20 percent, or 1,700 dealerships. The goal was to consolidate Pontiac and GMC franchises under one roof by 2000 to create a "one-stop shopping" experience for customers who were increasingly switching between cars, trucks and SUVs. This was good for customers; bad for the folks who would lose their jobs. Therefore, I vowed in the national media to proceed with respect, dignity and care. To do this, I dispatched teams to dealerships across America to assess how to embark on our new strategy.

This would occur in an increasingly competitive market, as the Big Three aggressively pursued the most coveted segment of the car market: young, sporty, upscale buyers. GMC was about to lose its monopoly on the full-size SUV market, because Ford was introducing the Expedition, a four-door SUV that would compete with Yukon buyers. Ford was also about to give GMC's top-selling Sonoma and Sierra a run for their money by presenting the entirely redone 1997 F150 pickup truck.

GM leadership was trusting me to implement changes that would beat our competition.

"Roy will have the primary role in the positioning, pricing, advertising, promotion, retail environment and the way we distribute to that retail environment," Ron Zarella told *Black Enterprise*. "That's the scope of a general manager's role today in General Motors. It's an enormous job, and Roy is the right guy to run it."

Meanwhile, I was making progress with my campaign to persuade Pontiac people to embrace the merger. Money talks! My presentation comparing the financials of each division shocked Pontiac people when they learned how much money GMC was making. They were tuned to Channel "What's In It For Me?" and the answer was, "Big money!" I could almost hear them exclaiming, "It's bonus time!" One of the Pontiac guys said it best: "If you have to get married, marry rich!"

What a union it was: Pontiac-GMC became the third-largest car and truck franchise in America.

And Roy Roberts was running it.

My Definition of Success Evolves Over Time

My new job kept me working at breakneck speed, and I loved it because I truly believe that my work had value and would help GM resume its dominance in the marketplace.

Four months into the job, my attendance at the Pittsburgh Auto Show exemplified the pace: I flew in that morning, addressed the media, lunched with dealers, spoke at Carnegie Mellon University, and then flew back to Detroit!

"He plays down speculation that he's being groomed for even loftier positions within General Motors Corp," said a February, 22, 1996, article in *The Pittsburgh Post-Gazette*. A large photograph of me at the Pittsburgh Auto Show accompanied the article by Steve Holvonik that illuminated how my definition of success had evolved.

"There were times in my past where I was concerned about my career," I said in the article. "What I learned over the last several years is that if you just focus on the next job, you'll probably make a big mistake."

I echoed this statement during many media interviews by saying that the best way to get ahead was to focus on doing my very best in my current job. That was more important than being wholly focused on attaining a particular position.

"What I really want to do is make a difference in this corporation," I told the Pittsburgh paper. "I want to help GM get back its preeminent position, its success. This promotion is important. It gives me a chance to help move the corporation forward."

This mindset inspired me to always take the spotlight off Roy Roberts and shine it on General Motors. I did this literally by changing the location of the Pontiac-GMC offices during the merger. At first, we operated from the old Pontiac headquarters in Pontiac, Michigan. The building was beautiful, and I inherited John DeLorean's former office. Embellished with enough marble to build a Roman palace, it was an ostentatious tribute to his flashy, glitterati persona.

From a car perspective, the former GM engineer and executive had been one of the best car guys ever in the American automotive industry. But in 1982, he was arrested for drug trafficking and later proved entrapment by federal agents. In 1985, he enjoyed Hollywood celebrity when his *DeLorean DMC-12 sports car* was featured in the film *Back to the Future*. That same year, he divorced former model Christina Ferrare. For many reasons, John DeLorean did not work out at GM.

Likewise, his decadent décor did not represent me or my values. So I announced that the Pontiac headquarters would close and relocate to GM's Detroit headquarters. Our move reflected what the corporation as a whole was doing. General Motors decided in 1996 to leave its classic headquarters building on West Grand Boulevard, which the company had occupied since its founding in 1908.

Working Toward a Renaissance in New Corporate Headquarters

With the urging and support of Detroit Mayor Dennis Archer, we moved our corporate headquarters to the Renaissance Center, a sleek, soaring complex of five skyscrapers on Detroit's International Riverfront. Offering breathtaking views of Windsor, Canada, the Detroit River, downtown Detroit and beyond, the complex boasts the Western Hemisphere's tallest, all-hotel skyscraper. At the time, the central tower was occupied by the Westin Hotel; now it's the Marriott. Bill Marriott, Executive Chairman and chairman of the Board of Marriott International, was on the GM Board of Directors at the time.

As Michigan's tallest building, the RenCen was built in 1977 after Ford Motor Company Chairman Henry Ford II conceived the idea and partnered with business leaders to construct it. The complex symbolized the beleaguered Motor City's quest for a "renaissance" of economic revival. Ford and other city leaders hoped that this development would recapture Detroit's glory as the thriving "Emerald City" that it had been during the auto industry's heyday in the 1950s. The RenCen did help drive a resurgence in Detroit's economy, but the economic recession of the 1990s prompted Ford to sell the complex.

When GM purchased it in the fall of 1996, we got a deal because nobody wanted it; the occupancy rate was extremely low. Concerns arose when Ford moved thousands of its employees back to its world headquarters in Dearborn, about thirty minutes southwest of Detroit.

GM's relocation to the Renaissance Center was a bold, monumental move, and I was central to making this strategy work. At the time, we had people scattered all over southeast Michigan in leased properties.

"Roy, we can't save Pontiac, Flint, Lansing and all these cities," the chairman told me. "We've got to make a stand and that stand ought to be in Detroit." His statement also applied to other divisions that had employees throughout Michigan.

I moved the Pontiac-GMC offices into one-and-a-half floors of the new GM World Headquarters downtown Detroit. Mine was the first functional area to occupy the new space; the chairman and vice chairman preceded me with their staffs.

By moving everyone into one GM-owned property, we no longer wasted money on renting office space. And we significantly boosted productivity by enabling employees to communicate face to face.

This process, however, was not without critics or concerns. We invested significant time and money into strategizing how to move people from Lansing and Pontiac and different cities where people lived. Detroit was perceived as a very undesirable place where residents had to pay high city income taxes. Critics warned that the move would cost GM a significant amount of talent.

"Mr. Roberts," one young man told me in the beginning, "you've got to put some lipstick on this pig." To his credit, six months later, he came back to me and said, "This is the best professional environment I've ever worked in at General Motors. So we did not lose talent. Instead, we cultivated a new spirit of bold innovation.

My job required me to attend racing events nationwide. And I worked with GM's design team to create fantastic displays for General Motors vehicles at auto shows worldwide.

I also worked with our designers to conceive a fantastic display area whose gleaming GM vehicles remain today as a centerpiece of the sprawling, modern space of the Renaissance Center. We unveiled the display area with a beautiful reception emceed by local broadcaster Lauren Sanders, who was married to Detroit Lions star Barry Sanders. Events like this injected excitement into every division, especially GMC-Pontiac.

Our successful execution of the merger made me proud that I was able to unite people and products in ways that advanced the corporation.

Awards and Press Coverage Enhance My Clout at the Corporate Table

My success as head of Pontiac-GMC, and my continuing rise at General Motors garnered prestigious honors and celebratory reports in the national media. While this was tremendously flattering, I leveraged these accolades to teach people on a multitude of levels.

Before I explain, let me list some of the honors involved.

In 1995, I received the Distinguished Alumni Award from Western Michigan University.

I was named Executive of the Year by *Black Enterprise* magazine in 1996. Correspondent Caroline V. Clarke wrote, "As someone who has beaten the path from the assembly line to the executive suite, [Roberts's] story is accessible to virtually everyone. And his warm, gregarious manner only makes it more so."

During a gala awards ceremony at the Detroit Athletic Club, I was honored for my leadership, charisma and accomplishments in the corporate world.

In 1997, *African Americans on Wheels* magazine selected me as its Executive of the Year. Also that year, *Automotive News* named me to the All-Star Team of the Automotive Industry. And the Sales & Marketing Executives of Detroit, partnering with *The Detroit Free Press*, honored me as the 1997 Marketing Statesman of the Year. The souvenir program from the Sales Success Recognition Awards Banquet contains the ultimate compliment from the global advertising agency D'Arcy Masius Benton & Bowles. Its full page in the booklet says, "Congratulations, Roy Roberts." Beneath my photo is it reads: "His leadership, enthusiasm and high standards make him the ideal candidate for this award. Or for cloning."

Another honor came in August of 1997, when *Fortune* magazine profiled me in a special edition called "New Black Power." A plethora of media reports during this period consistently lauded me as one of America's most powerful black executives.

In 1998, I received the Distinguished Service Citation from the Automotive Hall of Fame.

I was also honored with the invitation to serve as a Director of Abbott Laboratories in 1998. It was thrilling to join the Board for the Chicago-based pharmaceutical and health care products company that has 90,000 employees and does business in more than 130 countries.

I celebrated these honors in the context of three main points that carry far more weight in society at large than the heady excitement of receiving an award.

First, my stature and the praise that it attracted continue to show people of every race, around the globe, that African Americans are capable of innovative, excellent leadership that contributes to the success of a huge corporation.

Second, positive press reports and awards amplified my value and influence within General Motors. When GM's leadership witnessed my popularity in the black community and in the mainstream, they understood that Roy Roberts represented a public relations coup for the corporation.

This is an often misunderstood dynamic amongst black professionals and executives, so I used my celebrity to explain it as often as possible. My message emphasized that it is imperative for black professionals, especially high-ranking executives, to remember that their value at the corporate table is rooted in their credibility with and connections to the black community.

"Don't think the corporate leaders elevated you to this position because you're just like them," I continue to warn today. "Don't get there, and forget where you came from. Don't disassociate from your people. That is the kiss of death for your career. Instead, know that you were hired because you are different. You are the corporation's link to a coveted demographic in the marketplace. Black people spend billions of dollars every year as consumers, and purchasing cars and trucks are their big ticket items."

This is a message that I share from podiums before thousands of people, as well as with individuals and small groups.

"So don't take your fancy job title and big salary and turn your back on your people," I warn. "Embrace them, cherish your relationships with them. Stay active in the community. In church. In civic groups. In civil rights organizations. That's where your power lies. And while you're at it, reach back and help other blacks advance in their educations and careers."

I shared this wisdom in many national media articles, including *Ebony,* the glossy, monthly magazine that highlights successful

African Americans in business, politics and entertainment. When Reporter Lynn Norment wrote a four-page spread about me for the January 1999 edition, she reported that I was one of the first blacks admitted to the Bloomfield Hills Country Club, and that I played golf at some of the world's most prestigious clubs.

That was the perfect segueway for me to use *Ebony's* global platform to talk about the importance of bringing my black experience into the predominantly white corporate world, where it is valued.

"If I belonged to Black clubs only, I'd cut myself out of their lives and the other executives that make decisions," I told *Ebony*. "Put yourself in a position so you can participate. You've got to be able to mix it up with people everywhere, at all times. If you don't, people aren't going to be comfortable with you and you don't have to compromise yourself in the process."

I continued to say, "When I go to the corporate table, I have to be as technically competent as anybody or better than most. And if I don't bring the Black experience to the table, then I hurt this company. And I would be disrespectful of myself. You don't run away from who you are and what you are. That's why you were hired… Don't be confused about why you are there."

I have seen many blacks fall from grace because they distance themselves from the black community. In this sense, a black person can become consensual validation for negative behavior. When that happens, I'd rather see a white guy in the executive position. The truth is that an African American who relinquishes his or her "street credibility" and racial accountability at the corporate table is ultimately giving up the clout that secured the job in the first place. They are often replaced with someone who understands this truth.

"I will tell people any day that affirmative action got me into management, but it didn't keep me there," I told *Ebony*. "Performance will keep you there, and working to build coalitions and to build relationships."

Chairing the 60ᵗʰ annual National Scout Jamboree of the
Boy Scouts of America in 1997, where I greeted and conversed with
President Bill Clinton at Fort A.P. Hill in Bowling Green, Va.
BSA photo by Randy Piland

The third way that I continue to leverage my value is by helping children, teenagers, college students and young professionals. I wanted to be the "Sticks Green" for new generations. I hoped that young people would see me in the media or interface with me in a variety of arenas, and feel motivated to achieve their absolute best in life.

That's why, during the mid- to late 1990s, my involvement with youth became increasingly broad and influential. After many years of volunteering with the Boy Scouts of America, my level of service intensified after I became a GM vice president. At that time, a high-ranking executive advised: "Roy, you've got to get more involved with Scouting. Everybody needs something outside of the company to get involved in. Scouting is safe. Education is safe."

My involvement with this wholesome American institution reflected well on General Motors. And my presence before a majority white membership of millions of boys, parents and volunteers enabled me to serve as an example of African American success like they had probably never seen. I wanted to set an example for more minorities to join.

This had never been more true than on July 30, 1997, when I chaired the Boy Scouts' Jamboree, at Fort A.P. Hill, the U.S. Army base in Bowling Green, Virginia. We hosted 350,000 youths, ten thousand volunteers, and 290,000 guests — including President Bill Clinton.

Many people did not want him to visit. Some were Republicans. Others wanted to avoid the cost and commotion. When the President's aircraft landed, I was the only person designated to walk out and greet him. We shook hands and I escorted him on stage, where we took pictures. Within twenty minutes, he owned that crowd.

"I want to say to Jere Radcliff, Roy Roberts, Jack Creighton, to all the officials of the Boy Scouts here, thank you for what you do with our young people," President Clinton said in a speech published on the U.S. Government Printing Office website.

"It's a great privilege for me to be here to celebrate the sixtieth anniversary of the first national Scout jamboree, a pleasure to serve and an honor to serve as your honorary president. As has already been said, ever since 1910, when William Boyce founded the Boy Scouts of America, every President has proudly served as your honorary president, for every President has recognized what a great contribution Scouting has made and is making to the character of our young people and, therefore, to the character and future of the United States of America."

President Clinton was only supposed to stay for half an hour, but after he spoke, he approached the crowd to shake hands and kiss babies. It was incredible to watch that crowd respond to him with such reverence.

That day was a highlight of my service with the Boy Scouts, and chairing the Jamboree was a huge honor. After that, I worked my way up to executive vice president, and ultimately president.

My commitment to young people led me, over the years, to

support the Boys and Girls Clubs, enabling me to mentor many young people. I became a board member of the Morehouse School of Medicine. I chaired the Executive Committee of the Education Achievement Authority of the state of Michigan. I became a Trustee Emeritus at Western Michigan University.

I also served as a board member for the National Urban League, the United Negro College Fund, and the local NAACP. My commitment to civil rights underscored my message to young people about getting the best education possible. With that, I became a popular commencement speaker at such places as Florida A&M.

"The keys to success are preparation, a quality education, and a belief in yourself," I told young people then, and continue to do so today. "Hard work is the fuel that propels success. The harder you work, the faster and higher you'll go."

My message for young women and people of color continues to be that the folks doing the hiring didn't care about color or gender; they care about performance, and how a good worker of any race can impact the company's bottom line. I also talk about Silent Killers.

"You may think it's okay to wear hip and trendy hairstyles or tattoos, or if you're male – pierced ears. But those are silent killers. The person interviewing you won't tell you, but radical clothing, hairstyles and bodily adornments appear rebellious and therefore clash with corporate culture. You won't get the job."

Imparting my wisdom to young people always included the topic of a strong work ethic: "I work 12- and 14-hour days. You need to spend as much time as necessary preparing, and it will pay off."

I have shared these messages with my six grandsons for as long as they have been old enough to speak. Since they have grown up during an era when African Americans are reaching the highest heights in business, politics, entertainment, and sports, their generation has tended to believe that anything is possible.

With this belief, however, comes a failure to understand that old-fashioned hard work and values are still required to achieve great success. The foundation of achievement, I explain, begins with an impeccable appearance. I don't care what company adopts a "business casual" dress code or who says it's cool to wear "eclectic" clothing in the workplace.

"You are young black men," I say. "You must be neat. Well-groomed. Sharply dressed. If you're overdressed, you can take something off. Looking your best at all times says everything about who you are and where you are going in life."

I also emphasize that punctuality is a key to success. It shows that you're responsible with your own time, and that you respect other people's time. My motto is: "Early is on time. On time is late."

Honesty is imperative: "When you say something, speak the truth, and mean it. Stick to it. The same applies to commitment. When you make a commitment, honor it."

I stress the importance of education: "If you have a bachelor's degree, you need a master's degree as well. Without a good education, this world is going to chew you up and run circles around you. You are not competing with the person next to you. You're competing with the entire world."

Hard work, I repeat, is key to success: "Don't let anybody out-work you. And be prepared. You've got to be the best."

On Top of the World, Traveling with Family

I sacrificed time with my family for my career. Every major corporate executive I ever worked with invested more time in his or her job than in their families. The jobs were that demanding. But what I lacked in quantity, I made up in quality when it came to family time -- and Maureen will back me up on that.

The births of our six grandchildren were especially joyous occasions. By the mid-1990s, three of them were teenagers. They included Robin and Roger's two sons: Roger, Junior, who was born on April 21, 1980; and Rory, whose birthday is July 6, 1981. In addition, Ronald's first son is Ryan, who was born on December 9, 1981. After he married Cynthia in Grand Rapids, they had two sons: Ronald, Junior, born on March 12, 1985; and Randyll, whose birthday is June 22, 1994. Our youngest grandchild is Katrina's son, Jeremy, who was born on August 1, 1996.

Family gatherings at our home, especially on holidays, provided time to relax, reflect, and talk to the next generation about focusing on school and being their best.

I shared the same messages when my children visited me occasionally at work. My daughter Robin recalls her childhood visit to the office of the president of Lear Siegler when I declared, "Someday I'll have an office just like this."

"When GM moved to the RenCen," Robin recalls, "Daddy invited me to meet people there and see his office. I remember he met me downstairs, and when we got into the elevator, we heard this chorus of people saying, 'Hello, Mr. Roberts,' and 'Nice to see you, Mr. Roberts.' Then they stepped aside and whispered. Upstairs, people were running ahead and opening the doors for us, constantly saying, 'Mr. Roberts' with the utmost respect. I met his secretary, then saw his office."

On the Thirty-Sixth floor of GM's world headquarters in the Renaissance Center downtown Detroit, my office was furnished with sleek, pine furniture with black trim. Its wall of windows revealed the Detroit River and the green island park called Belle Isle to the north, with the Ambassador Bridge to the south.

At the time, an upscale restaurant on the seventieth floor of the Renaissance Center was called The Summit. It was first class, and its rotating floor offered 360-degree views of Metro Detroit, the Detroit River, Lake St. Clair and Canada. The Summit was a favorite meeting spot, and its name described how I felt in my new office.

"My father's office was bigger than the president's office at Lear!" Robin exclaims. "I thought, 'Gosh! What Daddy said when I was a little girl, came true.' But he actually had an office that was better than the one where he'd declared his future success. Seeing the tangible results of how he had achieved this self-fulfilling prophecy through his hard work was so powerful, it still brings tears to people's eyes when I tell the story."

While my office made me feel on top of the world, Maureen

and I had the privilege of traveling the world.

In 1997, I headed up General Motors' dealer association, comprised of 8,000 dealers across America and Canada. The divisions awarded trips to the top performing dealers, as incentives to help sell the five million vehicles that General Motors sold every year. As a result, Maureen and I had the pleasure of choosing from several trips and getting to know dealers and their spouses on very personal levels. This really enhanced our ability to grow our business.

My favorite trip took us to a luxurious safari resort in Tanzania, Africa. When the organizer said, "We're going to camp two nights," I envisioned a rustic, outdoors experience. Not so! Maureen and I were stunned to arrive at the resort where our opulent guest cottage had crystal chandeliers and rose petals sprinkled around a huge bathtub. At night, a guard carrying a spear escorted us to the main house for dinner. The people were so beautiful, smart and friendly, that we took about 1300 pictures! Many of our photographs captured the breathtaking terrain and animals that we encountered during excursions into the wild.

Another memorable trip was a cruise to Alaska, with one thousand couples filling the entire ship as we beheld the beautiful islands, coves and bays of the Alaska Intercoastal Waterway. Helicopters took us to a glacier and an island, where we were treated to eating fresh-caught and cooked fish. We also visited a hospital for wounded eagles.

While this may sound fun and adventurous, I was constantly in work mode because every dealer wanted to consult with me about workplace challenges.

Taking three major trips every year, Maureen and I traveled to Spain, Italy, France and many other countries. On one occasion, we had breakfast in Athens, lunch in Paris, and dinner in Monaco, where we spent a few days. Now, Maureen and I are revisiting these amazing places without the pressure of work.

TWELVE

The World's Most Powerful Black Auto Executive

Like professional athletes who retire after winning a championship, I wanted to depart from GM at the top of my game. That was my feeling in 1997, after two glorious decades at General Motors. However, I was a star player, and the team needed me to score victory during a critical competition. Our opponents were the Big Three and the foreign automakers, and the trophy was a bigger market share.

To win, the chairman of General Motors was introducing a revolutionary plan to restructure the North American Group into a more streamlined and financially efficient entity. Jack Smith wanted me to play a role in this endeavor. In August of 1998, he and the Board elevated me to vice president in charge of Field Sales, Service and Parts for the Vehicle Sales, Service and Marketing Group.

Two months later, in October of 1998, I was promoted again, to Group Vice President for North American Vehicle Sales, Service and Marketing. This promotion occurred after Ron Zarella became President of North America. I was thrilled and honored that Chairman Smith and General Motors leadership were entrusting me to execute an enormous restructuring for sales and marketing for the entire corporation.

In this job, I took over GM's $100 billion North American operation, which included Mexico and Canada. All of the marketing divisions of General Motors came under my responsibility. This included a $3.2 billion advertising budget. From this pinnacle of power, I commanded control of a fortune that was greater than the Gross National Product of many countries. It was extremely rare for an African American to wield this kind of financial control in a one of the largest Fortune 500 companies.

"Roy Roberts: GM's $100 BILLION DOLLAR MAN," announced a headline over a four-page spread in *Ebony* in January of 1999. Full-page photographs showed me standing beside a Cadillac in front of the Renaissance Center, talking with Chairman Smith, and meeting with my communications staff in my office.

"The changes at GM's North American Vehicle Sales, Service and Marketing will help dismantle a system created by GM President Alfred Sloan, GM president from 1937 to 1956, by eliminating hierarchy and driving the decision-making process down into the organization—closest to the customers," Jack Smith told *Ebony*. "This is the second most significant change in GM's history."

It would cut 800 jobs and save $200 million annually. To accomplish this, I was charged with the revolutionary task of decentralizing the sales, service, parts and marketing workforce from the traditional hub in Detroit, to five regional distribution centers throughout the United States. A regional distribution system would save time and money, and accelerate the availability of our vehicles in the marketplace. This was radical! Since the founding of General Motors in 1908, vehicles had always been marketed and distributed from The Motor City.

As the brainchild of a strategy to execute this momentous project, I led a research team to study the marketplace. We learned that people in different regions of America had distinct preferences for the types of vehicles they drove. Our study determined that New York, Chicago, Atlanta, Dallas and Los Angeles were the ideal locations for these distribution centers.

236

At the time, each division of General Motors marketed and sold its vehicles as a separate entity. If you visited our sales and marketing offices in Chicago, for example, you'd see that Cadillac had a floor. Buick had a floor. Oldsmobile had a floor. Every division had its own floor. The problem was that the divisions were competing internally with each other. For example, Buick wanted to usurp Cadillac's dominance as America's top-selling luxury car for nearly sixty years. Marketing teams were so proud of their individual divisions, they lost sight of our true competitors — Ford and Chrysler. When Toyota, Honda and other foreign car companies came along, our people didn't even see them.

When you make love in the family, as the saying goes, you have crazy kids. That was exactly what was happening at General Motors. It was costing us market share, profitability, efficiency and dominance in the American automobile market.

So how would I convince these internal competitors to form one team to market with equal vigor every vehicle that General Motors manufactured?

This daunting task would require me to lead a radical shake-up in corporate culture. I had done it before during the GMC-Pontiac merger. Now I needed to replicate that strategy on a huge scale, for every division of General Motors. When you start trying to change the culture in an institution, you're asking for war! As a result, getting all of the people to sell all of the products was the toughest thing I've ever done.

First, I rearranged staffs so that people from each division were forced to interact and work together. Second, and very importantly, I implemented a quota system for the five regional sales and marketing offices that both held everyone accountable for failure and rewarded success. I captured their attention by blasting WIIFM. If anyone wondered "What's in it for me?" the answer was, "Money!" I established a reward structure that paid X-number of dollars if someone sold X-number of Cadillacs, Y numbers of Buicks, and so on. Money talks loudly and clearly, and it inspired people to get with the new program that ultimately helped General Motors reduce costs and boost profits.

I also gave frequent pep talks to my team of 9,000 employees in Detroit and around the country. I often warned, "The competition will eat your breakfast and your lunch, then drink your martini for dinner. They'll leave you wondering what happened." To avoid that, I drilled into everyone the importance of aggressive marketing and sales, so that car buyers chose General Motors over the hundreds of other vehicles that were available.

"There isn't anybody on the face of the earth who needs our product to live," I frequently said. "You've got to win our customers every day, and the next day, and the next day. Remember, you're only as good as your last sale."

As I succeeded at changing the corporate culture, Ron Zarella was pushing the regional distribution system from a brand management standpoint. One major aspect was integrating the technology to support this massive endeavor. This required us to install computer systems to allocate products to each region. Getting this system up and running efficiently was a monster of a challenge. Before we were ready, in my opinion, my boss forced me to give it the green light. I and several of my people begged him not to do it.

"We need more time to ensure smooth distribution," I insisted. "Delivery of these automobiles in a timely, efficient manner is the lifeline of a dealer. This is how they meet customers' needs. We can't afford any glitches!"

I further emphasized that the national media would chew us up and spit us out — all over newspapers, radio stations and television broadcasts, if we launched a flawed system. Even worse, customers would be furious if vehicles were not available or delayed. And dealers would suffer exponentially.

Ron Zarella forced us to proceed before we were ready. It was a colossal mistake that almost brought GM to its knees. Dealers were complaining everywhere. Of course my boss ducked. The back-story was that Ron Zarella was close with a few dealers who were misleading him about the readiness of dealers as a whole to launch our new process. It was really disheartening; it hurt a lot of dealers.

In the midst of this, my desire to retire became acute, and I told the chairman.

"Roy," he said, "we really need you to stay another year to see this through."

Grieving Family Losses; Nose to the Grindstone

That was a tough period. In 1998, my father died of diabetes and heart failure. He was 76 years old. The death of a parent always brings into focus one's own mortality and leaves grown children to shoulder the leadership responsibilities in a family. Though at age 59 I was not the oldest sibling, my professional and financial stature established me with authority amongst my brothers and sisters.

I had experienced this when lupus put my sister Minnie Ruth into a coma for ten days. Doctors were trying to save her. Ultimately, she was on life support. My sister Ludine, along with Minnie Ruth's husband, Jeff, were both wringing their hands. In this highly emotional situation, I demonstrated a tenet of my value system that applies both personally and professionally: It's not about me, it's about doing the right thing for the larger entity that I served, whether it was General Motors or my family. After two hours of listening to the doctors, it was clear that Minnie Ruth was brain dead.

"Pull the plug," I said.

Her husband and my sister were so relieved. They couldn't do it. They didn't want the accountability or accusations of being heartless or giving up. I didn't care about any of that. I wanted to do the right thing.

No matter what I was enduring personally, I reported to work with a zest and a zeal to make things better. The status quo was never an acceptable option. I was driven to make improvements. I also walked into General Motors' world headquarters every morning fully aware that I had a fiduciary responsibility to the corporation to do my best.

Therefore, I set aside my desire to retire and shouldered the responsibilities of helping the company succeed. My twelve-and fourteen-hour days continued into evenings at home, as I studied reports about sales, service and marketing in our five sections of the country. These reports detailed what dealers were saying about business, what customers were saying to dealers, and what was happening technically with our products in the marketplace. The reports also revealed what kinds of recalls we were having.

As group vice president, every issue was my issue. I was the interface with the dealer body. If the chairman was going to ask any questions about them, this was in my bailiwick, and I had to be on top of it. As such, I was required to thoroughly understand the issue and offer solutions to every problem. You can't help your organization improve if you don't understand what's going on.

Service is an overlooked but major aspect of an automotive company, because that's typically the root source of information about recalls. That's why I would drive a different car every two weeks. I specifically requested any vehicle that was causing a problem, because I wanted to experience it first hand.

This was such an effective practice that I proposed to the chairman that instead of having our new vehicles delivered to corporate headquarters, all executives would be required to physically go to dealerships, order a car and pick it up ourselves. Rather than being pampered and detached from the front lines of General Motors, we needed to understand the buying experience. My proposal was not approved.

Meanwhile, I was responsible for all auto shows. This was not a glamorous job. In 1998, the General Motors display at the Detroit auto show was horrible. Business was weak, and Ford was strong. This resulted in a lackluster auto show, because you can't make your displays ultra-exciting unless you're winning market share and making money. If your employees are suffering through a year without bonuses, or worse, facing potential lay-offs, it would kill morale, productivity and quality for the company to give a glitzy auto show to impress potential customers. Employees would accuse GM of throwing money away at their expense.

Thankfully, our efforts to turn the company around were bearing fruit, and subsequent auto shows in New York and Chicago were significantly better. GM was using aggressive marketing tactics to attract new buyers. Under the headline, "Promotions to Go: If Buyers Won't Come To GM, It'll Bring Its Cars To Buyers," a December 06, 1998 article in *The Wall Street Journal* focused on how we were jazzing up our marketing plan. The article by Fara Warner explained that GM had lost market share, even though it was America's biggest advertiser, spending billions on multimedia advertising.

The article highlighted our innovative "Motorama" displays, which were first introduced during the 1960s. These were small "take the product to the people" auto shows – with a dozen or so vehicles – at multiple venues nationwide.

"Every day, we're looking for opportunities for eight-tenths of (market) share here or one-tenth there," I told *The Wall Street Journal*. Our reorganization and marketing were useless if our vehicles lacked the "Wow factor," and these mini car shows made GM shine.

Bad Bosses at GM: Few and Far Between, but Miserable Nonetheless

The thrilling successes of the Pontiac-GMC merger and subsequent assignments were tainted by something that I experienced only twice at General Motors: a bad boss.

My first one was the head of Rochester Products Division. The second one was Ron Zarella.

Bad bosses were the exception. In fact, I prided myself on working with extraordinarily ethical, principled people like GM Vice Chairman Harry Pearce, who was in the running to become president and chairman.

Unfortunately, my new boss who was hired from the outside was from a different world. This caused a lot of consternation and pain. A person who cheats at one thing, will cheat at many things. Likewise, if a manager or executive lies and cheats at one level, they do so at every level, becoming more brazen as they rise.

During the Christmas season of 1998, General Motors was basking in celebration and positive press after releasing sales figures in one of our luxury vehicle divisions. The numbers indicated that GM's Cadillac division had beaten sales for Ford's Lincoln division — by just 222 cars.

This was big news for General Motors. First, Cadillac and Lincoln were fierce competitors; Cadillac had been America's top-selling luxury car for fifty-seven years, and was fighting to maintain its dominance. Yet sales had been sputtering throughout the financially turbulent 1990s. Still, news that Cadillac had once again beaten Lincoln was cause for celebration at General Motors. The celebration, however, was short-lived.

"Roy, you need to know that your people lied to you about their sales," said a fellow in the corporation who approached me during Christmas break. "They did not beat Ford Motor Company." He then proceeded to tell me the whole story that hinged on two unscrupulous executives who had manipulated the numbers and lied to the world about Cadillac beating Lincoln.

I called my boss, Ron Zarella, and told him what had transpired.

"I'm going to go to the opposing company and tell them we made a mistake," I said. "I'm going to tell them what the numbers were. Then I'm going to go to the media and tell them. After that, I'm going to back off and figure out what we should do with these two executives who lied."

My boss shook his head. "No, Roy, no you don't! You don't do a thing. That was good news for us at General Motors. We don't have a lot of good news. People have been writing good news lately. You just stand down. Don't you do a thing."

A bad feeling crept through me. By colluding with the lie, my boss was being just as unscrupulous as the two executives who had falsified sales figures for the sake of bogus glory for GM.

"Careful," I said. "You know what you're saying. My responsibility is to tell you, and tell you what I want to do. If you tell me not to do it, then I can't do it, but I think that's wrong."

Ron Zarella vehemently reiterated: "I'm telling you, Roy, don't you do a thing."

242

Two or three weeks passed, and all of a sudden, an auditor came to my office. He wanted to know precisely what had happened with the sales for Cadillac and Lincoln. I told him exactly what transpired. I described the fellow who came to me and told me that my people had cheated. I divulged that I told my boss, and that my boss told me not to say or do a thing.

The auditor turned to me and said, "Vice Chairman Harry Pearce said that you would tell me the truth."

That was a powerful moment, because I felt that my commitment to honesty and integrity was recognized and appreciated by the most ethical individual in the corporation. In the end, the truth was revealed in the world media, and this debacle tainted General Motors' public image.

"After reporting almost unbelievable sales results in December, Cadillac eked out a come-from-behind victory by just 222 cars," *The New York Times* wrote on May 6, 1999, in an article by Robin Meredith. "Apparently the numbers were pulled from thin air. Today, the General Motors Corporation said that its Cadillac division sold 4,773 fewer cars in December than it had reported at the time, acknowledging four months late that Lincoln was the nation's best-selling luxury car for the first time since 1939," the article said.

The Times then quoted a statement released by GM: "The December sales results were 'overstated due to an improper reporting process.'"

The appearance that General Motors was lying and cheating was extremely embarrassing, and it hurt the corporation's image with customers and our competitors.

On a more positive note in May of 1999, I was profiled among *Ebony's* 100 Most Influential Black Americans. As such, I felt a personal responsibility to do my part to preserve the integrity of General Motors. That's why, internally, I recommended that General Motors should fire the two executives who had lied about Cadillac's sales figures. Unfortunately, top management gave them a mere slap on the wrist by penalizing their bonuses. That bothers me to this day. I'm convinced that they were rewarded for negative behavior.

Ironically, their sneaky behavior would ultimately benefit General Motors in a significant way. These two individuals bypassed traditional protocols for introducing new products. They hatched the idea of making a GMC Suburban into the very popular luxury Cadillac Escalade that is extremely popular today. They went around the system to do it. It was a very good outcome, but they cheated. You can't cheat the system and get rewarded for it. That becomes consensual validation for unscrupulous acts. And I don't believe that their contribution will exonerate them.

As for Ron Zarella, he later returned to Bausch & Lomb. It was revealed that he had falsified his resume, claiming that he had a master's degree in business administration when, in fact, he did not.

These individuals illustrate a crucial tenet in business and in life: honesty is the best policy. What's done in the dark always comes to light in a way that's detrimental to the person who did it.

A Powerful Moment with a Prestigious Peer

Sometimes one simple experience can encapsulate a complicated intersection of history, emotions, socioeconomics and accomplishment. I enjoyed one such moment with one of my few black counterparts in the automotive industry.

My good friend Elliott S. Hall was a pioneer. He became the highest-ranking African American executive at Ford Motor Company in 1987, when he was named as vice president of Washington Affairs. He directed Ford's Washington office after a distinguished career as a prominent attorney in Detroit. His story was somewhat similar to mine because he was an autoworker's son who became the first in the family of eight children to complete college.

One day, Elliott invited me to lunch at Ford World Headquarters in Dearborn, about thirty minutes outside Detroit. I was escorted to his office on the twelfth floor, which housed the Executive Offices and offered sweeping views of the metropolitan region.

"Good afternoon, Mr. Hall, Mr. Roberts," said a uniformed waiter who entered, pushing a cart that carried our lunch. With the meticulous decorum that one might expect in a royal palace, the waiter transferred china plates, crystal glasses, silverware and our gourmet lunch onto a table. Meanwhile, Elliott and I chatted about our families and the auto industry. After a few minutes, the waiter rolled the cart away and closed the door.

As soon as we were alone, Elliott looked at me, laughed exuberantly, and exclaimed, "Ain't this some shit!?"

His recounting of this experience inspired a standing ovation from hundreds of people attending a Roast and Toast in my honor in September of 2013 in Detroit.

That moment, as he and I had basked in the luxurious pampering of the inner sanctum of one of the world's greatest corporations, was so powerful because we were the first African Americans to enjoy the kind of royal treatment that white executives have always experienced.

No Bad Apples: Winning Casino Partnership Approval

One of the secrets of my success has been a refusal to dwell on anything negative. Instead, since childhood, I have focused my time and attention on how to improve and advance in any situation. This has served me well, but almost landed me in big trouble with state regulators in 1999.

The issue arose amidst an exciting and lucrative investment prospect: casino gambling in Detroit. After years of debate, the legal ground was finally softened to build three casinos. They promised to attract thousands of jobs, tourism, and millions in revenue for cash-strapped Detroit.

The casinos needed investors, so I teamed up with nine other African American and Mexican American professionals to form Partners Detroit LLC, which would hold an unstated interest in MGM Grand Detroit.

State gaming investigators scrutinized every investor to ascertain whether he or she had the financial prowess, moral character, and history of ethical business practices to receive a casino license.

These investigations included a criminal background check. State casino laws required investors to disclose any crimes that involved them, even if charges were dropped.

When asked whether I had ever been arrested, I disclosed that I had been arrested during high school for driving without a license. However, I did not recount the incident involving stolen apples. I did not consider that an arrest, and my positive mindset had erased the memory of being detained by police and driven to jail with my friends.

"Mr. Roberts, is there anything else you want to tell us?" asked a Michigan Gaming Control Commissioner.

"No," I said.

A Commissioner called a second time and asked, "Mr. Roberts, do you want to share anything else with us about your past?"

When I said "No," no, the Commission reminded me that in 1956 I had been arrested for stealing apples. I suddenly recalled that the police had informed us that the incident would be ex-punged from our records, so I had dismissed it. Now, it appeared to the Michigan Gaming Commission that I had been dishonest. At the same time, the local media was reporting about the teenaged arrest that I had disclosed.

A *Detroit News* headline announced: "Old crime risks casino bid: Petty larceny committed as teen may hurt MGM investor and GM exec Roy Roberts." The June 17, 1999, report by Judy DeHaven said, "A petty crime more than forty years ago may prevent General Motors Vice-President Roy S. Roberts from owning a part of the MGM Grand Detroit casino. The prominent African American, who worked his way up to the inner sanctum of the world's largest company, pleaded guilty to stealing $100 from a high school friend's family when he was 17 years old."

The News reported that it had obtained police documents de-tailing the August 3, 1956, incident when I was a junior in high school. It said Bobby Tates' mother reported to police that I had snatched small amounts of cash over a one-year period when I was a guest in their home. Mrs. Tates also told police that I had taken Bobby's wallet and used his driver's license.

Here's what really angered me: the article said, "Roberts admitted to police and to the Tates family that he had taken the money, the police report said, and he pleaded guilty in Muskegon Municipal Court to larceny."

I had never admitted to stealing, nor had I pled guilty to anything! Thankfully, the newspaper was told that Judge Michael Nolan in the 60th District Court in Muskegon had suppressed my court file.

This arrest was being combined with the one concerning the stolen apples to cause a major glitch. "Michigan Gaming Control Board Executive Director Nelson Westrin would not say Wednesday if Roberts disclosed the larceny in his application," *The News* reported, regarding the cash missing from Bobby Tate's house.

Meanwhile, the media was also reporting that two members of our investment team were encountering last-minute obstacles to approval. Oakland County real estate developer Tony Gramer had been arrested in 1990 for assaulting his wife. Regal Plastics Inc. Chairman William Pickard had donated money to politicians after a new state law barred casino investors from making campaign contributions.

For the time being, the three of us transferred our shares to our seven partners. Otherwise, the entire group risked being ousted from this investment opportunity. Our lawyer advised that this was the best option, and that we would be allowed to reapply at a later date.

Meanwhile, members of the state legislature took my side, saying, "You can't do that to a man who's done everything right for fifty years. You're talking about something that happened when he was 17 years old." In fact, the state legislature was so incensed that this was being used to block my casino investor application that they proposed a piece of legislation in my defense. We asked them not to do that because it was drawing too much attention. Fortunately, the problem disappeared when the Gaming Commission realized that neither I, nor my partners, owned a large enough percentage of the casino to require the Commission's approval at that level.

When the MGM Grand Detroit Casino officially opened on July 29, 1999, the gala was terrific.

The following year, on October 3, 2000, the Michigan Gaming Control Board voted to permit me, Bill Pickard and Anthony Gramer to rejoin our investment partners. Today, the MGM Grand Detroit Casino is a premier destination with its first-class restaurants, hotel, ballroom, entertainment, spa and gaming. I have been extremely pleased with my participation in what has become an absolute gem for Detroit.

THIRTEEN

Retirement Invites New Opportunities

In 1999, I felt strongly that my boss was making decisions that were hurting the corporation. Operating in that environment and taking damaging directives became intolerable. It was time for me to leave General Motors, so I alerted the chairman. I also spoke with Harry Pearce about opportunities after my retirement.

"Would you like to become a supplier to GM?" he asked.

"I'd like to explore that." I knew people who had done well at that, and I thought that might be a great option.

Harry was instrumental in arranging for some legal staff to counsel and advise me as we analyzed the possibilities. We explored several scenarios that would benefit me and General Motors. It was clear that being an effective supplier required a proprietary product and the technology to make it successful. Otherwise, when the company caught cold, the supplier would get pneumonia. It would be deadly. So I shied away. We ultimately did not find anything that really fit.

"Roy, would you like to own the five dealerships that GM now owns?" Harry asked. "It would include ownership of a plane."

These dealerships remained a bone of contention with our dealers, who felt that we were competing with them. I had never liked the idea of GM-owned dealerships. Purchasing them had been an idea forced by Ron Zarella, who thought he knew it all, but really caused a lot of consternation. As for owning the dealerships, I was not convinced that GM insiders would treat me fairly or give me a proper shot at succeeding. I decided it was not the right move for me.

Announcing My Retirement at the Right Time, for the Right Reasons

I once heard a professional basketball player say practice cannot end until a succession of baskets are made, and the athlete feels good about his performance.

"Never leave on a miss," he said.

Such was my feeling about retiring from General Motors. Though I was eager to liberate myself from a boss whom I did not respect, and the succession of debacles that I endured under his direction, I could not rest or leave until my work had generated better sales and profits.

Fortunately, my successful sales and marketing reorganization ushered General Motors into one of its most impressive years in decades, with sales spiking 9 percent as GM's market share increased 3 percent in important areas, including mid-size vehicles and full-size pickup trucks. That was the proverbial icing on the cake of my service at General Motors, which earned me to continuous prestige in the media and the mainstream as "the most powerful black executive in the global auto industry."

As such, I felt that my service had concluded at General Motors. My sixty-first birthday was approaching, and I was excited to conquer new professional territory.

This was foremost on my mind on Tuesday, January 18, 2000, as I delivered a powerful speech at the Automotive News World Congress in Detroit. I spoke about the urgency for GM to heal relations with its dealers. Their sales and service staffs interfaced with customers, and those relationships could make or break the company's success. For that, I told the huge audience, dealers should be valued, celebrated and supported for their starring role in the organization.

Unfortunately, many dealers were still outraged about the previous year's botched computerized system for ordering cars. They were also angry that GM had withdrawn its plan to purchase and operate 10 percent of its dealerships. I urged GM to seek forgiveness and aggressively campaign to repair relationships. It was a poignant speech, punctuated at the end with an announcement that surprised many in the media and global automotive industry.

I announced my retirement from General Motors Corporation, effective February 1, 2000.

"While my tenure at General Motors has enabled me to fulfill a lifelong dream of serving in leadership positions for the world's top manufacturer," I said, "the time has come for me to pursue another dream: investing in and running my own business. I believe that my future promises many decades of exciting business challenges that will enable me to continue to contribute to our global marketplace in a positive, powerful manner."

I explained that I would stay on board at General Motors until April 1 while I trained my successor, William J. Lovejoy, vice president for SPO – Service Parts Operations. Our first joint venture would occur soon, when we would travel on a good will mission to Orlando, Florida to attend the National Automobile Dealers Association convention. At the conclusion of my announcement, reporters from around the world surrounded me.

"Were you forced to retire?" one journalist asked.

"No," I answered. "I've wanted to retire for some time, but the chairman asked me to remain on board so that I could supervise the implementation of our sales and marketing reorganization."

Still, the media fixated on the idea that I was forced out. A *Chicago Tribune* article by Jim Mateja on January 19, 2000, exemplified this: "A few weeks ago, Vice Chairman Harry Pearce raised some eyebrows by saying GM management had to be held accountable for the automaker's failure to reach its goal of a 30 percent market share for 1999 after finishing a shade over 30 percent in 1998."

The article, under the headline: "GM Sales Exec Roy Roberts To Retire," continued: "Last week, the GM board held an unexpected meeting at the Detroit Auto Show at which time Roberts' resignation was accepted. The speculation is that as head of sales and marketing, Roberts became the target of accountability." The article quoted me as saying that I had kept my retirement a secret so that my team could stay focused on boosting market share and mending relations with dealers.

Still, a lot of people thought I was fired. They believed I was younger than I actually was, so they could not understand why I was leaving. A lot of questions were being asked. My answer was, unequivocally, that I was leaving of my own volition.

At the same time, my retirement focused media attention on another issue at General Motors: diversity.

"Mr. Roberts has been the most powerful black executive in the global auto industry," said a January 19, 2000, article in *The New York Times,* entitled, "A Top Official Has Plans to Leave G.M."

"With his departure," said the report by Keith Bradsher, "the only black manager in G.M.'s top five levels is Roderick D. Gillum, who is the vice president for public policy and diversity."

I told Keith that GM was hiring more people of color as managers below the rank of vice president. This was occurring in the wake of criticism by Reverend Jesse Jackson, who founded The Wall Street Project in 1996. In doing so, he had slammed Wall Street and the automotive industry for failing to integrate their highest ranks. The deputy director of the Detroit office for the Rainbow/PUSH Coalition, Glenda Gill, told *The Times* that the organization was "saddened and dismayed" by my retirement.

A short time later, *Black Enterprise* ran a story by Hersh Doby on May 1, 2000, with my photo and the headline: "Roy Roberts retires from GM: Highest-ranking black executive aided automaker's turnaround." The article described me as "one of the highest-ranking and most influential African Americans in the automotive industry." It quoted me as saying: "I'm proud of what my team has achieved in the past year, and I expect greater gains lie ahead. I had considered retiring some time ago, but decided to see the reorganization through."

GM President and CEO Rick Wagoner told the magazine: "Roy has been a huge contributor to the past decade's turnaround of General Motors. When glitches arose, Roy acknowledged them and worked with our dealers to fix them. The end result was a faster and more responsive organization. That's a tribute to Roy's tenacity and skill." Rick also praised my unwavering commitment to quality as well as my ability to envision and implement better ways for the corporation to operate.

A quote that I shared with the *Wall Street Journal* has been frequently reprinted in many places because it summarizes my career with simplicity and poignancy: "I've never had a job that I disliked. I've never had a job I did not grow from. It's been a good journey."

I absolutely loved General Motors. I thought it was one of the classiest companies in the world, and I am forever grateful for the glorious, ground-breaking career that I enjoyed there.

When you spend nearly a quarter of a century with a company, it becomes a part of you. As a result, my retirement was an extremely emotional time. What could possibly be as exciting and fulfilling as the career I was leaving? I was not ready to retreat to a beach and lounge for the rest of my life. Instead, I had many more years of good health and vitality to excel in another endeavor. At the same time, I reflected on something that my father had said long ago: "Someday you have to look in the mirror and answer the question, 'Did you do the very best job that you could possibly do?'"

When I looked at my reflection in April of 2000, my answer was a resounding, "Yes!"

The corporation and various employee groups showed their agreement by hosting *twelve* retirement parties! First was the company-wide extravaganza, amidst shiny new GM vehicles in our showroom in the Renaissance Center. My family joined hundreds of people from every level of the company, who gathered to bid me farewell as a band played. Then, every functional area where I had worked — including Human Resources, Pontiac-GMC and Cadillac — threw parties so that people could say goodbye. I was overwhelmed and overjoyed.

Internet Start-Up Designed to Connect Companies with Minority Firms

As I explored career options, I was approached by a fellow whose wife and Maureen had orchestrated a major event at the Detroit Institute of Arts. Gary Wasserman owned Allied Metals Corporation and had done well in business.

"Roy," he said, "I'd like to talk with you about starting an internet company that will connect Fortune 1000 companies with minority-owned businesses."

Gary explained that this Internet trade exchange would provide one-stop shopping through online catalogs for companies in any industry to purchase goods and services from minority-owned and women-owned businesses. For example, if a company needed steel, we would connect it with a minority steel supplier. If a business required ice cream cones, we would find a company that made ice cream cones and was owned by a racial minority or a woman.

General Motors had a similar company without the minority perspective. They tried to convince us to sell our company or partner with them. But we preferred an independent venture.

This innovative concept had huge potential: initial financial data suggested that our company could facilitate electronic commerce between businesses ranging into the billions of dollars.

Duly impressed, I partnered to launch M-Xchange.com in March of 2000. I was chairman, owning 51 percent of the company; Gary was president, with a 49 percent stake. When we opened our downtown Detroit offices, we held a press conference that prompted the local and national media to write and broadcast reports about the business. Under the headline: "Former G.M. Executive Forms Web Site for Minority Suppliers," a *New York Times* article quoted me as saying: "We want to ensure that minority businesses are not left behind in the migration to online marketplaces."

After I spoke about the uniqueness of our business, the March 22, 2000, article by Robin Meredith noted that Reverend Jesse Jackson was on hand. He admonished corporate America to support our business by saying, "There is nothing you want to procure that we cannot supply."

At the time, Reverend Jackson was aggressively challenging the business world "to end the multi-billion dollar trade deficit with minority vendors and consumers," according to The Wall Street Project's website. Reverend Jackson's backing boosted our success! We raised money so fast that we had to stop people from coming in the door. Delphi Automotive Systems — with offices in Troy, Michigan, Paris, Tokyo and Sao Paulo, Brazil — was the first to join our network.

"Having Delphi, the world leader in providing innovative, high-tech solutions to global automotive manufacturers, on board signals the potential value of our portal," I said in a statement released on PRNewswire. "M-Xchange.com will level the playing field for minority companies in the New Economy; partnerships like the one with Delphi will get us there faster."

However, working with my partner became very difficult. My legal counsel warned that the best way to extricate myself from the partnership was to shut down the company. After we did that in September of 2000, I had to return money to everyone who had invested with me. The company's final financials determined that each person would recoup 72 percent of his or her investment dollars.

I then wrote a personal check for the 28 percent difference, so that each investor received 100 percent reimbursement. *Inc.* magazine subsequently published an article saying that I was the only known company in the United States that had done that. Legally, it was not required. But these individuals were invested in Roy Roberts, so I felt a moral responsibility to repay them in full.

On a Sunday when I wrote the last check, I told Maureen, "This was one of the best days of my life."

Reliant Equity Investors: "We Were Hot!"

In 2001, I co-founded a private equity firm called Reliant Equity Investors. This venture began when I received a call from a woman who had an impressive position in a prominent financial organization; we had met at Harvard when she was an MBA student. She had worked with Thomas E. Darden, Managing Director for Wind Point Partners, a private equity firm in the Detroit suburb of Southfield. Thomas had told her that he wanted to start his own firm.

"If you do," she suggested, "you need to partner with someone who has gray hair. Money lenders value wisdom, and they fear that a young person like you doesn't have it yet. I know the perfect guy for your partner: Roy Roberts."

Thomas called me and made an excellent impression. He was highly ethical, capable and intellectually bright. His wife was a patent attorney; they had two children. With a bachelor's degree in Engineering from the General Motors Institute, he earned an M.B.A., cum laude, from Babson College, where he was awarded a Kauffman Fellowship. Thomas suggested that two others join us:

★ Carr T. Preston, J.D., a principal at Allied Capital of Washington, D.C., who had an MBA from the Wharton Business School at the University of Pennsylvania, a law degree from George Washington University, and a B.A. in Economics from Morehouse College.

★ Omar L. Simmons of Boston, who graduated with honors from the Harvard Business School's MBA program, after graduating from Princeton University.

The four of us had nearly sixty years of executive level operating experience with top Fortune 100 companies and businesses financed by private equity investors. But most private equity firms failed during the first year because people did not know each other well enough. When money starts to flow, all hell can break loose. To avoid that, the four of us held weekend meetings at an airport hotel where we spent hours asking deeply personal questions:

"How big is your mortgage?"

"How much does it cost for your kids to go to private school?"

"How long have you been married?"

After reaching a sufficient level of confidence in each other, we co-founded Reliant Equity Investors. It was based in Chicago, and I was adamant about not moving to the Windy City. With each of us serving as a Managing Director, we developed a strategy to focus on buyouts of growth-oriented and middle-market American businesses in a variety of industries that included light and heavy manufacturing, food, packaging, consumer products and business-to-business services.

On March 23, 2001, we opened our downtown Detroit office. In a statement that generated many national media interviews, I said, "Traditionally, Michigan-based businesses are fundamentally strong and offer huge potential for organic growth coupled with strategic investment initiatives. Despite the current economy, we see tremendous value in focusing our resources in this market and on companies that are looking for capital to grow globally."

We soon discovered that few people were willing to give money to minorities, especially in private equity. Then Reverend Jesse Jackson essentially saved the day with his on-going condemnation of the financial community on Wall Street and across the nation. He criticized them for blocking minorities from opportunities for employment, investment and prosperity. Thankfully, his efforts elicited guilt that spurred the financial community to do business with minorities.

By 2003, Reliant Equity had raised $126 million. Our limited partners included Illinois Public Employees, Illinois State Teachers, and Calpers, the largest pension fund in the United States. General Motors invested with us, as did Wells Fargo Bank. When we were ready to operationalize our company, we were probably the hottest African American private equity firm in the United States, with the fourth largest in investable dollars.

We were hot! Wherever we went, whatever we did, we were successful! In time, Reliant Equity Investors was profiting and expanding. We hired young analysts and vice presidents who had worked on Wall Street. By giving them a percentage of the company, our attitude was, "If we do well, we want everyone to do well."

We had a staff of about a dozen people, including a brilliant female office manager. Each of us played roles that utilized our individual strengths. Omar Simmons, for example, was responsible for asking the hard questions before money was exchanged. All the while, our professional code of conduct was so exemplary that people still talk about "doing business the Reliant way."

My partners and I then helped our six young employees get into graduate school to earn MBAs. Five attended Harvard. One went to Northwestern University. All graduated with honors.

As business continued to improve, we were planning to market a new vehicle, but our investors did not support the idea.

At one point, we explored the possibility of partnering with a highly accomplished investor in Chicago. At the time, he had several billion dollars under management, and was looking to partner with private equity firms. He liked that our company's culture was similar to his.

Unfortunately, our people overstated our value. When this individual met with companies, he spoke directly with CEOs. Reliant interfaced with CFOs at best. Exaggerating our clout tainted the possibility of a partnership, so I called it off. Relationships and friendships are more important than business deals. In the end, this individual invested with us personally.

Meanwhile, as the first decade of the new millennium passed, I continued to work on corporate boards, and I truly enjoyed that. From 2007 until 2010, I was a Director at Thermon Manufacturing Company. The Texas-based company manufactures cooling wiring systems. From 2008 until 2011, I served on the Board at Enova Systems, Inc., an alternative energy technology company in Torrance, California. My service on the Burlington Northern Santa Fe Board concluded in 2010 when it was sold to Warren Buffett. Also during this period, I served on the Aspen Institute's Board of Directors.

In 2012, after Abbott Laboratories split into two companies, I joined the board of directors for the new research-based pharmaceutical company, AbbVie. I continue to serve on the AbbVie Board.

I was also serving as executive vice president and chairman of the Strategic Plan Committee of Boy Scouts of America.

Meanwhile, at Reliant Equity Investors, some of our members wanted to make it a family business. I did not favor that. When families are in business, management gets muddled. Our disagreement caused friction. At the same time, it was time to raise another fund, because each fund has a 10-year lifespan. Raising another fund would require me to move to Chicago. Now in my early seventies, I did not want to commit to another ten-year fund — or relocate.

These factors fractured the organization; we closed in 2011. In hindsight, my mistake was failing to be more involved in daily management. Likewise, my refusal to move to Chicago was a missed opportunity.

Overall, I really enjoyed private equity. We still get together every year, and it's been a joy to watch my former partners build their families and excel professionally.

FOURTEEN

National President
of Boy Scouts of America

In May of 2002, I embarked on one of the most meaningful experiences of my life: I became president of Boy Scouts of America. It was historic! I was the first African American to lead 2.7 million youth members and 1.3 million adult volunteers in the respected organization founded in 1910.

"I am looking forward to the next two years because we're going to do great things together," I told thousands of people during my inaugural remarks at the National Annual Meeting in New Orleans. Outgoing President Milton H. Ward and Chief Scout Executive Roy L. Williams officially welcomed me to my new post. Joining us via video was President George W. Bush, whose recorded message praised Americans' continued dedication to serving as Scout leaders across the country.

It was deeply meaningful to become president as the organization aggressively campaigned to make Scouting accessible to all children — rich or poor, urban or rural. As I made my inaugural speech, I was impassioned by my boyhood memory of seeing a Boy Scouts meeting, and concluding that any group with such a spiffy uniform was way out of my family's reach. Now, I had the power to prevent little boys from suffering that same self-rejection.

"I am proud of this movement," I told the crowd that included the Executive Board, dignitaries, parents, Scout leaders, Scouts and volunteers. "I am proud of our work for young people, and I am proud to serve as your president."

I was a natural fit because the Scouts' values echo my personal code of conduct.

"The mission of the Boy Scouts of America is to prepare young people to make ethical and moral choices over their lifetimes by instilling in them the values of the Scout Oath and Scout Law," according to Scouting.org. Each boy takes the Oath to follow Scout Law, which is this: "A Scout is trustworthy, loyal, helpful, friendly, courteous, kind, obedient, cheerful, thrifty, brave, clean, and reverent." I had been helping Scouts develop these qualities during my 35 years of service that included: serving on the Detroit Area Council's advisory board; working as vice president of Scouting's coed program, Venturing; and joining the National Executive Board in 1992.

My service had earned me the Boy Scouts of America's highest honor for outstanding volunteer service and unwavering commitment to helping young people succeed: the Silver Buffalo Award. I had also received the Silver Antelope Award, which recognizes extraordinary service on a regional level.

During my first year as president, I visited Scout councils all across America.

"Everywhere I've been, the support for Scouting has been overwhelming," I told the crowd at the National Annual Meeting in Philadelphia, Pennsylvania. "That's a credit to you, and I want to thank you for what you do for Scouting and for young people."

From the day I was appointed, I was inundated with support from important allies. My dear friend and longtime Scouting supporter George Francis III, senior vice president at Blue Cross Blue Shield of Michigan, was really moved and congratulated me. Likewise, the number two leader in the Morman Church, who is its current leader, approached me with a several members and said, "We like the way you manage. We've watched you. If you ever want any help, let us know." With this kind of support — along with parents and volunteers — I never had a bad day in Scouting.

One key responsibility was to implement the 2002-2005 National Strategic Plan. This four-year strategy encompassed five key areas: traditional unit and membership growth, Scoutreach, leadership, marketing and strategic positioning, and financial development. But I focused on something more basic, yet fleeting in our hectic lives: quality time with our young people.

"What every parent wants—and every child needs—is time," I said in remarks that are published on the Boy Scouts of America's website. "[But] more and more it seems the hands of the clock are pushing against young people." I added that Scouting "has a lot to offer children: leadership skills, values, character, fun, and so much more. But at its most basic level, Scouting is about time ... with a caring adult. That's part of the magic of Scouting. For at least an hour a week, boys have our undivided attention. And in that sacred period of time between a child and a caring parent or volunteer leader—whether it's over a service project, on a hike, making a pinewood derby car, or a simple lesson in knot-tying—that's where character is formed."

During my tenure, the controversy about openly gay Scout leaders and youth was boiling under the surface, and the Boy Scouts of America's legal team was working on it. Interestingly, no one ever verbally accosted me about the organization's refusal to allow openly gay adults to become Scout leaders. Nor was I asked my opinion about the organization's prohibition against openly gay adults in such roles. In January of 2014, the organization lifted the rule that denied openly gay boys membership in Boy Scouts of America. Openly gay adults, however, remain banned from membership.

Had I been asked, my response would have been that I am pro-gay and-lesbian. People should do what they want, as long as they don't bother me. However, we conducted three surveys during my tenure that showed 78 percent to 84 percent of parents declared that if gays were allowed to become Scout leaders, they would withdraw their children from Boy Scouts of America.

At the same time, recruiting new members was a major priority. In January of 2003, we launched a national, six-month campaign called "Character Connections—Reaching Youth with Scouting" to partner with religious and community organizations. I introduced it by co-hosting a national videoconference with National Commissioner Rick Cronk and Chief Scout Executive Roy L. Williams that was broadcast to Boy Scouts groups across America, providing an inspiring message from President George W. Bush, as well as testimonials and commentaries.

As part of this endeavor, we set recruitment goals for the Boy Scouts of America's four regions to add 1,082,134 new members by the end of 2004. I was especially motivated to increase membership after our survey showed that 60 percent of parents had not considered enrolling their children because they had simply never been asked. In addition, a startling 88 percent of non-Scouting parents said that no one had ever talked with them about getting their children to participate in Scouting.

"We have to ask," I announced, "and we have to ask effectively."

Another priority for me echoed a motivation that drove my management style in the plants at General Motors: boosting quality scores. I am quoted in the article in Scouting's online magazine as saying: "In 2003, we had only 59 percent of our Scouting units achieve the Quality Unit Award, and only 38 percent of our direct contact leaders were trained."

My presidential term ended when I passed the baton to my successor at the National Annual Meeting in Chicago. I have remained active, serving as honorary vice president in 2012. Today, I continue to serve the Boy Scouts of America as a member of the National Executive Board.

FIFTEEN

Roy Roberts: Emergency Manager for Detroit Public Schools

Maureen and I purchased a serene retreat in Scottsdale, Arizona, where we play golf, socialize with friends and family, and truly enjoy retirement. Our lovely 5,800 square-foot home in an exclusive golf community celebrates the American Southwest's sand-colored, adobe architecture. We have a large, infinity-edge pool amongst multiple outdoor living spaces that offer spectacular views of the golf course and the mountainous terrain of the High Sonoran Desert. Our guests are close friends and family, and we maintain a low-key, relaxing lifestyle in Scottsdale. We remain true to the purpose of that home: relaxing.

In early 2011, we were at our home in Scottsdale, golfing, spending time with our grandchildren, relaxing by our swimming pool, and enjoying dinners at the country club.

"Roy, this is Richard Baird calling," said the man on a voicemail message. "I'm Special Assistant to Michigan Governor Rick Snyder. I'm calling because the governor would like to meet with you. Detroit Public Schools Emergency Manager Robert Bobb will be leaving, and the governor would like to talk with you about this."

I listened to the message, then went golfing. Rick Snyder was an accomplished, millionaire businessman and Republican who had recently become Michigan's forty-eighth governor on January 1, 2011. I was extremely impressed with his inaugural pledge to use "Relentless Positive Action" to reinvent economically battered Michigan—which had suffered one of America's highest unemployment rates during the Recession. His goal was to create good jobs, improve the education system, and overhaul government to serve Michigan's ten million residents.

A top priority was to fix the public school system. As private investors revitalized downtown Detroit to create a vibrant, world-class metropolis, young professionals were moving back into the city. But the deplorable public school system has been a persistent deterrent to attracting the demographic to sustain Detroit's future: young, upwardly mobile families.

Detroit had suffered one of America's most dramatic population losses in history — 61 percent — after plunging from a high of 1.8 million in 1950 to about 701,000 in 2010, according to the U.S. Census. Unfortunately, the financial crises afflicting the auto industry drove the depopulation of Michigan, the only state to lose residents between 2000 and 2010, according to U.S. Census statistics.

People left Michigan because they could not find work in the sputtering auto industry. This helped push the Motor City toward bankruptcy and devastated Detroit Public Schools, which deteriorated behind a revolving door of nine superintendents and emergency managers. As a result, one hundred school buildings were empty in Detroit. Ravaged by strippers and covered in graffiti, these architectural gems became dangerous eyesores that worsened Detroit's globally notorious blight problem.

Meanwhile, the population drain was pulling ten thousand students from Detroit Public Schools *every year*. The school's deficit became so dire, that in March of 2009, when 85,000 students attended 172 schools, Democratic Governor Jennifer Granholm appointed Robert Bobb, a New Orleans native, former president of the Washington, D.C. board of education, and longtime Washington city manager, as Emergency Financial Manager of Detroit Public Schools.

Bobb's appointment sparked outrage, protests and death threats from Detroiters who claimed that white state officials were taking over the mostly black district. In addition, Bobb's $425,000 annual salary drew accusations that he took the job for the money, not to help the kids.

During his first year, the district's deficit spiked from $219 million to $363 million. Bobb closed dozens of schools. His attempt to consolidate others sparked fears of violence by mixing gang rivals from warring neighborhoods. He fired teachers, tried to eliminate music, and hired expensive consultants. In March of 2011, Michigan Governor Rick Snyder needed to replace him with someone who could mastermind a dramatic turnaround for Detroit Public Schools.

Five days after Richard Baird's call, I was contacted by Darrell Burks, a CPA who worked for PricewaterhouseCoopers and is a friend of Richard Baird and Governor Snyder.

"Roy, the governor thinks you would be ideal for this leadership role," Darrell said.

Intrigued, I took Richard Baird's second call. "Roy, can you come back to Michigan and meet with the governor?"

When I met with Governor Snyder in his conference room in the Capitol Building in Lansing, he entered two minutes late — then apologized profusely. I am a stickler for punctuality; one of my favorite "Roy-isms" is that: "Early is on time. On time is late." Tardiness disrespects the person who's waiting — and the subject matter. So, Governor Snyder's regret for tardiness impressed me.

The meeting began, with Michigan State Treasurer Andy Dillon joining us.

"Michigan runs through Detroit," the governor said, "and if I can't turn Detroit around, I'll never re-invent Michigan. The biggest single problem I have is Detroit Public Schools. The kids in Detroit are not being educated. Finances are turned upside down. And I can't send a white guy down there to fix it."

"You're right," I said.

"I can't pay you what you're worth," Governor Snyder said.

"You're right again," I said in jest. "Want to go for a trifecta?"

As the meeting continued, Governor Snyder and the Treasurer made it clear that they were committed to improving education for Detroit and Michigan by implementing innovative strategies. Their apparently genuine commitment excited me. After I shared some opinions and ideas, the Treasurer said, "Roy, we're talking to you about the wrong job. You should take over the City and be Emergency Manager of Detroit."

"Not me!" I exclaimed. "And whoever takes it over, they better do that job correctly, and they better leave town when it's over."

I steered the discussion back to Detroit Public Schools. Governor Snyder and Treasurer Dillon described the mission that would take me out of retirement for one year. As they spoke, I contemplated that I was at a stage of my life where I did not need money. I was free to do anything I pleased if my wife agreed to do it as well. I also reflected on my father's prophecy: "You're going to get a good education. You're going to be somebody. And you're going to help other people."

This opportunity would bring my life full circle, by integrating my father's directive into one powerful endeavor to help mankind by giving the 65,000 young people in Detroit Public Schools a better chance at life.

Back in Arizona, I shared Governor Snyder's proposal with Maureen. Interestingly, she and I had a relatively short conversation.

First, we agreed that I was healthy and that we had always believed in the importance of education. Second, we were disturbed by Detroit's 70 percent drop-out rate, abysmal standardized test scores, and the fact that less than TWO PERCENT of students were considered college-ready, according to a *Detroit Free Press* report. This was robbing the children of a future, and handicapping the city's future workforce. In the global marketplace, our kids would get eaten alive by their peers from countries that provided excellent schooling for all children.

"Who are we to say, 'We have ours and you people better get yours the best way you can?'" I asked hypothetically.

268

Maureen and I announced our $1.1 million gift to the Detroit Institute
of Arts for the establishment of the Maureen and Roy S. Roberts
Gallery of Contempory African American Art in May 2011.
Photo courtesy of the Detroit Institute of Arts

Maureen and I agreed that I should take the job, even though it
would require major personal sacrifices: spending less time with our
grandchildren, and leaving retirement in sunny Scottsdale to work
through Michigan's grim winter.

Plus, this job was dangerous. After death threats, my predecessor had three bodyguards and a driver. I was advised to have a
bodyguard and a driver, and to wear body flak.

Still, Maureen and I concluded that helping the children out-
weighed the risks. "If we can help," Maureen said, "We have to go
help. You can't have thousands of kids who are not being educated.
We have received a lot of help along the way. It's time to give back."

"Then let's do it," I said.

Next, I told Governor Snyder and Richard Baird: "I would be
honored to serve as the Emergency Manager of Detroit Public
Schools."

However, I had one caveat: to keep my decision it secret because
Maureen and I were going to make a historic announcement that we

did not want overshadowed. It would show the community that Roy Roberts was not becoming the Emergency Manager of Detroit Public Schools because he needed the $250,000 salary. I wanted everyone to know that my motive was altruistic: to help the children.

The DIA: A Convergence Of Philanthropy, Art and History

In early 2011, Maureen and I were attending a gala at the Detroit Institute of Arts. We were chatting with my dear friend, Nettie Seabrooks, who was executive adviser to the DIA's director.

"Nettie," I said, "I told somebody I wanted to donate some money, and they never called me back."

Nettie shared my dismay. "Roy, you're aware that GM has the General Motors Center for African American Art in the DIA. It has four sections, and the largest and best section is available."

That piqued my interest. Maureen and I love art; we display many beautiful paintings and sculptures in our home.

"You ought to acquire that gallery," Nettie said. "Following your career at GM, it would be a perfect, natural fit for you."

This idea also intrigued Maureen. She had served as co-chair for the DIA's annual gala fundraiser, Under the Stars. She had also served for many years on the DIA's Volunteer Information Committee.

Later, Maureen and I discussed Nettie's proposal. We concurred that philanthropy had always been one of our top priorities. Most recently, we had been major contributors to a campaign to rescue Detroit's celebrated Charles H. Wright Museum of African American History. We were proud to help the world's largest museum of its kind remain open after a financial crisis threatened to close it. Likewise, over the years, we had donated generously to the United Negro College Fund, the NAACP, the National Urban League, Western Michigan University and many endeavors.

Maureen and I agreed that we often saw no tangible results of where the money went or how it was used. However, having our names on a gallery in one of the world's most prestigious museums would enable our children and grandchildren to see our contributions well after our deaths.

"Let's do it," we agreed after visiting the gallery at the DIA. Nettie arranged for Maureen and I to meet Rosemarie Gleeson, the DIA's Major Gifts Officer.

On Tuesday, May 3, 2011, the DIA announced that we donated $1.1 million to create the Maureen and Roy S. Roberts Gallery of Contemporary African American Art. As part of the GM collection that exhibits modern and contemporary African American art, our gallery showcases works by prominent artists who include Benny Andrews, Elizabeth Catlett, Sam Gilliam, Alvin Loving, William T. Williams, Joyce Scott, Richard Hunt, Charles McGee.

We were naïve about the historic and pioneering magnitude of this undertaking. Though many African Americans, such as comedian Bill Cosby, have impressive art collections, we became the only black couple in the United States to have an art gallery of this size and stature named for us. This endeavor highlights my motto, "Always the first, never the last." I hope that our donation inspires other African Americans to follow suit.

My family was among the one hundred guests at a reception as we unveiled the collection.

"I can't tell this august body anything," I told them. "You're all accomplished. I want to talk to my family and I want you to bear with me and listen." I faced my six grandsons and said, "You have to get the best education possible. After that, you have to work hard. There are no silver bullets, no shortcuts. And when you rise high enough to where you can help others, you have to help the community." My grandsons listened with rapt attention.

Gethered for our family's DIA announcement were Maureen and I (seated),
and (standing L-R) son Ronald Roberts and his wife Cynthia Roberts,
daughter Robin Rene Huff and her husband Roger Huff,
and son Ricky Roberts.

This experience thrilled Maureen. During her years of volunteering
at the DIA, black students often approached her and asked, "Why
don't any black people do anything to support art and artists?"
Now, our gallery shows our grandchildren and the world that black
artists do, in fact, create beautiful art that is supported by philan-
thropic African Americans.

Three months later, Maureen and I were honored at the DIA's
Forty-Seventh Annual Bal Africain Gala, a fundraiser hosted by the
DIA's Friends of African and African American Art. The museum
was transformed into a Caribbean paradise. As we dined and
danced amongst dignitaries, business and civic leaders, it was a joy
for us to receive this honor.

Public Announcement of My Appointment as DPS Emergency Manager

One day after our DIA gift was made public, Michigan Governor Rick Snyder announced that he had appointed me as the Emergency Manager for Detroit Public Schools. Media packed the press conference in his Detroit office on May 4, 2011.

This was huge news, and my phone blew up! Friends were calling, almost in a panic: "Roy, have you lost your mind?" A good 20 percent of these individuals were worried about my mental state. Others made it clear that trying to save DPS was like re-arranging deck chairs on the Titanic. Why try to rescue something that was doomed to crash and sink?

Because those 65,000 kids in Detroit deserved a good education. And Roy Roberts was ready to help create a prototype for re-inventing and revitalizing public school education across America. The governor believed I could do it. The U.S. Secretary of Education believed I could do it. And most importantly, I believed I could do it.

Right-Size Roberts Comes Full Circle

When I officially began my term on May 16, 2011, I reported to Cadillac Place, the former General Motors Headquarters building on West Grand Boulevard in Detroit's New Center district. After GM bought Detroit's downtown Renaissance Center complex in 1996 and moved its headquarters there, the former GM building was renamed and the State of Michigan moved in several of its agencies.

You'll recall that West Grand Boulevard was where I had stood — as GM's vice president of Personnel Administration and Development — during a 1988 *Wall Street Journal* interview, as I coined the term "right size" and my nickname, "Right Size Roberts," came into being. How ironic that I was returning to the same street to "right-size" Detroit Public Schools, change the culture, and transform the district into a shining star of urban education.

"You're not an educator!" critics protested. "What are you doing in this job?"

My response was that education is a business, and the two are so alike, it's unreal. If you have a quality problem, you look at the data. If you have a non-performance problem, you look at the data. The problems arise when people fail to follow the data. Follow the data and you'll fix the problems in Ford, General Motors and the school system as well. As I analyzed the problems in Detroit Public Schools, my experience at Lear, and GM and Navistar helped me to develop strategies to fix all of those problems.

Therefore, anyone who wondered why the governor had anointed a retired automotive executive with carte blanche to do whatever he pleased to improve Detroit's schools, my answer was that Rick Snyder knew exactly what he was doing. He was doing the same for Michigan. The millionaire who once chaired the board of directors for the Gateway computer company, had also founded a venture capital company. Now he was applying his business skills to government to improve the state's economy.

Two months before I was sworn in, Governor Snyder signed Michigan's Public Act 4 of 2011, the Local Government and School District Fiscal Accountability Act. The law ramped up 1988 laws that allowed the governor to appoint emergency managers who had the power to break union contracts, fire elected officials and privatize or sell public assets.

"I came here under Public Act 4," I told four hundred leaders from business, government, the community and the media at the *Michigan Chronicle's* popular Pancakes & Politics Breakfast on June 23, 2011, at the Detroit Athletic Club. "I could have gotten rid of all labor contracts. I could have gotten rid of the school board, slash and burn, but I didn't. That's not what I came to do."

I reiterated that I came to ensure that Detroit children received quality educations, with at least a 90 percent graduation rate and a 90 percent college placement rate, while also restoring the district to fiscal stability and balance.

"Superman's not comin'," I told the crowd. "But I would have to put forth a superhuman effort. I knew it was a bad situation, but I was literally shocked to witness the rampant chaos that reigned in Detroit Public Schools.

It was unbelievable! And it was no secret.

Shortly before I took the job, U.S. Education Secretary Arne Duncan called Detroit Public Schools "Ground Zero for education in this country" at the 2011 Education Summit in the Los Angeles. When he was appointed in 2009, Duncan said, he lost sleep over Detroit's "devastating" drop-out rate. America had a "moral obligation" to provide our boys and girls with a quality education, he said, expressing optimism that Detroit could surpass the progress that New Orleans public schools had enjoyed during revitalization following Hurricane Katrina.

During the 1950s, Detroit Public Schools were praised as stellar, one of the most exemplary public education systems in the nation.

An Action Plan Focused on Accountability

My remedy for the Detroit Public Schools' chronic lack of financial accountability was to implement a Zero Based Budgeting plan. If we took in $1, we spent $1, not $1.50, as had been the practice that spawned a crippling $327 million deficit.

Making matters worse, non-financial people were managing the district's $1.2 billion annual budget. Rampant corruption in the school system — Detroit's the biggest employer — included employees setting up businesses inside Detroit Public Schools, hiring unqualified friends and relatives, and awarding lucrative, unnecessary contracts.

To my dismay, people tried to continue this when I took office by saying, "Roy, I'm black. Can I get a job?" On my second day, a prestigious, accomplished professional said, "Roy, feed the herd!" That meant, "Give people jobs." One minister tried to sell me his churches' goods and services. I refused! The money was for the children, no one else.

As this behavior had persisted under prior leadership, the elected School Board members had played to the voters — not to the kids. As a result, administrators, teachers and students suffered in chaos, crime, crumbling buildings, bathrooms that lacked soap and toilet paper, classrooms without books, school offices and district head-quarters lacking technology for proper record-keeping, horrible morale, and a terrible attendance rate — 55 percent on the first day of school!

It was the worst, most shocking institution I had ever seen in my professional life. For example, systems were nonexistent for Human Resources and Finance. People in those areas were working with pencils and paper! The district was too bankrupt to purchase up-to-date computers. This invited rampant human errors and corruption. Procurement, for example, was an open sieve for thieves. Abysmal or non-existent record-keeping provided no accountability for huge sums paid to employees and for unnecessary contracts.

To stop this financial hemorrhaging, I cancelled every contract that DPS had with outside contractors because the numbers were all wrong. Many were written when the district had 150,000 students. Now we had less than half that, so the district was paying more than double what it needed for services and supplies!

To right-size our expenditures, I teamed up with brilliant CPA Darrell Burks, senior partner at PricewaterhouseCoopers. I ordered that all contracts be rebid to accurately address the district's current needs. That immediately saved $44 million dollars.

Additional Cost-Cutting and Team-Building Measures

I also had to right-size Human Resources, which was in complete disarray. When I came on board, thirty people reported to me. Half were contract employees. They included nine people in top academic and financial positions who were working part-time and getting paid full-time! It was outrageous!

With Darrell Burks' help, I eliminated these contract employees, saving the district $14 million. Then I needed to assemble a talented team that was as fast-moving and committed to helping the kids as I was. Sadly, DPS employees were incredibly downtrodden. My goal was to give people a chance to be successful. This epitomized one of my favorite Roy-isms: "When you find people who can leap tall buildings, don't step on their capes!"

I legitimized the Procurement & Logistics Department by hiring a woman who had provided exceptional service for Ford, GM and a global pharmaceutical company. She introduced a top-notch system at DPS that ensured efficient ordering and purchasing of quality goods and services while eliminating extraneous expenses and employees. This would save more than $5 million as of Fiscal Year 2013. My overhaul of the Procurement & Logistics Department was a prototype for improving every area of the district.

Technology was one especially crucial area. I hired a talented woman who introduced a technology program to streamline the entire system, including Finance and Human Resources. Her work was key in getting the business systems right as I shrunk and reorganized the staff.

She exemplified how I utilized my HR experience at GM by matching people's skill sets with the best jobs. I fired unnecessary people. Then I elevated smart, dedicated people to leadership positions. I made each person aware of goals, responsibilities and accountabilities. After that, I had people double up in jobs. For example, Gwen DeYoung headed Labor and Human Resources. As an incentive, I offered a quarterly stipend until I hired someone to take over the second job.

I received the shock of my life when I walked through DPS-owned office space that epitomized astounding waste. Years ago, the school board purchased four floors in the Fisher Building in Detroit's midtown. With its trademark gold roof, this celebrated tower houses the Fisher Theatre, which features traveling Broadway shows such as *The Lion King* and *Fiddler on the Roof* The thirty-story building — across West Grand Boulevard from the State of Michigan offices — also contains restaurants and office space.

Unfortunately, the school board paid more for those six floors than the property's owner, The Farbman Group, paid for the entire building! This was flagrant waste! Plus, the layout was horrible and the space was piled with boxes, or empty. Even more unbelievable, I found $20 million worth of computers and equipment in the basement. It was enough to run the entire city! (Kevyn Orr, who served as Detroit Emergency Manager, later identified the city's outmoded technology and lack thereof as Detroit's Achilles heel).

District management had failed to relocate employees to the Fisher Building. Instead, DPS employees were scattered in four buildings on three blocks. To create a cohesive, efficient workforce, I upgraded the facilities with new paint and carpeting, and moved everyone into the Fisher building. This cost $1.7 million, which saved the district $2.2 million per year in perpetuity. Uniting the staff facilitated a better information exchange, effective problem-solving and higher morale.

As I gained momentum, I expanded my staff. I appointed DPS graduate, teacher and longtime administrator Karen Ridgeway as my Superintendent of Academics. She continues to thrive in that position today. I selected Kevin Smith, an outstanding attorney with an impressive background in politics, city government and law, as my chief of staff. For my general counsel, I chose Jean-Vierre Adams, who had worked at the prestigious Detroit law firm, Miller, Canfield, Paddock and Stone PLC.

Key Meetings Intensify My Urgency to Succeed

This was the toughest job I'd ever had, in part because I often felt I was fighting everybody. Several meetings early in my tenure provided jarring reminders that I had committed to a colossal, seemingly impossible challenge.

One of those meetings was with Governor Snyder. Early on, I was convinced that a number of leaders in government, business and the civic arena wanted to implode Detroit Public Schools. They were tired of the school system's poor performance, and were convinced that it could not be fixed.

Detroiter magazine, a publication of the Detroit Regional Chamber, featured me on the cover of its September 2011 issue, which focused on reform of Detroit Public Schools.

This was déjà-vu for that 1986 day when I concluded that GM had sent me to Tarrytown to shut the plant down. Similarly, the 65,000 children in DPS would not lose their school system under my watch! I called the governor's chief of staff and demanded a meeting with the governor.

"Look, this is crazy!" I said. "You want me to run the school system, but you don't really want me to do it, because it's public education."

I had reached this boiling point because the governor, his chief of staff and other members of his team were touting the virtues of charter schools. They had removed the limit on the number of charter schools that a district could have, which

279

signaled a trend for exponential expansion into that direction of education.

"Detroit didn't ask for an unlimited number of charter schools controlled by outside entities," I said. "They ultimately won't help Detroit. Bloomfield Hills, Birmingham and Troy asked for that because Detroit had the schools. Detroit had the kids, and they wanted them."

I was not going to allow capitalistic scavengers to come in and profit on Detroit's children!

"Where in the hell is the money going to go for charter schools?" I demanded. "Follow the money trail! It's going right up to those wealthy, white suburban communities! It's not going to stay in our community. Name the last time white people wanted to save black people. That's a bunch of bullshit!"

The governor tried to explain. "Roy—"

"No, no, that's where I am!" I exclaimed. "Every time I make a move in Detroit Public Schools and improve it, they change the goal line. So I don't understand this ball game!"

That ended the meeting. I returned to my office on the fourteenth floor of the Fisher Building and dictated to my first chief of staff, Bob Boik, a letter for the governor and his people. In it, I detailed every point that I had made in that meeting.

"Tell me which part of this is wrong," I challenged in writing. "I need to be correct. If I'm wrong, tell me which part is wrong."

I never heard a response. I was right, no question about it. After that, monthly meetings with the governor and his team enabled me to showcase everything that I was doing to resuscitate DPS. I was tough-minded and action-oriented. I didn't care what anyone thought, or what their motives were. I just kept my nose to the grind until they finally started to realize:

"This guy is going to save this school district!"

The State Board of Education affirmed that I was steering DPS toward success by complimenting our work.

But another tense meeting occurred three weeks into the job, when Darrell Burks and I met with State Treasurer Andy Dillon and his top two lieutenants at the Detroit Athletic Club.

"I'm not going to say a word," Darrell said beforehand. "I'm going to let them do all the talking."

When we entered the meeting room, they were sitting at a table with their attaché cases before them; one had his feet on the table.

"You've got a deficit problem," Andy said tersely. "What are you guys going to do about it?"

"We've been on the job a day," I quipped. "We've barely learned where the bathroom is."

"We have an urgent need to address this deficit problem," Andy said.

Darrell immediately answered, "I think we can eliminate $200 million by reducing long term bonds to pay off the short term note at one half of the interest rate and save debt service."

"That's not true," Andy snapped.

Darrell Burks is not one to challenge on who's the smartest when it comes to financial matters. If you do, he's going to keep you around for awhile. When Darrell got through with them about what they should have been doing and had not done, we had some new friends. They really worked with us after that.

Another time, I had the coldest meeting ever with Michigan Senator Phil Pavlov. Chairman of the Senate Education Committee, Pavlov was spearheading reform of the state's public education system and the governor's staff recommended that I meet with him.

He glared at me as if he wanted to say, *Yeah, scumbag, what do you want?* in his office with my communications person and his assistant. The senator's demeanor reminded me that some state leadership wanted me to "blow up" Detroit Public Schools and replace DPS with charter schools.

Undaunted by Senator Pavlov's hostility, I enthusiastically described the aggressive actions we were taking to improve Detroit Public Schools. With each point, I inched closer to him at the other side of the table. Before I finished with him, I was in his face, and he gave me his business card with his cell phone number on it. We've been friends ever since.

Darrell and I had another tense meeting with eight members of the Michigan State Board of Education. For two hours, they ranted about how horrible Detroit schools are, and how the leadership was not cooperative with the state. All I could do was sit there and cry inside.

"What do you think?" Darrell asked me afterward, in private.

"The people we just left are right," I answered, "and my people are wrong."

I called a meeting that night for DPS leadership. I relayed everything that I had heard, silencing anyone's attempt to give a retort.

"Each and every one of you is going to operate with the highest level of professionalism or you're going to leave here," I announced. "I want you to work and be proud of yourselves and what you've done, so the kids can be proud of you. When you ladies go to the beauty shop, I want you to hear people saying good things about you and Detroit Public Schools."

Introducing the Education Achievement Authority

A few weeks into the job, I joined Governor Snyder and U.S. Education Secretary Arne Duncan to announce a bold new concept to reinvent and rescue public education across America. The Education Achievement Authority mirrors the same coalition-building, culture-changing, restructuring strategies that I had implemented to achieve unprecedented successes at General Motors.

"To get this right has the potential to be a model not just for the city, not just for the state, but for the entire country," U.S. Education Secretary Arne Duncan said via Skype from Washington, D.C., during the June 20, 2011, press conference with school administrators, community members and media at Detroit's Renaissance High School.

"We're not fighting just to save children and save the public school system," he added. "We're fighting to save the city of Detroit." He said the EAA could reverse the "massive exodus out of Detroit," adding, "I think you'll see a massive influx of families back into Detroit," and that the EAA could be "an amazing economic development tool for the city."

Though he called Detroit "the bottom of the barrel in terms of education," he said it could "be leading the country as a model of education reform and as a model of achievement."

That invigorated me, and I loved having the power to make that happen.

"I'm appointing Roy Roberts to chair the executive committee of this new (Education Achievement) Authority," Governor Snyder announced. "He'll have the Emergency Manager role for Detroit Public Schools, as well as chair of this executive committee."

Governor Snyder explained that the EAA is an inter-local agreement between Eastern Michigan University and Detroit Public Schools. It allows two governmental entities to form a third, separate entity called the EAA. It would oversee the lowest-performing 5 percent of Detroit's schools, forty-five in all, offering: longer school days and school years; principals empowered to hire and train teachers; principals and teachers held accountable for student performance; a challenging curriculum; high expectations for student achievement; more resources in the classrooms; academic success that attracts and retains students and families in Detroit; and more parental input, through a Parents Advisory Council at each school.

While only 55 percent of school funding reached the classroom now, Governor Snyder announced that the EAA would aim to get 95 percent of funding to the classroom level. It would begin as a pilot program for the 2012-2013 school year.

"This system is broken," I said. "And I can't fix it. You can't fix it. We've got to do something different. So today we change the game. Today we announce a new system that drives vastly more resources into the classroom, offers more school autonomy and increases student performance."

The Michigan Chronicle covered the press conference with a two-page report called "A Giant Step for DPS: Why saving children in poor performing schools matters." It quoted me in large print:

"Every time I walk through these several communities and I see little brown, black and white children not being properly educated, I see myself when I was a child. This is really important. This is my life's work, as far as I'm concerned."

I explained that the EAA could help me achieve my goal of making 100 percent of Detroit students college- and career-ready, and to ensure that 100 percent of third graders were reading at grade level. The EAA was one strategy in my two-pronged plan to use bonds to eliminate the deficit within five years, while educating the kids *first* on our way to achieving that goal.

For the next year, the executive committee — comprised of appointees who included civic, business, community and religious leaders — would plan how the EAA would operate. We agreed that any school that showed dramatic progress would return to the traditional public school system.

Understanding High Student Absenteeism and No-Show Parents

Detroit kids lapsed into a ritual of skipping school in September. The state required 75 percent minimum attendance for the district to receive full state aid. But in September of 2011, the first back-to-school season of my tenure, the 55 percent attendance rate prompted the state to withhold $25 million from DPS!

We negotiated with them, and they reduced the charge to $7 million. That was still too much — $7 million worth of books, school supplies or computer equipment that our students would not receive.

I set a major goal to boost enrollment numbers for September 2012. To solve the problem, we had to understand it. Though DPS had doctors, lawyers and PhDs, we remained baffled, frustrated and even angry about why kids would not attend the first few weeks of the school year.

"Let's gather all the student council leaders from each school in one spot," I proposed to my team, "so five or six of us can meet with the kids."

We did, and the students eagerly and honestly ticked down a long list of reasons why kids skip school. For critics who believed kids just didn't care about getting their education, they were dead wrong.

"Momma didn't get her ADC check," one student said, "and I didn't have clean clothes, so I didn't go to school."

I was embarrassed. This reason had not crossed my mind. But it was so prevalent, several schools had purchased washing machines so that students could wash their clothes. We ended up buying more washing machines to help more schools address this problem.

We also heard stories about destitute parents working two and three jobs, preventing them from meeting with teachers, attending parent-teacher conferences or helping kids with assignments. Some parents were illiterate and, because they were embarrassed, they hid that from their kids. Some students even asked us to include in our Strategic Plan a class to teach their parents how to be parents. These kids were dealing with horrible conditions at home, all related to poverty, hunger, abuse, crime, addiction, unemployment and the plethora of problems that stem from those tragic circumstances.

I'll share the story about an incorrigible kid who was going to get kicked out of school.

"Let's find out what's wrong," I cautioned. Administrators had called the child's mother to school on four occasions to discuss the student's bad behavior. She never made it. So we visited her home. She was twenty-eight years old, and had this kid when she was fourteen, then two more children. Unmarried, she worked two part-time jobs. Every time she attempted to come to school, her old car broke down. To school officials, it appeared that she didn't show up because she didn't care. Quite the contrary. Our response was, don't expel the child. Work with the student to address the problem.

That was not an isolated story. It fueled my outrage toward critics who said Detroit parents didn't care about their children earning a good education.

Recognizing Good Educators, Confronting a Broken System

It also angered me when people blamed the district's problems on teachers, by calling them apathetic toward whether the children learned, attended school or graduated. Any teachers who were still in the Detroit school system — after not getting a raise for ten years — were clearly there for one reason: they cared about the kids!

"We believe there's a war on children, a war on education," many teachers told me. "And we refuse to give up on the kids. We're going to keep fighting to help them get the educations they deserve." These devoted teachers were so generous and compassionate, they spent their own money on the kids and on supplies.

Unfortunately, these teachers were caught in a broken system with terrible leadership. The head of the School Board had done despicable things that landed in a courtroom. Board Members fought, ostracized parents and community members on live television, and took limousines to eat chicken dinners.

Meanwhile, the majority of the teachers and principals were good. Some were outstanding. Some were bad. Because it was my moral obligation to put a qualified teacher in front of every student, we purged the system of hundreds of teachers and several principals. That, like every single action that I took in that job, was motivated by one question: "How do you improve life for these kids, provide a quality education, and prepare them for college and careers?" Anything or anyone that did not help me achieve that goal was eliminated.

Therefore, since Michigan law endowed me with total authority to run the school district, I cancelled labor agreements if we could not reach an agreement. Then I imposed labor agreements on all of our unions, in the process removing rigid work schedules and anything else from our teachers' contracts that impeded a teacher from doing his or her job.

This sparked fury. The national president of the American Federation of Teachers demanded to meet with me. When she and her team came to my office in the Fisher Building, hundreds of protesters crammed the parking lot, holding signs and beating drums. After she gave me a thorough "who do you think you are!" scolding, I simply handed her the contract. To this day, it's still in place!

Unfortunately, I had to use my authority under Public Act 4 to impose a 10 percent pay cut on the district's ten thousand district employees — including myself. When the teachers' contracts expired on June 30, 2011, I tried to negotiate a new contract with the American Federation of Teachers. One of my enticements was that when we beat the budget, I would give 2 percent of the money back before Christmas. At first, the teachers' union refused to accept it. They would not even talk to me about it.

"School's about to start," I said. "Teachers are upset. They've had no raises for ten years tomorrow. If you don't make an agreement with me, tomorrow at 8 a.m., I'm going to give the money back to the teachers and you get no credit!"

That got their attention.

"When we save $5 million," I vowed, "I'll give 10 percent back to the teachers." We made the announcement and people received their money before Christmas. They were thrilled! This simple act boosted morale and reflected what I had learned at Tarrytown: it's about the people.

Unfortunately, the teacher's union sued me and State Treasurer Andy Dillon on behalf of three union locals affected by the contract. The following March, Federal Judge George Steeh settled the case, awarding the workers a 2.5 percent pay bonus that year.

All the while, I refused to get sidetracked by criticism, such as when the district purchased a new Chevy Tahoe for me to do my job. The previous vehicle, a 2005 Chrysler Durango, had broken down during a recent trip to the annual policy conference on Mackinac Island. It had 111,000 miles and was in total disrepair; fixing it cost one thousand dollars. My retort to critics was that the new vehicle would save the district money by eliminating costly repairs and breakdowns that prevented me from doing my job in a timely fashion.

I enjoyed an extremely proud moment in education, eight months into my tenure as the Detroit Public Schools Emergency

Manager. I was invited to speak at the December commencement for Michigan State University, where I addressed undergraduates from the colleges of Agriculture and Natural Resources, Communication Arts and Sciences, Engineering, Natural Science and Nursing, as well as Lyman Briggs College. Awarded an honorary doctorate of business, I was in good company: also speaking that day was *Detroit Free Press* Columnist Mitch Albom, author of the best-selling memoir *Tuesdays with Morrie*.

Calling On Ministers for Help

If you want to know who holds the power in the black community, go to church. The ministers run our community, because they are viewed as respected leaders whose word about any issue can persuade masses of people. Therefore, Maureen and I invited 71 ministers and their wives to our home to enlist their help in saving Detroit Public Schools.

Our guests knew me only as a prominent General Motors executive. When I described my background, they were shocked that I had been poor, on welfare, and well-versed with the ways of ghetto street life.

"This guy knows how to cry," one minister exclaimed.

"We didn't know your story!" another minister said in awe. "Why didn't you tell us all that?"

"We saw you as the face of General Motors," someone added. "Now we see a man who's more like the community you're serving than most people know."

The ministers' and first ladies' warm acceptance convinced me that they viewed me as an ally, and they wanted to serve in the same capacity for me. First, the wives gave me an award for my efforts with DPS. That garnered positive attention in the media and amongst their congregations where DPS families attended. Then they led the "First Ladies — First Day!" campaign by visiting churches to spread the word about attending school. They also showed up on the first day of school to greet students and parents.

"It is not cool to skip school!" ministers proclaimed from their pulpits. "Without an education, you will get nowhere in life!" They praised me as a passionate leader who was working hard to improve the district. "Now you have to do your part," the ministers said, "by making sure our young people show up to receive the education that Roy Roberts is trying to provide."

Other efforts included DPS' first-ever open enrollment in March of 2012 to allow parents to select schools early. In August, parent organizations knocked on the doors of 2,000 families affected by school transitions and mergers to answer questions and encourage children to attend school. In addition, I held a back-to-school parade and made media commercials encouraging Detroit students to attend school in September.

Two-Year Results: Improved Public Perception of DPS, Tangible Signs of Progress and Hope

After I had served my one-year term as Emergency Manager for Detroit Public Schools, Governor Snyder appointed me to a second, one-year term. While I was being sworn in, the governor's team provided a document that said: "City of Detroit Emergency Manager."

"Guys!" I exclaimed. "I'm not doing that!"

The local and national media's daily chronicle of how I was turning around the system provided tangible evidence that I was making a difference. The community was beginning to believe that my reforms I could save DPS.

As a result — and I say this with the utmost humility — people began to treat me like a rock star. Wherever I went, people were complimentary, expressing their desire to help. These were some of the same people who had been critical and suspicious of my appointment. This turnaround in public sentiment made me really proud. This was the toughest — but most rewarding — job I had ever had.

In July of 2012, I presented the proposed budget for the 2012-13 school year. Very importantly, it was balanced, reducing overall expenditures by 25 percent, or \$250 million. It maintained class sizes for kindergarten through third grade. It also allocated academic resources for students in the district's ninety-eight schools.

This budget was based on enrollment of 51,927 students. The lower number was due to the fact that 11,020 students attended fifteen schools that were absorbed into the Education Achievement Authority and were no longer counted in the DPS system. I stressed our "relentless focus on accountability" and my commitment that, "we will never again accept failure as long as I'm leading this district." I listed exciting innovations for DPS: strong programs for science, technology, engineering and math; pre-algebra for seventh graders; nine languages, including sign language; Advanced Placement classes at every high school; music programs that included instruments, vocal and dance; and business partners that were providing reading and volunteers.

"Mr. Roberts, do you have any good news?" a reporter asked as I headed into a press conference at Ivan Ludington Magnet Middle School on September 6, 2012.

"It's my honor to report that Detroit Public Schools had reached nearly 85 percent attendance on the second day of the school year, which is unprecedented!" I said we were well above the state's required 75 percent attendance. Still, 8,000 students had not returned, so I issued a plea for parents to get their children to school, all day, every day, all year. Then I shared the exciting evidence that people were coming back to Detroit Public Schools: 860 students enrolled from outer district schools and 694 transferred from charter schools.

"When I put on my old historic automotive hat for a minute," I said, "that's like selling quality, new General Motors products to folks who previously owned Toyota products. There's nothing more exciting than convincing people that your product is the right product for them."

More good news: the district's sixteen new and renovated schools were at capacity and we put a cap on enrollment. Stunning renovations and new construction of school buildings, I said, "send a message to the kids that they're important and that education is important."

When a reporter asked what I tell parents about my commitment to DPS, I answered, "I was one of these kids once upon a time. My wife was one of these kids. We were poor. I didn't have books in my home, but along the way, I've gotten a lot of education and it made a difference in my life. My coming here wasn't a job. It was a personal commitment." I added, "The day I graduated from Western Michigan University, I couldn't attend graduation. I had to work. But I went to the highest point on campus and shouted at the top of my voice, 'Nobody is going to stop me from being successful!' These kids will do the same."

Nine Detroit Rising College Preparatory Schools promised to help them do that by grooming every student to graduate and attend college. These self-governing schools aimed for 90 percent of incoming ninth graders to graduate and head to college. This education model showed success quickly at the Benjamin Carson School of Science and Medicine. And Osborn High School had 100 percent of classified seniors admitted to a postsecondary institution.

Time to (Actually) Retire

After what felt like a nonstop race to save Detroit Public Schools, I crossed the finish line in the spring of 2013, and I was exhausted. The proverbial gold medal was U.S. Education Secretary Arne Duncan's declaration that Detroit was one of the most improved urban school districts in America.

At the same time, the data indicated that I had achieved a significant cultural change while building a sound, sustainable financial foundation to guarantee the district's future success.

We reduced the deficit from $327 million as of June 30, 2010, to $76 million on June 30, 2012. That was a 76 percent reduction! Then we established a three-year Deficit Elimination Plan, approved by the State of Michigan, to eradicate the $76 million deficit by Fiscal Year 2016. In addition, during my tenure, we provided the district with two consecutive years of balanced budgets and operating surpluses. The FY 2012 budget reduced total expenditures by 25 percent and directed 85 percent of resources to school and related resources and programming. My administration also completed an audit of financial statements on time and achieved the best outcome in decades, reducing findings by 33 percent.

Very importantly, academic achievement was on the rise. In March of 2013, I announced on NBC's Education Nation Detroit Summit that Detroit Public Schools had exceeded the Michigan average in fourteen of eighteen categories for the MEAP standardized test in the Fall of 2012. Flanked by EAA Chancellor John Covington and Detroit Parent Network President/CEO Sharlonda Buckman, my accounting of Detroit's educational progress impressed moderator Chelsea Clinton so much that she said she would consider sending her children to Detroit Public Schools.

Graduation rates increased to 64.74 percent— the highest since 2006. DPS bested the statewide graduation average by 3 percent. Five schools had graduation rates of 90 percent or higher. And thirteen schools surpassed the statewide graduation rate!

We improved school security, dramatically reducing serious on-campus incidents — arson, robberies, and concealed weapons incidents. Parental engagement in school programs and student activities soared, and 49% percent more parents attended parent-teacher conferences during my tenure than in prior years.

A few weeks before my contract expired on May 16, 2013, I announced that I would conclude my service as Emergency Manager for Detroit Public Schools.

"Detroiters and Michiganders alike can be thankful for Roy's leadership," Governor Snyder said. "He has been successful in restoring fiscal responsibility, including reducing spending, saving money and balancing budgets. Schools are safer, more parents are involved, attendance is up, test scores are improving across the board, and more seniors are graduating."

I stayed on board until Governor Snyder named my successor,

Jack Martin, a CPA experienced in presidential administrations. My duties officially ended on July 15, 2013.

Three days later, the city filed for bankruptcy. I was hopeful that Detroit Emergency Financial Manager Kevyn Orr would engineer a turnaround for Detroit that was as successful as the one that I had designed for Detroit Public Schools.

Respect and Laughter at a Roast & Toast

More than one hundred dignitaries, business leaders, government officials and school employees honored me at the Detroit Public Schools Foundation's Second Annual Roast & Toast at the Detroit Golf Club on September 26, 2013.

Dr. Glenda Price, President of the Detroit Public Schools Foundation, thanked the corporate sponsors, led by the Lear Corporation and Global Automotive Alliance. WDIV-TV News Anchor Rhonda Walker emceed as speakers confessed that they respected me too much to "roast" me.

"So I'm simply going to toast him," said Nettie Seabrooks, holding up a champagne glass as I sat in an armchair on stage near the podium. Applause punctuated her touching remarks about our symbiotic relationship as two of few blacks at GM during the 1980s.

My friend Detroit Mayor Dave Bing expressed similar admiration at the event, which far surpassed the Foundation's fundraising goals to benefit DPS, its authorized charter schools, and the EAA.

"When we see people like you every day," said Mayor Bing, who was dealing with the city's bankruptcy, "doing what you do, we can't give up."

He praised my rags-to-riches success story. "Roy comes from a tough, tough background… If you look at his ascendance… he was the top-ranking African American in the automobile industry… unparalleled at that time."

Mayor Bing continued: "He set the bar very high. It was more than just being a first. He pulled a lot of people along. Because I was a supplier for twenty-nine years in the industry, I knew first-hand how instrumental he was, not just within General Motors, not just in the automotive industry, but all across this country. He was an idol to a lot of young people, male and female, in terms of not only what he achieved, but how he went about it: first class, all the time."

The former Detroit Pistons star and Hall of Fame player re-counted how he founded Bing Steel LLC and was trying to penetrate the automotive market as a supplier. He and other black suppliers boldly assembled a group of black executives from GM, Ford and Chrysler, with the goal of being mentored on how to excel as minority suppliers to the Big Three.

"We called ourselves the Six-Thirty Group," Mayor Bing said, "because we would meet at six-thirty in the morning or six-thirty in the evening. I feel so proud and honored to know that Roy and others gave of themselves to help us grow and survive." The audience laughed when he revealed my nickname: "Short Timber," while he was "Tall Timber."

After that, the mayor lauded my dedication to DPS: "He at-tacked this job, and I don't think he looked at it as a job. I think he looked at it as an honor."

My successor, Jack Martin, praised my nonstop work ethic that inspired me to leave retirement to help the children.

"He looked like he stepped out of the pages of GQ," said Rich-ard Baird, representing Governor Snyder. "Here's a man who showed up, I'm told, at a school blight reduction flower planting activity in designer jeans! Most in attendance that day had never seen anyone plant flowers without ever having a knee touch the dirt!"

He turned to me and said, "My friend, you do look great: tai-lored suits, silk ties, pocket squares, exquisite cufflinks. This is a man who probably wears monogrammed pajamas." Richard added, "I told Roy that far and away, he is the youngest seventy-something — in mind, body and spirit — I've ever known."

Sharing some of the more spirited moments of my tenure, Richard said: "He can string (words) together in a way that makes Richard Pryor look like an altar boy. You do not want to be on the wrong side of Roy's rant! We've had some conference calls where there was an unexpected *click!* followed by sudden silence on the other end of the line. Roy's hang-ups were frequently preceded by, 'I don't have to sit here and listen to your friggin' stuff anymore, and you know what? I'm not going to!' *Click!* Spoiler alert: he didn't always say friggin or stuff." The audience roared!

A Detroit Public Schools classroom visit with students, parents, faculty and administrators.

Then Richard read, in its entirety, one of the most touching letters I have ever received. It was from Governor Snyder, thanking me for my service as Emergency Manager of Detroit Public Schools. Here is an excerpt:

"Your accomplishments over the past 2.5 years are unparalleled...

Since becoming Governor, I have often said that the best way to move forward is to stop worrying about placing blame or taking credit — and just focus on Relentless Positive Action ("RPA") to solve problems and create opportunities.

Therefore, it gives me great pleasure to bestow upon you, my very first 'RPA Champions Award of Excellence' for your incredible service to the people of Detroit and Michigan.

I cannot adequately express how much I appreciate your leadership, integrity, and your friendship. Please accept my sincere best wishes to you and Maureen and your family for a retirement that exemplifies good health, good times, and the satisfaction of knowing that you made an incredible difference in the lives of a great many people."

Sincerely,

Rick Snyder, Governor

Next, Darrell Burks described how Governor Snyder and Richard had asked him to convince me to take the job. "When I called Roy, I asked, 'What do you think about taking the emergency manager job?' I thought he was going to say, 'Are you on drugs? Get the heck outta here!' But he was willing to talk about what he wanted to achieve in public education. He said all the right things." Then Darrell added, "I didn't know that what Roy was going to say to the governor was, 'I will take this job only if Darrell comes with me.'"

My friend Dr. Bill Pickard, Chief Executive Officer of Global Auto Alliance, an automobile parts supplier, recalled our days as "The Fabulous Five" at Western Michigan University. Then he said, "Maureen, you and Roy represent the very best that not only the black community has to offer, but that America has to offer."

The next speakers were my dear friends Rod Gillum and his wife, Dr. Linda Gillum, Founding Associate Dean of Academic and Faculty Affairs and Associate Professor of Biomedical Sciences at Oakland University's William Beaumont School of Medicine. Linda began by quoting the late author Maya Angelou: "You didn't go through life with a mitt in both hands. You threw something back."

The Gillums praised my service: "You believed that every child mattered. That they deserved to be hugged and embraced. That they liked to have someone put their arm around them, put a book in their hand, and put a good thought in their head and in their heart, and move forward believing that they could become worthwhile contributors like you and Maureen."

Then they said, "We're in partnership with the Detroit Public Schools Foundation to announce tonight the establishment of the

Roy and Maureen Roberts Scholarship."

As the audience exploded with applause, Maureen and I were overwhelmed.

Next, Kevin Smith, my chief of staff, shared a hilarious rendition of how I can switch gears from fast-talking furious to the epitome of charm. As he was driving us to a luncheon, he was terrified that he might be fired because I was ranting and raving at him until we arrived and the car door opened. "It was like a light switch goes on," Kevin said. "Roy is saying, 'Hey, hey, how you doin'? Did you meet my chief of staff? He's a smart guy.' We go in, we have lunch, we have a good time, and I'm thinking, 'Okay, Roy is good. I'm not fired.' We get back in the SUV. As soon as the door closes, he turned to me and says angrily, 'And another thing—'"

The audience roared. Kevin added that he was amazed at how I finessed the art of firing and demoting people: "People were thanking him as they went out the door. And Roy would always say, 'Fifty years, baby! I've been doing this for fifty years!'"

Roy-isms like that inspired my staff to print a beautiful hardcover book, presented by Kevin and Karen Ridgeway. The cover features a photo of me beside the title: *Fifty years of wisdom: The sage musings of Roy S. Roberts*. The back cover shows a photo of children laughing, and says: "Thank you for caring so much about the children of Detroit. Presented to Roy Roberts on September 26, 2013, by his forever-in-awe Cabinet." Kevin and Karen then playfully interpreted each Roy-ism as it flashed on a projection screen.

"Fifty years, baby... fifty years," Karen said, means: "You really don't know what you're talking about. Now get out of my office!"

Kevin translated, "If you're early, you're on time. If you're on time, you're late!" to mean, "If you're late to my meeting one more time, you're going to be an alumnus by choice!"

The book lists other Roy-isms: "Bold problems require even bolder SOLUTIONS!"

"We must be willing to change and make ourselves uncomfortable."

"If you want to start a fight, you have to pick another subject."

"Lead with your head, guide with your heart."

"It's all about the kids, folks... it's about THE KIDS."

"What you expect, you must inspect!"

"I've got my suspenders on *with* my belt."

"I've got enough friends; I don't need any more!"

Here's one that I repeated incessantly, especially at press conferences: "Kids don't fail... adults fail kids."

"Culture will eat strategy for breakfast every time!"

"You better not let me walk off a cliff." Kevin added that this really means: "Because if I fall off, I'm going to be firing back at you!'"

"It's great to be the first, but it's more important not to be the last."

The final Roy-ism was: "At my age, I don't even buy green bananas." Karen and Kevin explained that this means, "Stop wasting my time!"

Their presentation ended with Karen saying, "Roy, you helped us to build a team and earn back credibility. You gave DPS hope. I hope you learned a little bit from us. We sure learned a lot from you."

The program concluded with my friend, Elliott Hall, sharing the story about how we enjoyed lunch in Ford Motor Company's executive offices when he was the corporation's first African American vice president. After he recounted how he turned to me and said, "Ain't this some shit!?" the audience exploded with a standing ovation.

I could not have felt more proud and honored that I had dedicated two years of my life to helping the children of Detroit.

That same week, I began the privilege of serving as Detroit's Chief Land Officer to strategize how to remove and repurpose Detroit's 85,000 abandoned, burned-out and boarded-up houses and vacant lots. President Obama's administration provided $300 million in federal and private funds to eradicate blight, stimulate business development, improve public safety, and revamp the beleaguered bus system. That position enabled me to "help people" in another important way.

SIXTEEN

Tribute and Legacy

A Special Tribute to Maureen

My accomplishments were made possible by the love and support of my wife, Maureen. She has been the perfect partner during our forty years of marriage. I truly lack the words to express the gratitude and joy that I feel for having been blessed with such a wonderful, supportive wife.

My praise for her top quality — an outstanding value system — remains the same today as when I met her. Now I tell my grandsons that choosing a wife should not be based on looks or style.

"When you find a wife with a strong moral compass and good value system," I tell them, "you will find true and enduring happiness."

I speak from experience. During my corporate life, my wife's intellect enabled her to interface with anybody. Her quiet personality is an asset because she's cordial, not catty, and respectful to everyone.

"Nursing taught me discretion," Maureen says. "Back during the 1960s, the nurses would listen to the doctor's instructions at the nursing station, then we would go to the patients' rooms to take care of them." Male doctors enjoyed an all-knowing, god-like stature, whereas the female nurses were treated as subordinates. "When I was in training, and a patient asked, 'What medications are you giving me?' I would always answer, 'You'll have to speak with the doctor.' Discretion was rule number one."

Maureen learned to guard confidential information and avoid gossip or petty behavior. With a kind and considerate personality that is authentic and innate, she has always treated everyone equally. In fact, the General Motors chauffeur always sang Maureen's praises because she treated everyone so well.

Very importantly, her support of my career helped me to excel, and I've supported everything Maureen wanted to do, including earn her Bachelor of Arts in Education from Aquinas College in Grand Rapids, and a Master of Arts in Health Education and Occupational Education from the University of Michigan.

Our unified approach to success required compatible and complimentary personality types. I'm a pretty aggressive guy, the polar opposite of Maureen's passive and demure nature. If I had a wife with my temperament and aggressiveness, the marriage would explode.

Maureen and I treasure the artwork in our home, including this painting by Paul Collins, an internationally renowned artist from Grand Rapids, Mich.

I must also praise my wife for never being motivated by material pursuits. When she is safe and her basic needs are being met, Maureen is happy. If you see her wearing extravagant jewelry or a designer evening gown, that's by my insistence. I could never treat her to enough of the finer things to express my appreciation for her love and dedication.

Now we are demonstrating our faith in the future of Detroit's renaissance by selling our Bloomfield Hills home and moving into a condominium tower in Detroit. At the same time, we are planning many vacations around the world.

Maureen, I am excited to spend the rest of my years at your side, cherishing every minute of the gift that I consider our marriage to be.

Reflecting on My Life's Legacy

During the reception for my Roast & Toast at the Detroit Golf Club, I was chatting with Richard Baird, Bill Pickard and Skillman Foundation President and CEO Carol Goss.

"What do all of you think your grandkids will say about you fifty years from now?" Richard asked.

Bill Pickard answered: "I think they'll say, 'Grandpa was a talented, fair and good business person.'"

Carol Goss added, "I hope my grandkids will say that I was loyal to my family."

Then they looked my way.

"Me?" I smiled. "Fifty years from now, I hope they say, 'Grandpa is still lookin' pretty damn good!'"

The crowd laughed, a short time later, as Richard recounted our conversation during the program. In truth, I will be long gone from this earth in fifty years, but my legacy will remain, as written in this book. It boils down to my father's prophecy: "You're going to get a good education. You're going to be somebody. And you're going to help other people." I live by those tenets, and I encourage everyone — especially young people — to do the same.

When you're blessed to reach my age, you realize that you can't go back to relive, repair or replay any of the best or worst moments of your life. Even the most analytical hindsight cannot change the vision of your earlier years that brought you to retirement.

That's why I'm asking you to experience *My American Success Story* to excel. Model your mindset after mine; emulate my courage and boldness to innovate and stand out from the pack. Believe that hard work and a strong moral compass will guide you to the top. Develop a code of conduct to cultivate an outstanding personal and professional life.

Interestingly, my grandsons have taught me that young people today are looking for external events to propel them into prosperity and prestige. However, my life demonstrates the power of a process-driven formula. I adhered to the same process — preparation, self-evaluation, hard work, discipline — day in and day out, for years, in every position at Lear Siegler, Navistar and General Motors. Rather than wishing for or waiting on external events to push you forward, seize your own power by adhering to a *process* that guarantees success.

Likewise, I cannot over-emphasize to black professionals that your race and your connection to your people is your power at the corporate table. You were invited there because your organization's leaders value the influence and reach that you possess amongst this important sector of our economy.

Do not take your seat at the corporate table and forget what got you there. If you do, your lack of racial allegiance — and therefore lack of influence — will forfeit your privilege of being there. The company will replace you with someone who understands and values the power of staying connected to his or her people.

General Motors valued that Roy Roberts was lauded in the global media as the world's top-ranking African American in the automobile industry. When *Black Enterprise* named me Executive of the Year in 1996, that was a feather in GM's cap, because my success reflected a positive image for General Motors in the eyes of millions of black people who read that cover story about me. That was just one of so many articles and accolades — including the

American Success Award, personally handed to me by President George H. W. Bush in the White House Rose Garden.

I recount these examples to drive home the power of my formula for pioneering my way to the pinnacle of corporate America. It worked for me, and it can work for you. My desire now is that you use my experiences to create your own *American Success Story*.

Index

About the Authors

Roy S. Roberts

Roy S. Roberts is a businessman and philanthropist who became the highest-ranking African American executive in the history of the global auto industry. Roberts served as Group Vice President for North American Vehicle Sales, Service and Marketing at General Motors Corporation from October 1998 to April 2000, the pinnacle of his 24-year career with GM.

Roberts held other positions of strategic and historic importance at General Motors. During the 1990s, a highly productive decade in his career, he served as Vice President and General Manager in charge of Field Sales, Service and Parts from August 1998 to October 1998; General Manager of the Pontiac-GMC Division from February 1996 to October 1998, during which he led planning and oversight of the merger of Pontiac and GMC; and was General Manager of the GMC Truck Division from October 1992 to February 1996. Roberts also was Manufacturing Manager of GM's Cadillac Motor Car Division from 1990 to 1992.

He joined General Motors in 1977 as a salaried employee-in-training at GM's former Diesel Equipment Division in Grand Rapids, Michigan. In 1983, he became the first African American plant manager of GM's assembly facility in North Tarrytown, New York. Roberts served as vice president and corporate officer in charge of Personnel Administration and Development at GM, from 1987 to 1988 – a position that made him only the second African American vice president in the corporation's history. Roberts left GM to become vice president for truck operations and chief operating officer at Navistar International Corporation (1988-90), but was recruited back to lead Cadillac manufacturing.

Before joining General Motors, Roberts spent 17 years with the Aerospace division at Lear Siegler Inc., serving in a variety of positions ranging from engineering to manufacturing to labor relations. After retiring from GM, Roberts served as managing director and co-founding member of Reliant Equity Investors, a private equity investment firm. He was appointed Emergency Manager of Detroit Public Schools by Michigan Governor Rick Snyder, serving from 2011 to 2013.

Roberts earned a bachelor's degree in Business Administration from Western Michigan University in Kalamazoo, Michigan, and completed graduate work at WMU and Detroit's Wayne State University. He completed the Executive Development Program at Harvard Graduate School of Business, and the General Motors Advanced International General Management Program in Switzerland. He also has been awarded honorary doctorates from Michigan State, Florida A & M, Grand Valley State and Central Michigan universities.

Roberts is trustee emeritus at WMU and has served on numerous corporate boards, including Burlington Northern Santa Fe Corporation, Abbott Laboratories, and Enova Systems Corporation. He served as president and president of the national board of the Boy Scouts of America, president of the Grand Rapids NAACP, and has been a board member of the Morehouse School of Medicine, the United Negro College Fund, The Aspen Institute and the National Urban League, where he chaired national conventions in San Diego and Atlanta.

Roberts and his wife Maureen donated $1.1 million to the Detroit Institute of Arts in 2011 to create the Maureen and Roy S. Roberts Gallery of Contemporary African American Art. Roberts was presented the American Success Award in 1989 by President George H.W. Bush in the Rose Garden at the White House. He was named 1996 Executive of the Year by *Black Enterprise* magazine and was awarded the Automotive Hall of Fame's Distinguished Service Citation in 1998. Among his many other honors, Roberts received a 2014 Legacy in Motion Lifetime Achievement award from the *Michigan Chronicle* newspaper.

Elizabeth Ann Atkins

Best-selling author, actress and award-winning journalist Elizabeth Ann Atkins uses the power of the pen to inspire people to unlock infinite potential and live with passion, prosperity, health and happiness.

Atkins' desire to empower others springs from the colorblind love and courage of her mother, an African American judge, and her father, a former Roman Catholic priest who was English, French Canadian and Cherokee. Her parents taught Atkins to challenge the status quo by bucking convention through literary endeavors.

Atkins has written 14 books that include the novels *White Chocolate, Dark Secret and Twilight* (with actor Billy Dee Williams) Other books have included collaborations with executives, a surgeon, a networking expert and a family that triumphed on NBC's *The Biggest Loser.*

Atkins' work as a journalist, much of which has focused on issues involving mixed-race Americans, has appeared in *The New York Times, The San Diego Tribune, Essence, Ebony* and other publications. She has been a guest on *Oprah, Montel, NPR, Good Morning America Sunday* and other national TV shows.

Atkins created POWER JOURNAL, a program that teaches people to unleash their creativity for life enrichment. More information is available at MyPowerJournal.com.

Atkins is a public speaker represented by The American Program Bureau who has spoken to the NAACP, General Motors' World Diversity Day, Gannett, Columbia University, 100 Black Men, the University of Michigan and many other organizations.

In her acting debut, Atkins played a major role in the feature-length film *Anything is Possible*, nominated for "Best Foreign Film" by the Nollywood and African Film Critics Association. She has also written an original screenplay, *Redemption*, which is a suspenseful, gritty drama about a gangster and a writer.

Atkins earned a master's degree in journalism from Columbia University and a bachelor's degree in English Literature from the

University of Michigan. She has taught writing at Wayne State University, Oakland University and Wayne County Community College District.

ElizabethAnnAtkins444.com

CPSIA information can be obtained at www.ICGtesting.com
Printed in the USA
BVOW07*1400060315

390023BV00001B/1/P